THE
HISTORY OF
GREAT BRITAIN

THE
HISTORY OF
GREAT BRITAIN

Anne Baltz Rodrick

The Greenwood Histories of the Modern Nations
Frank W. Thackeray and John E. Findling, Series Editors

Greenwood Press
Westport, Connecticut • London

Library of Congress Cataloging-in-Publication Data

Rodrick, Anne B.

The history of Great Britain / Anne Baltz Rodrick.

p. cm. — (The Greenwood histories of the modern nations, ISSN 1096–2905)

Includes bibliographical references (p.   ) and index.

ISBN 0–313–31968–5

1. Great Britain—History.   I. Title.   II. Series.

DA30.R625   2004

941—dc22   2004012485

Library of Congress Catalog Card Number: 2004012485

ISBN: 0–313–31968–5

ISSN: 1096–2905

First published in 2004

Greenwood Press, 88 Post Road West, Westport, CT 06881
An imprint of Greenwood Publishing Group, Inc.
www.greenwood.com

Printed in the United States of America

The paper used in this book complies with the
Permanent Paper Standard issued by the National
Information Standards Organization (Z39.48–1984).

10   9   8   7   6   5   4   3   2   1

For Julie Margaret Xiaolei Rodrick

Contents

Series Foreword

The *Greenwood Histories of the Modern Nations* series is intended to provide students and interested laypeople with up-to-date, concise, and analytical histories of many of the nations of the contemporary world. Not since the 1960s has there been a systematic attempt to publish a series of national histories, and, as editors, we believe that this series will prove to be a valuable contribution to our understanding of other countries in our increasingly interdependent world.

Over thirty years ago, at the end of the 1960s, the Cold War was an accepted reality of global politics, the process of decolonization was still in progress, the idea of a unified Europe with a single currency was unheard of, the United States was mired in a war in Vietnam, and the economic boom of Asia was still years in the future. Richard Nixon was president of the United States, Mao Tse-tung (not yet Mao Zedong) ruled China, Leonid Brezhnev guided the Soviet Union, and Harold Wilson was prime minister of the United Kingdom. Authoritarian dictators still ruled most of Latin America, the Middle East was reeling in the wake of the Six-Day War, and Shah Reza Pahlavi was at the height of his power in Iran. Clearly, the past 30 years have been witness to a great deal of historical change, and it is to this change that this series is primarily addressed.

With the help of a distinguished advisory board, we have selected nations whose political, economic, and social affairs mark them as among the most important in the waning years of the twentieth century, and for each nation we have found an author who is recognized as a specialist in the history of that nation. These authors have worked most cooperatively with us and with Greenwood Press to produce volumes that reflect current research on their nations and that are interesting and informative to their prospective readers.

The importance of a series such as this cannot be underestimated. As a superpower whose influence is felt all over the world, the United States can claim a "special" relationship with almost every other nation. Yet many Americans know very little about the histories of the nations with which the United States relates. How did they get to be the way they are? What kind of political systems have evolved there? What kind of influence do they have in their own region? What are the dominant political, religious, and cultural forces that move their leaders? These and many other questions are answered in the volumes of this series.

The authors who have contributed to this series have written comprehensive histories of their nations, dating back to prehistoric times in some cases. Each of them, however, has devoted a significant portion of the book to events of the last thirty years, because the modern era has contributed the most to contemporary issues that have an impact on U.S. policy. Authors have made an effort to be as up-to-date as possible so that readers can benefit from the most recent scholarship and a narrative that includes very recent events.

In addition to the historical narrative, each volume in this series contains an introductory overview of the country's geography, political institutions, economic structure, and cultural attributes. This is designed to give readers a picture of the nation as it exists in the contemporary world. Each volume also contains additional chapters that add interesting and useful detail to the historical narrative. One chapter is a thorough chronology of important historical events, making it easy for readers to follow the flow of a particular nation's history. Another chapter features biographical sketches of the nation's most important figures in order to humanize some of the individuals who have contributed to the historical development of their nation. Each volume also contains a comprehensive bibliography, so that those readers whose interest has been sparked may find out more about the nation and its history. Finally, there is a carefully prepared topic and person index.

Readers of these volumes will find them fascinating to read and useful in understanding the contemporary world and the nations that comprise it. As series editors, it is our hope that this series will contribute to a heightened sense of global understanding as we embark on a new century.

Frank W. Thackeray and John E. Findling
Indiana University Southeast

Timeline of Historical Events

55–54 B.C.E.	Caesar's expeditions to the Isles
47–84 C.E.	Roman conquest of southern and northern England, Wales, Scotland
409	End of Roman Rule in Britain
450–495	Saxons settle in Kent, Sussex, and Wessex
597	Arrival of St. Augustine; spread of Christianity begins
664	Synod of Whitby
731	Bede's *Ecclesiastical History* completed
790s	Danish raids begin
878	King Alfred defeats the Danes
910–920	Much of Dane-law reconquered
1002–13	Renewed hostilities in Dane-law
1016	Danish Cnut becomes king of all England
1066	William of Normandy invades
1086	Domesday survey

1139–53	Civil war
1169–72	English begin invasion and conquest of Ireland
1173–74	King William of Scotland invades northern England
1215	Magna Carta
1276–77	War with Wales
1282–83	Edward I conquers Wales
1296	Edward I invades Scotland
1306	Robert the Bruce rebels
1314	Scots victorious over English at Bannockburn
1321–22	Civil War in England
1337	Hundred Years' War begins
1347	English capture Calais
1348	Bubonic plague reaches England
1381	Peasants' Revolt
1400	Rebellion of Wales begins
1415	Victory at Agincourt
1455–85	War of the Roses
1485	Henry VII
1509	Henry VIII
1513	War with Scotland
1525	Peace with France
1527	Henry seeks divorce from Catherine of Aragon
1533	Henry marries Anne Boleyn; Princess Elizabeth born
1534	Act of Supremacy
1535	Thomas More executed
1536	Monasteries dissolved; Pilgrimage of Grace; England and Wales formally unified
1543	War with France
1547	Edward VI

1553	Mary I
1554	Mary begins reunion with Roman church
1558	Elizabeth I
1559	Religious settlement
1570	Pope excommunicates Elizabeth, calls for her death
1580	Jesuits arrive in England
1585–1604	War with Spain
1587	Mary Stuart executed
1588	Defeat of Spanish Armada
1601	Essex's rebellion
1603	James VI of Scotland becomes James I of England
1605	Gunpowder Plot
1607	Settlers to Virginia
1609	Plantation of Ulster begins (Scots and English Protestants)
1620	Pilgrims travel to "new world"
1624–30	War with Spain
1625	Charles I
1626–29	War with France
1628	Petition of Right
1629	Personal Rule begins
1633	William Laud becomes Archbishop of Canterbury
1637–40	Crises in Scotland over religious observance; first and second Bishops' Wars
1641	Grand Remonstrance of Parliament to King; rebellion of Ulster Catholics
1642	First Civil War begins
1646	King surrenders to Scots; Presbyterian Church established as bishops abolished
1648	Second Civil War

1649	Charles I tried and executed; England becomes a republic
1649	Drogheda Massacre
1650	Oliver Cromwell's armies to Scotland: Scotland conquered 1652
1652–54	War with Dutch
1653	Cromwell becomes Lord Protector
1655–60	War with Spain
1658	Cromwell dies; Richard Cromwell succeeds
1660	Charles II restored
1662	Church of England restored
1665–67	Second Dutch War
1665	Great Plague
1666	Great Fire of London
1672–74	Third Dutch War
1685	James II
1687	Isaac Newton, *Principia Mathematica*
1688	James abdicates; William III and Mary II
1689	Bill of Rights; Toleration Act
1694	Bank of England established; Mary dies
1701	Act of Settlement; War of Spanish Succession (till 1713)
1702	Anne I
1707	Union of England and Scotland
1714	George I
1715	"The 15" (failed Jacobite rebellion)
1720	South Sea Bubble
1721	Walpole's ministry begins
1727	George II
1738	John Wesley "strangely warmed" by religious experience

1739	War of Jenkins' Ear (vs. Spain)
1740–48	War of Austrian Succession
1745	"The 45" (failed Jacobite rebellion)
1746	Battle of Colloden Moor
1752	Britain adopts Gregorian calendar
1756–63	Seven Years' War against France, Austria, and Russia
1759	English capture Quebec
1760	George III
1765	Stamp Tax in American Colonies
1769	James Watt patents steam engine
1773	Boston Tea Party
1776	Declaration of American Independence; Adam Smith, *Wealth of Nations*
1783	Peace of Versailles recognizes independent USA
1784	East India Act
1790	Edmund Burke, *Reflections on the Revolution in France*
1791	Thomas Paine, *The Rights of Man*
1792	Mary Wollestonecraft, *Vindication of the Rights of Women*
1793–1802	War with France
1795	Outdoor poor relief ("Speenhamland system") begins
1796	Smallpox vaccinations begin
1798	Income tax introduced; Thomas Malthus, *Essay on Population*
1801	Union with Ireland
1803–15	War with France
1805	Battle of Trafalgar
1807	Slave trade outlawed
1811	Luddite uprisings
1815	Napoleon defeated at Waterloo; Congress of Vienna

1819	Peterloo massacre
1820	George IV
1825	Trade unions legalized; first railway line opens
1829	Catholic emancipation
1830	William IV
1830–32	Cholera epidemic
1832	First Reform Act
1833	Factory Act regulates child labor; slavery outlawed in British empire; Oxford Movement in Anglican Church
1834	New Poor Law; Grand National Consolidated Trades Union (GNCTU)
1837	Victoria
1839–42	First Opium War
1840	Penny post
1840s	Railway boom: 5,000 miles of track by 1845
1845–48	Famine in Ireland
1846	Abolition of Corn Laws
1848	Failure of People's Charter
1848	Cholera epidemic
1851	Great Exhibition
1854–56	Crimean War
1857	Indian Mutiny/Sepoy Rebellion
1857	Second Opium War
1858–59	Fenianism emerges in Ireland
1858	India Act
1859	Charles Darwin, *Origin of Species*
1861	Albert, Prince Consort, dies
1866	Cholera epidemic
1867	Second Reform Act; Dominion of Canada Act

1868	Benjamin Disraeli's first government
1868–74	William Gladstone's first government
1869	Suez Canal opened
1869	Irish Church disestablished
1870	Irish Land Act; Education Act (England and Wales); Married Women's Property Act
1872	Education Act (Scotland)
1874–80	Disraeli's second government
1875	Disraeli buys majority stock in Suez Canal; Trades Disputes Act
1876	Victoria becomes Empress of India
1878	Congress of Berlin
1879	Zulu War
1880–85	Gladstone's second government
1880–81	Anglo-Boer War
1881	Irish Land Act
1882	Britain occupies Egypt
1884	Third Reform Act
1886	Gladstone's third government; first Irish Home Rule bill (fails)
1887	British East Africa company chartered
1888	Founding of Scottish Labour Party
1890–91	Parnell scandal splits Irish National Party
1892–94	Gladstone's fourth government
1893	Gaelic League founded
1893	Second Irish Home Rule bill (fails); founding of Independent Labour Party (ILP)
1898–1902	Second Boer War
1901	Edward VII

1903	Land Purchase Act (Ireland)
1905	Sinn Féin founded
1906	Formation of Labour Party
1908	Old Age Pensions Act
1909	Union of South Africa
1910	George V
1911	National Insurance Act
1911–12	Strikes by railway, mining, coal workers
1912	Titanic sinks
1912–14	Third Irish Home Rule Bill (passed but suspended); Welsh Church Disestablishment Act (passed but suspended)
1913	Ulster Volunteer Force founded
1914–18	World War I
1916	Easter Rising
1918	Representation of the People Act
1919	Dáil Éireann; Irish Volunteer Army becomes Irish Republican Army (IRA)
1920	Government of Ireland Act creates Irish Free State and Northern Ireland
1921	Anglo-Irish Treaty (effective January 1922)
1921	Threatened strike of "Triple Alliance" (miners, dockworkers, railwaymen) averted
1922–23	Civil War in Irish Free State
1924	First Labour government under Ramsay MacDonald
1926	General Strike, May 3–12
1929	Second Labour government
1932	Ottawa Conference (protective tariffs for empire); Stormont Government
1935	Government of India Act

1936	Edward VIII abdicates; George VI
1938	Munich Accords
1939–45	World War II
1940	Winston Churchill becomes prime minister; Battle of Britain (till 1941)
1942	Beveridge Report
1944	D-Day
1947	India, Pakistan, Burma independent; program of nationalizing industries begins
1948	National Health Service
1949	NATO founded; pound devalued
1951	Festival of Britain
1952	Elizabeth II
1954	Withdrawal from Egypt
1956	Suez Crisis
1963	First bid to join European Economic Community (EEC) denied by France
1967	Pound devalued
1968	Immigration from Commonwealth restricted
1972	National miners' strike; Stormont government replaced by direct rule from Westminster
1973	Britain enters EEC
1974	National miners' strike
1979	Zimbabwe granted independence as Rhodesia; Margaret Thatcher leads new Conservative Government
1982	Falklands' War
1984–85	Miners' strike
1985	Hillsborough Agreement between Britain and Irish Free State
1989	Poll tax (Scotland)

1990   Poll tax (England and Wales)

1990   Britain joins Exchange Rate Mechanism (ERM); That-
              cher resigns; Maastricht Treaty

1991   Gulf War

1992   Britain leaves ERM

1994   IRA cease-fire in Northern Ireland

1996   Prince Charles and Princess Diana divorce

1997   Labour under Tony Blair wins sweeping victory; de-
              volution in Scotland and Wales; withdrawal from
              Hong Kong

1998   Good Friday agreement in Northern Ireland

1999   Britain refuses to join new Economic and Monetary
              Union; elections in Scotland and Wales; abolition of
              hereditary peers in House of Lords

2000   Millennium Dome; new elected lord mayor of London

1

Great Britain Today

Perhaps the most important question facing the reader of this volume is one of identity. What do we mean when we refer to "Great Britain"? The "United Kingdom"? This is an especially crucial question now, in the early twenty-first century, as Britain is juggling the tensions of a historical past that literally spanned the globe with a European future that includes membership, however reluctant, in the European Union. Britain has always meant more than "England," although for many English and for many outside England this meaning has been allowed for centuries to assume a role of singular importance. Yet Britain has always encompassed much more than England, and the often difficult relationships between England and the rest of Britain, on the one hand, and the British Isles themselves and the rest of the British Empire, on the other, have shaped the identity of all those peoples touched by Britannia.

This book will try to briefly account for the reasons that this question is so important. At one time or another in history, Britain has incorporated England, Wales, Scotland, Ireland, the smaller islands surrounding these larger isles, parts of what is now France, great chunks of North and South America, large portions of both Africa and Asia, and the whole of Australasia. Britain has also, by choice or by compulsion, divested itself of many of these holdings, but has left indelible traces of British culture behind.

Perhaps the best place to start is with a quick geographical primer. England (capital London), Scotland (capital Edinburgh), and Wales (capital Cardiff) are all part of the contemporary entity known as Great Britain. All three of these, along with Northern Ireland, are part of the "United Kingdom of Great Britain and Northern Ireland," or U.K. Very often, the United Kingdom is also referred to as simply "Britain," and today "British" is held to describe and refer to the entire United Kingdom.

Ireland, which was part of the United Kingdom of Great Britain and Ireland from the 1801 Act of Union until 1921, was divided in that year by the Anglo-Irish Treaty into the Irish Free State and Northern Ireland. The Irish Free State changed its name to Éire in 1937 before becoming the Republic of Ireland in 1948. It includes the 26 southern counties of the former larger Ireland, and its capital is Dublin. Northern Ireland is made up of the six northeastern counties, including Ulster, and its capital is Belfast.

Within the geographical perimeter of the British Isles, the Channel Islands (Jersey, Guernsey, Alderney, Sark, and several smaller islands) and the Isle of Man are crown dependencies, governed by lieutenant governors but with relative autonomy, and not included in the formal United Kingdom. The Shetland and Orkney Isles, by contrast, are each counties of Scotland, and Anglesey is a county of Wales.

But "Britain" is not and has never been limited to these areas. The British Empire at its peak spanned the globe, and in the years after the First World War, as the empire began to be dismantled, commonwealth status replaced colonial status for much of the empire. The British Commonwealth of Nations was formally established in 1931 to include the white-settled dominions that had been self-governing for decades: Canada, Newfoundland, Australia, New Zealand, South Africa, and the Irish Free State. As decolonization progressed in the years after the Second World War, commonwealth status was granted to those new nations that chose to belong. Today, some 50 former members of the empire belong to the Commonwealth, recognizing the British monarch as the symbolic head of the organization but sharing little else except a common history of British rule.

The British Isles themselves are, especially to Americans, quite small. Their entire area—93,000 square miles for the United Kingdom and 27,135 square miles for the Irish Republic—is only slightly larger than New England. Figures for 2002 estimate the U.K. population at 59,778,000 and that of the Irish Republic at 3,918,000.[1] Yet within this small area there is

THE BRITISH ISLES IN THE
NINETEENTH AND TWENTIETH
CENTURIES

From Walter Arnstein, *Britain Yesterday and Today: 1830 to the Present, Seventh Edition*. Copyright © 1996 by Hougton Mifflin Company. Reprinted with permission.

great geographic diversity, from the moors of Devon to the fens, or swamps, of the southeast and the highlands and lowlands of Scotland. The climate is tempered by the effects of Atlantic currents, so that while the varieties of weather include snow and heat, extremes of temperature or precipitation are rare (as with the heat wave in the summer of 2003). Certain areas, such as Scotland and Wales, receive some 200 days of rain a year, although most of England and Ireland is less perpetually soggy.

ETHNICITY AND CULTURE, CLASS AND RELIGION

Within the United Kingdom, most of the population is concentrated in urban areas—some 90 percent overall. According to 2001 census returns, 83.6 percent of the population lives in England, 8.6 percent in Scotland, 4.9 percent in Wales, and 2.9 percent in Northern Ireland. Some 21 percent of that number is over 60 years of age; another 20 percent is under 16 (in Northern Ireland, this number is 24 percent). While the population of Northern Ireland is almost wholly white and Roman Catholic, the numbers of those in the rest of the United Kingdom who claim mixed and nonwhite ethnicity have grown considerably since 1980. Indeed, the overall population of the United Kingdom increased by 4.4 percent between 1981 and 2001, and much of that was due to immigration. A generation ago, most of the nonwhite population would have been born abroad or would have immigrated to Britain when very young. Today, more than 50 percent list Britain as their place of birth, and many have parents who themselves immigrated there at a young age.[2]

The result of this influx is, not unexpectedly, a mixed bag. Many immigrant families have more children than native-born families and therefore are larger users of social services than non-immigrants. At the same time, these families—as in other parts of Europe and in the United States—tend to work very hard in their new countries, contributing to the local economy in ways that much anti-immigrant propaganda chooses to ignore. They also, inevitably, help reshape a British culture that has always included elements of empire, from the late-nineteenth-century craze for all things Egyptian to the twentieth-century Jamaican influence on popular music. Anti-immigrant sentiment has been an unfortunate part of British culture for the last century, worsening at times of economic stagnation—which includes much of the period beginning with the Cold War—and focusing on obvious differences in religion, race, and cultural habits.

These ethnic differences tend to complicate rather than to erase Britain's traditionally very strong class divisions. In many areas where there are fewer issues of race, class alone remains as divisive as it was at the height of the nineteenth century. Markers of class these days still include accent, although this has been complicated by the deliberate adoption of downscale pronunciation by university students rejecting the "BBC English" that was so ubiquitous in the 1970s and afterward. They also include leisure preferences: a preference for football (U.S. soccer) and the soap opera *Coronation Street* are still considered to be accurate markers of working-class status, while the middle classes are believed as a group to feel themselves superior both to those below them on the social scale and, more loudly, toward the "upper-class twits" above them. Attitudes are slippery things, of course, but to meet a 17-year-old girl behind the counter in a Birmingham tea shop who is both completely resigned to her life as a waitress and who also believes that "everything's different in America" is to realize that class dictates attitude in Britain in much more obvious ways than it does in the United States.

Talk about "upper-class twits" notwithstanding, the continued existence of a hereditary aristocracy is a source of endless fascination for Americans and often for the British as well. It is outlined in all of its complexity in both the annual *Debrett's Peerage* and the less-frequent *Burke's Peerage*. The highest rank within the peerage is duke or duchess, a title limited to the royal family. Dukes are territorial titles; that is, one is a Duke of Northumberland because the family territory is in Northumberland. Other titles often incorporate the family name rather than the territory. The highest rank held by an individual outside the royal family is marquess (sometimes "marquis") or marchioness. This is followed in descending order by earl/countess, viscount/viscountess, and baron/baroness. At the bottom of the ladder of hereditary titles is that of baronet, which is, essentially, an inherited form of knighthood. Knighthood itself is an honor conferred by the Crown to recognize service in various ways, ranging from traditional military service to popularity in the theater or sport, and is for life only.

Generally speaking, life peers hold the title of baron or baroness. Using Margaret Thatcher as an example, the former prime minister is now a baroness and called "Lady Margaret Thatcher." To confuse non-British readers of British history, when a son inherits a title, he is referred to by the highest of his honors. Thus, if the Duke of Bedford dies, his son, the Marquess of Tavistock, automatically becomes the new Duke of Bedford and is subsequently referred to as such. Historically, this may cause confusion, as when Benjamin Disraeli, the (untitled) nineteenth-century prime minister, was made the earl of Beaconsfield (a title that died with him) by Queen Victoria; he was "Disraeli" until 1876, and "Beaconsfield" thereafter. Similarly, the eighteenth-century man of letters Horace Walpole became the earl of Orford (a hereditary title) in 1742.

Since the 1950s, many politically minded sons of peers have renounced their titles, primarily because the inheritance of a peerage means immediate translation from the House of Commons, where political power is considerable, to the House of Lords, where it is not. Thus, for instance, the Labour politician Anthony Wedgewood Benn fought for the right to renounce the title of Viscount Stansgate, and has been known simply as "Tony Benn" for decades.

The Church of England is as complicated as the peerage. Also known as the Anglican Church, it is the traditional established, or state, religion of England. The church has successfully fought several battles against disestablishment, or the formal removal from its position as a part of the state. Until 1920, the Anglican Church was also the established, or state, church of Wales, but it was disestablished in that year. In Scotland, the state church is the Presbyterian Church. In Northern Ireland, there is no state church, but most of the 66 percent Protestant majority are either Presbyterian or Church of Ireland (Anglican).

Within the Anglican Church in England, the highest authority resides in the Archbishop of Canterbury, whose province now has 29 dioceses; his counterpart, the Archbishop of York, presides over 14. Each diocese is in turn presided over by a bishop within a cathedral. Below the bishop in each diocese are the archdeacon and the dean. Administratively, the Church of England is divided into parishes, each with its own church. Until the new Poor Law of 1834, one of the most important functions of the parish, in addition to religious care, was the care of the poor within the geographical boundaries of the parish. The priest of the church is referred to as the rector or the vicar.

In addition to the Anglican Church, England is home to both non-Anglican Protestantism (often still referred to as Nonconformism), Catholicism, and a variety of non-Christian religions. By 1994, in fact, a survey of the United Kingdom revealed that 24 percent of the population considered themselves to be "nonreligious"; of the other 76 percent, individuals listed themselves as Roman Catholic (9%), "practicing Anglican" (4%), Presbyterian (3%), Methodist (2%), Muslim (2%), Hindu (2%), and "other Christian" (4%). The remainder were considered by the surveyors to be "non-practicing Anglican," which may or may not adequately describe the 50 percent of the population not encompassed in these specific religious categories; it does not, for instance, reflect the 6,000 or more practicing Baha'i in Britain, nor the 0.7 percent who listed their religion in the census of 2001 as "Jedi."[3]

GOVERNMENT

Britain is a constitutional monarchy where most power now resides in the House of Commons, the lower house of Parliament. This was not always the case. The shift from "crown" to "crown-in-parliament" took many decades, a regicide, several civil wars, and an abdication. Today the queen, Elizabeth II, is a figurehead. However, for many her symbolic functions are crucial to the "Britishness" of Britain. Ongoing arguments over the wealth and responsibilities of the royal family erupt periodically in calls for the abolition of the Crown altogether. The personal disasters of many of Elizabeth's children—divorces, the affairs and then early death of Diana, the former wife of the Prince of Wales, other personal missteps that have provided ample fodder for journalists—have led some to argue that the royal family is more burden than boon. When a fire gutted part of Windsor Castle in 1992, the year Elizabeth herself referred to as an *annus horribilis*, the question of who should pay for the $62 million in repairs highlighted the larger question of whether the monarchy was anything more than a drain on the economy. Yet in 2002, when Elizabeth celebrated her Golden Jubilee, much of the British public warmly congratulated the queen on the 50 years of her reign.

Even the most cynical observers doubt that the monarchy will be abolished anytime soon, and are resigned to the continuation of a symbolic Crown that still wields important emotional and persuasive powers. Real political power is vested in the House of Commons, the lower house that along with the House of Lords constitutes the British Parliament, which sits in the borough of Westminster (London). Most political and government offices are located on Whitehall Street, many of them in Whitehall Palace. As a result, the government itself is often referred to as "Whitehall."

A series of reform bills in the nineteenth and early twentieth centuries extended the franchise to the entire adult population, although today election turnout tends to be quite small (59.4 percent in 2001).[4] Parliament is in session annually—often continually—and is structured so that a general election must be held every five years, although general elections are often held more frequently.

Although there are several smaller parties, the parliament in Westminster is essentially a two-party system. Today these parties are the Conservatives, still sometimes called the Tories, and Labour, dubbed "New Labour" with the rise of Tony Blair. Since 1945 the control of government has been in the hands of one or the other of those parties without much input from the smaller parties. Coalition government is the norm on the

Continent, but it is and has always been singularly absent in England. The devolved governments of Wales, Scotland, and Northern Ireland, on the other hand, which are responsible for all decisions not involving the United Kingdom as a whole, are much more dependent upon coalitions among smaller parties.

The House of Lords, until very recently populated by some hereditary and most life peers, is now limited to life peers and has lost some, but not all, of its power. Women have been sitting in the House of Lords as life peers since 1958 (they gained the right to sit as hereditary peers in 1963). The Labour government under Tony Blair has proposed that the House of Lords be reconstituted as an elected or appointed "second house," but so far neither of those proposals has met with approval. The House of Lords retains the power to debate important issues and to delay certain non-tax measures passed by the House of Commons, although any measure passed by the Commons in two successive years becomes law despite any vote by the House of Lords. The head of the House of Lords is the Lord Chancellor.

The powers of the Lords form only a very moderate check on the House of Commons, whose 651 members of Parliament, or M.P.s, represent Britain's 651 constituencies, including those in Wales, Scotland, and Northern Ireland. These M.P.s receive a salary, unlike the peers who sit in the House of Lords. However, real power is wielded not through the elected members of each district but rather through a ministerial system made up of approximately 20 cabinet ministers—with specific duties and responsibilities, such as Education and Housing—and some 70 non–cabinet ministers, or "ministers without portfolio," who lack these specific departmental responsibilities and serve primarily as advisors at large. These ministers, both with and without portfolio, are chosen by the prime minister and make up the cabinet. The prime minister is technically only "first among equals," but in reality wields tremendous power.

The prime minister's residence and offices are located off of Whitehall Street at 10 Downing Street; 11 Downing Street is the site of other ministerial offices, and references are often made simply to "Downing Street" as the source of ministerial decisions. A whip system maintains party unity. Members who do not vote as directed by the party whip—an individual chosen for his or her powers of persuasion—may lose all influence and support from the party and may not be nominated by the party to run for subsequent election.

One of the oddities of the ministerial system that has grown up over the course of the twentieth century is the so-called Shadow Ministry. The party not in power appoints members to form its own government, and each of these members "shadows" the party in power. Thus, a shadow secretary of education would research and recommend policies regarding education for the minority party, thus enabling a relatively smooth transition when government power changed party hands, based upon a strong working knowledge of the various aspects of administration and policy. Many party leaders rise through the ranks in this way. Conservative Prime Minister Margaret Thatcher, for instance, served in several shadow cabinet posts while Labour was in power in the 1970s.

To complicate matters further, all ministers are politicians rather than experts in their field. Every department of government—Education, Housing, and the like—is staffed by a bureaucracy led by the Permanent Secretary, an individual trained in the field and with deep working knowledge and experience that may be lacking in the minister.

Despite the location of most real power in the hands of ministers, the House of Commons remains for many the public face of the parliamentary system. Debates are often televised and the formal divisions and votes are open to the public. Within the chambers of the House of Commons, the Speaker of the House (elected by the M.P.s as a body) is located at the top of the chamber; the M.P.s whose party is the majority—"the government"—sit to the right of the Speaker, and the M.P.s in the minority party sit to the left. Ministers and shadow ministers sit on the front benches on their respective sides, with non-ministers on the back benches where they are known, not surprisingly, as "back-benchers." Minority M.P.s are known as Her Majesty's Loyal Opposition, and have the right and duty to harangue the majority M.P.s in debate and in the twice-weekly question-and-answer periods held in the chambers. The Speaker of the House presides over these debates and Q-and-A sessions and is responsible for ensuring that both majority and minority opinions are presented.

In 1997, referenda in Scotland and Wales set up a Scottish parliament and a Welsh assembly. (M.P.s continue to be elected from Scottish and Welsh constituencies to sit in the Commons at Westminster.) The Welsh Assembly has 60 members; the Scottish parliament has 129 members.

INDUSTRY AND THE ECONOMY

While British literature and poetry have always celebrated the idyllic qualities of the countryside, Britain—especially northern England—was the first major area in Europe to industrialize. Today only the south of England is still primarily rural. Scotland, with its often daunting terrain, still depends on fishing, oil, and sheep farming. Wales and Northern Ireland remain agricultural. All of the areas of Great Britain and Northern

Ireland, as well as the Irish Republic, enjoy and depend upon significant tourist traffic for economic health.

The United Kingdom's primary industries include petroleum, cars and planes, textiles, food processing, paper products, and chemicals, although as the international economy has turned from manufactured goods to intellectual capital, Britain and Ireland have made a similar shift. Coal mining, long a staple of the British economy owing to significant coal reserves in northern England and in Wales, has declined in recent years even as North Sea oil reserves have allowed Britain to emerge as a major fuel exporter. Not surprisingly, and reflecting the decline in trade and industry, union membership has fallen, to about 29 percent of all employed adults in Great Britain, with the lowest levels of membership in the south and southeast and the highest—some 41 percent in 2003—in Northern Ireland. In 2002, overall unemployment rates were 5.3 percent in the United Kingdom (4.7 percent in the Republic of Ireland), with inflation at 2.1 percent (4.5 percent in the Republic of Ireland). The per capita income in the United Kingdom for the same period was US $25,300; in the Republic of Ireland, it was US $28,500, reflecting a boom in computer-based business and technology in the "Celtic Tiger."

RELATIONS WITH EUROPE

As the major imperial power in the nineteenth century, Britain entered the twentieth century looking away from the Continent and toward the rest of the globe. This perspective was forced to shift with decolonization. Today, the question of Britain's relationship with the rest of Europe remains controversial, despite the fact that Britain's primary trading partners are the European Union and the United States.

Over the past decades, those advocating closer union with the rest of Europe have gradually become the dominant voice, although the voices raised against union and in favor of continuing special relationships with the Commonwealth have been loud and often very persuasive. Today Britain occupies an odd place within the international community, juggling close ties with the United States and long-term relationships with many of its former colonies, on the one hand, and with a dip-the-toe-in relationship with the Continent, on the other. While Britain is a member of the European Common Market, it has often been a reluctant participant, and while the Republic of Ireland has embraced the common currency of the euro and has joined fully in the European Union of the twenty-first century, the United Kingdom as a whole remains a holdout even as popular opinion in Scotland and Wales tends to be more in favor of closer relations with Europe than it does in England.

NOTES

1. All figures for this chapter are drawn, except where noted, from E. Gene Franklin, *Global Studies: Europe. Eighth Edition* (Guilford, Conn.: McGraw-Hill, 2004).

2. National Statistics Online: *Census 2001* at http://www.statistics.gov.uk/default.asp

3. National Statistics Online: *Census 2001* at http://www.statistics.gov.uk/default.asp

4. Tony Wright, *British Politics: A Very Short Introduction* (Oxford and New York: Oxford University Press, 2003), p. 99.

2

Roman and Anglo-Saxon Britain

PRE-ROMAN AND ROMAN BRITAIN

Little is known about the British Isles before written records, which generally began with the Roman invasion of 55 B.C.E. However, archaeological expeditions have uncovered some evidence of human settlements dating back to as early as about 17,000 B.C.E. More evidence—including the remains of ornamental pottery, flint arrowheads, and agricultural artifacts—exists for settlements beginning about 3000 B.C.E. These groups are thought to have migrated from northern Europe to what is today the southeastern part of England adjacent to the English Channel, and then to have spread northward into Yorkshire and westward into Ireland. Among the traditions of these early inhabitants was the practice of burying their dead in "barrows," or long mounds. A later wave of migrants, identified as the Beaker People based on their pottery, joined these earliest barrow peoples before the Bronze Age (about 2000 to 1000 B.C.E.). Several groups of migrants crossed the English Channel during the Bronze Age, the most important of which has been named the Wessex Culture. By the time of the Iron Age, settled farming sites were scattered throughout the south, with life organized around both animal husbandry and crop farming.

Perhaps the most immediate image of pre-Roman Britain is the famous site of Stonehenge, a great stone circle now believed to have originated as early as 2500 B.C.E., during the time of the Beaker People. "Henge" means "hanging" or hinged, and Stonehenge was so named because the giant circle on Salisbury Plain includes massive stones that appear to be hanging in air, balanced upon other stones in almost impossible ways. Although neither the details behind its construction nor the reasons for the circle are clear, evidence suggests the stones were quarried in Wales and then floated via riverways to their final destination, for use as an observatory or for religious practices that included sun worship. Other similar monuments were erected throughout the region, with one dubbed Woodhenge just a few miles from Salisbury Plain, and others scattered as far away as the Lake District and the islands off of Scotland.

The wave of pre-Roman migrants known as the Celts came from central Europe via northern Europe. Early Roman accounts link the Celts in Britain to the Celts in Gaul, and describe them as warlike, courageous, and aggressive. The Romans also describe two additional warlike peoples, the Picts in Scotland and the Scots in Ireland, who were believed to be related to the more widely scattered Celts. Fears that Celts in northern Europe would use the British Isles to launch an attack on Roman outposts prompted Julius Caesar to sail to England in 55 B.C.E. in a short-lived invasion. Not until 43 C.E. was Roman rule imposed in the southeast of England, by the emperor Claudius in a system that organized the new conquest into distinct areas, each under a client king. The system was rife with corruption, although it spawned only one major revolt, Queen Boudicca's ruthlessly suppressed uprising in 61 C.E. Between about 70 and 160 C.E., Roman rule was transformed under a series of leaders who gradually replaced the system of client kings with one of local administrators more closely tied both to the local inhabitants and to Roman bureaucracy.

The earliest Roman governors had focused on a small Britannia that encompassed much of southeast England, with a provincial capital established in Colchester. Within a few decades, however, Roman rule extended north and west to Hadrian's Wall (begun 122), which stretched roughly from Newcastle to Carlisle. Hadrian's successor, Antoninus Pius, ordered the construction of another wall farther north to extend Roman control and to present a defense against the Caledonian tribes of northern Scotland. Roman rule in the north and far west was, however, always less secure than in the southeast, and most Roman cities and towns were surrounded by defensive walls designed to protect Romans and Britons against the incursions of outlying tribes. The cities themselves—from London, which became the capital of Roman Britannia around 60 C.E., to the smaller centers of Colchester, Verulamium, Exeter, Chester, and Carmarthen—were characterized by a mix of market, government, and social functions, ranging from council chambers to public baths, all used in various degrees by populations that encompassed gentry and military officers, slaves and skilled laborers, businessmen and veterans. Rapid growth and development led to the division of Britain into two provinces during this period, with Britannia Inferior centered on York and Britannia Superior centered on London. Both cities were important centers not only of military defense and government administration but also—especially in the case of London—of international trade. A constant influx of immigrants contributed to the polyglot nature of Roman Britannia.

This period of peace, marred increasingly by tribal attacks along the northern and western frontiers and punctuated outside the borders of Britannia by chaos and breakdown within the Roman Empire as a whole, lasted until the middle of the third century. In 287 a senior military officer named Carausius seized control as a local emperor in his own right, and by the time the central Roman administration had regained control of Britannia in 293, significant changes had been initiated by the Emperor Diocletian. Economically, unprecedented levels of taxation were joined by new controls on labor that included the creation of a peasantry newly tied to the land. Diocletian also sought to replace the untrammeled power of the military with local and state government more firmly under royal control. Thus, he created new imperial offices, with two senior and two junior emperors, or caesars, serving under him. It was the senior caesar of the west, Constantius I, who presided over the reclamation of the rebel Britannia. Constantius embarked on a series of battles against mercenary troops from the Continent and against attacks by the Picts in Scotland.

Constantius's successor, Constantine the Great (c. 274–337), ushered in a golden age of prosperity and peace, during which Roman Britain enjoyed the growth of local arts and industries. Within the territory bounded by Hadrian's Wall, Britannia was subdivided into four separate provinces, with Lincoln and Cirencester joining the ranks of provincial capitals alongside London and York. London also became the official capital of the diocese—the new ruling unit—of Roman Britain. Villa culture flourished. Elaborate homes that included central heating and baths formed a central focus for a community of smaller homes and agricultural outbuildings, linked as a whole to main roads but providing a locus of aristocratic life separate from the towns and cities that were ruled by royal bureaucracy and imperial army. Within this villa culture, Christianity quietly took root and spread, although when Christianity became the state religion under Constantine certain elements of the villa aristocracy appear to have briefly embraced the old pagan cults as a way to establish resistance to imperial power. By the middle of the fourth century, however, heresy was a crime against the state and was punished as such. Despite this edict, Christianity appears to have been unevenly rooted in rural Britannia and even less securely established in urban areas.

Constantine's golden age ended with his own life; power passed violently from son to son until an army commander named Magnentius took control. The brutal program of suppression and murder after Constantine's death seriously impaired Britannia's villa aristocracy, and the diocese was further weakened when Picts and Scots launched a series of invasions along the borders, taking advantage of internal weakness to reclaim tribal ascendancy. In 367 a multipronged invasion of the empire took Roman Britain by surprise. Picts, Scots, and other tribes poured over the borders, looting and pillaging. Even famed city walls could not protect urban areas from invasion, and military troops deserted in large numbers until new forces were dispatched under the leadership of Theodosius, whose son would become Emperor Theodosius the Great.

Upon the death of Theodosius in 395, the Roman Empire fell into a period of further decay. Britannia was left largely to its own devices, with the result that by 409 it had thrown off nearly all its allegiance to a larger Roman Empire and was, at the same time, forced to defend itself against invasions by Saxons and other barbarians. The Roman machinery of central government was largely abandoned as Roman military troops were recalled to Gaul to repel trouble on the Continent. Britannia pulled itself inward, devoting its powers to self-protection, in a long but relatively steady slide away from the complex society of Roman Britain. The pottery industry collapsed by mid-century; local coinage ceased at about the same time, indicating that Britannia's role in an international trading community had faded. This does not mean that civilization ceased. Instead, local power was taken into the hands of local leaders, as regional, provincial, and imperial ties began to fray. By about 450 the Roman Empire was imploding, collapsing in upon itself. Roman Britain had been outside the orbit of the emperor for decades, and was ripe for invasion.

ANGLO-SAXON BRITAIN

In his famous *Ecclesiastical History of the English People*, the monk known as the Venerable Bede in 731 sketched the history of the Germani, the three major groups of Germanic invaders who began to enter the British Isles as Roman rule collapsed. Angles and Saxons and Jutes, all from northern Germany and the southern area of Denmark, came in great numbers.

Many entered Britannia as mercenaries in the last decades of Roman rule. Others were "invited" in to help protect settlements from the constant incursions of the Picts and Scots, now referred to generally as "Celts" along with other non-Roman Britons. By about 600, according to Bede's chronicle and other records, about half of the British Isles was under the control of the Germani. Celts retained control of the other half: Scotland remained in the hands of the Picts, while Ireland was home to settlements of Scots. Roman Britons had fled much of the southeast to escape the invaders, establishing three kingdoms in the north and a number of kingdoms in Wales. The word "Welshman," ironically, came to mean "slave" and referred to the Britons who had escaped to the west. Only traces of Roman rule and custom remained in the Anglo-Saxon settlements that covered most of the rest of the former Britannia.

Seventh-century England—the parts of the Isles now under the control of the Angles and Saxons and referred to as the land of the Angles, or England, in Bede's history—slowly organized itself into several large kingdoms. Wessex, home of the West Saxons, would eventually emerge as the strongest of these kingdoms, which included Essex and Sussex (east and south Saxons, respectively), East Anglia, Kent, Mercia ("middle Anglia"), and Northumbria. The Celtic areas formed their own kingdoms to the north and east. Thus, the Isles were a patchwork of kingdoms, each fighting first for its own survival and then for control over its neighbors.

This early period was one of shifting allegiances and power struggles among the kingdoms. Larger kingdoms meant greater wealth; greater wealth attracted greater military forces, which in their turn were used to enlarge boundaries even further. But the system was one that was constantly in flux, with kingdoms rarely enjoying prolonged periods of peace and stability. Kings followed kings in patterns that were not determined solely by kinship but that were instead often dependent upon the personal strength, charisma, and manipulative abilities of individual men. A military aristocracy was key to this system of kingship, and personal loyalty often trumped bloodlines. Both Bede's *History* and the most famous epic of the period, *Beowulf,* illustrate the centrality of warrior culture to the early Anglo-Saxon period. The purportedly more peaceful tenets of Christianity were not yet strong enough to balance out these essentially pagan notions of power and conquest.

In the countryside, peasants were generally free, rather than tied to the land as would be the case in the later Anglo-Saxon period. They were commonly responsible for a parcel of land called a hide, and with each hide came obligations to the king, usually obligations in kind such as grain or other commodities. Hides were themselves grouped into manors, or blocks of land, that were granted to servants or lords to the king. Blocks of land were also granted to the church as individual kingdoms converted to Christianity in the decades following 590.

THE SPREAD OF CHRISTIANITY

Christianity had gained hold of Roman Britain but lost numbers and influence in the waves of invasions by the Germani. The first attempt by the Roman church to re-Christianize the Isles came in 597 with the Roman monk Augustine, sent by Pope Gregory the Great who had purportedly seen young boys from England and had called them "angels, not Angles." Augustine entered the kingdom of Kent, where the king was married to a Christian queen from the continental kingdom of the Franks. The king, Aethelbert, converted to his wife's faith and Augustine went on to establish a monastery at Canterbury—the site of the first archbishopric, with Augustine himself as archbishop. Other conversions in other kingdoms followed, but initially these gains were offset by the rejection of Christianity in several royal households.

In fact, Christianity only regained its influence in the former Britannia owing to the enduring work of the Christians of Roman Britain, many of whom had fled westward to Ireland when the Roman Empire collapsed. Ireland had been dotted with monasteries since the fifth century, and it was the Irish monks who effectively preserved and then spread Christianity eastward through much of Britain, founding important monasteries in the process. By the 630s, the southern kings were willing to listen with new ears to the missionaries from these monasteries, and one king after another embraced the faith of the Irish church. Before the end of the seventh century, all of the kings of the British Isles were Christianized. As the ruler went, so also went his subjects. Monks traveled throughout the countryside to spread the faith and to establish new religious houses, for both monks and nuns, across the Isles.

The success of the Irish church posed serious problems for the Christian leaders in Rome, for the Irish ecclesiastics were organized differently and the Irish church calendar calculated differently than Rome's. The 664 Synod of Whitby was convened to address some of these discrepancies, imposing conformity with the practices of Rome, including the dates of church feasts and holy days. The allegiance to the new faith by English kings was crucial, especially because the tax assessments levied by the kings specifically for the churches provided essential financial support. By the early eighth century, many former Roman towns had been converted into sites for cathedrals and monasteries, often with forts built by the Romans used as the heart of these new religious communities and towns developing outside the gates of the church complex proper.

England remained a loose conglomeration of individual kingdoms, but over time certain kingdoms gained greater power than their neighbors and their rulers functioned as overkings to the entire region. The three main overkingdoms during the eighth century were Mercia to the west (encompassing much of Wales and the western Midlands of present-day England), Wessex to the south, and Northumbria to the north. Of these three, Mercia enjoyed the earliest supremacy, with kings Aethelbald (716–757) and Offa (757–796) recognized as the undisputed rulers of the region. Offa himself was regarded by Charlemagne as an equal counterpart to the king of the Franks, and was able to force Wessex to recognize his overlordship after 782. But Mercian supremacy did not last. Dynastic battles and bloody uprisings characterized all three of the major kingdoms. By 825 Offa's successors had been forced to cede much of Wessex back to the Wessex king, and by 830 much of Mercia had also been compelled to recognize the overlordship of Ecgberht of Wessex.

VIKING INVASIONS AND THE DANE-LAW

Internal dynastic disputes paled in comparison with the wave of Viking invasions that began in the 860s, however, as pirates and then settlers from both Denmark and Norway spread across western Europe and the British Isles. Population pressures at home and knowledge of English resources gathered from trade abroad fueled the waves of incomers. Norwegian Vikings tended to settle mostly in the west, in Scotland, Ireland, Wales, and Cornwall; Danish Vikings—the word signified "pirate" and was applied with equal vehemence to both groups of invaders—targeted the lands to the east. The Danish Vikings faced the combined forces of Aethelred and Alfred, the grandsons of Ecgberht of Wessex, but despite initial resistance the Danish armies appeared invincible.

Alfred, by 871 the king of Wessex, was able to forestall complete disaster through a series of money payments to the Danes, and in 878 he earned his reputation as the king who saved Wessex and the Angles generally by dealing a forceful blow to the Danish army. The Danish leader and Alfred came to terms that limited Danish settlements to the eastern half of England, an area known as the Dane-law that ran from London northwards to York. Alfred, for his part, continued to strengthen his Wessex kingdom, often by establishing fortresses that soon attracted trade and commerce. Towns sprang up around these defense strongholds. The marriage of Alfred's daughter to Aethelred of Mercia firmly and permanently attached that formerly independent kingdom to Alfred's own kingdom of Wessex, further consolidating the power of the English against that of the Danes.

The Danes for their part had established their own society in the Dane-law, with laws and religious practices that differed markedly from those in Alfred's England. When Alfred's successors, Edward the Elder, Athelstan, and Edmund, succeeded in reconquering and re-Christianizing the Dane-law by the early 900s, they had to accommodate a number of distinctive legal and social practices introduced by the Danish invaders. Alfred's heirs were powerful enough to compel the submission not only of the Danes but also of the kings of Scotland, Wales, and the formerly independent kingdom of Northumbria. A 973 pageant marked the formal "submission" of eight kings in the Isles to the overlordship of Eadgar, Edward's grandson. This fealty by no means precluded the consolidation of individual power under each of these kings; the Scots were developing a strong separate kingdom that remained relatively impervious to the influence of their Anglo-Saxon neighbors, and Wales remained formally independent, although bound by strong ties to the Wessex king.

THE DEVELOPMENT OF LOCAL GOVERNMENT

As the kings of Wessex gradually increased their kingdoms and secured their powers, they began to refocus their attention away from constant battle toward the establishment of systems of local government that would endure in peace. England was reorganized into a system of shires, each under the control of a local magnate called an ealdorman—later to be known as an earl. Each shire was further subdivided into portions generally called hundreds. Each hundred was itself split into 10 smaller units or households, known as "tithings," which were responsible for local law enforcement and administration of the laws of king and ealdorman. Within a generation, one of these administrators would become known as the shire-reeve, or sheriff, an office that would assume great power under Eadgar's heirs.

Peace, however difficult to establish, contributed to the further expansion of the monastic system throughout the kingdom. Monasteries and religious houses, particularly those under the Benedictine rule, were supported by royal patronage and formed the basis for a scholastic life as rich in its way as the religious treasuries were in theirs. Religious officials, from archbishop to bishop to abbot, held positions as royal advisors in the households of each of Alfred's successors, and by the time Eadgar was crowned in 973—at the same time during which he received the fealty of the eight kings of the Isles—the focal point of the coronation was the anointing of the ruler with holy oils. Indeed, the coronation had been delayed until Eadgar reached his thirtieth birthday, the earliest age at which a man might become an ordained priest. Thus the king had become nearly divine, an instrument of God on earth, recognized as such through elaborate rituals and association with the sacred.

NEW INVASIONS AND THE LAST OF THE ANGLO-SAXON KINGS

Eadgar, that divinely royal king, died in 975 and left behind two young sons. Within three years the heir, Edward, had been murdered and replaced by Aethelred, the younger son and the man doomed to be known throughout history as "the Unready." Aethelred ruled until 1016 over a kingdom once more preyed upon by Viking invaders, this time by a powerful military machine led by Swein, the king of a newly united Denmark and Norway. Heavy raids began in 991 and continued even after Aethelred paid large sums to forestall further invasion. The money itself only whetted the invaders' appetites, and by 1002 Aethelred ordered the massacre of all Danes living on English lands, even in those areas of the Dane-law that were by now peaceful regions of Aethelred's expansive kingdom. Swein retaliated by leading an invasion in person in 1003, inaugurating a decade of attack. By 1013, the residents of the Dane-law were ready to jettison the king who had been unable to protect them, and within the year Aethelred had been forced to flee to the Continent, where he sought the protection of the powerful duke of Normandy, his father-in-law. In 1014 Swein's younger son Cnut succeeded as king of the Dane-law. By 1017 he was the recognized king of all of what was now being referred to as England. The house of Wessex had been defeated.

Cnut divided England into four separate earldoms—Northumbria, East Anglia, Mercia, and Wessex—and replaced English earls with Danish noblemen. One result was that a period of serious political backbiting and intrigue followed Cnut's death in 1035, ending only with the restoration of the Wessex royal family under Edward (c. 1005–1066), who would be sainted as "the Confessor" for his piety. Edward's kingdom enjoyed efficient local government, especially under the office of the sheriff. Edward's grandfather, Aethelred, had already established a remarkably productive system of local taxation, first to pay the Danes to forgo invasion, and then to support Cnut's standing army. Edward used both of these tools, government and taxation, to great effect. He also continued his grandfather's emphasis on the sanctity of the king, further emphasizing the holy nature of his secular office by surrounding himself with clerks and advisors chosen from monastic houses. One of these clerical positions would evolve into the office of the royal chancellor. And he began the construction of a new abbey that would become Westminster Abbey.

Edward, the last of the Anglo-Saxon kings, presided over a kingdom that supported a rapidly growing population, an increasingly complex system of agriculture, and a vast increase in new towns and urban centers that supported not only local markets but also the guilds that sprang up to organize craftsmen and artisans. In the countryside small churches began to supplement the work of the cathedrals and monasteries, often built under the direction of the local aristocrat who wanted a priest to serve his extensive household and his tenantry. There was no parish system in the modern sense, but the foundation was laid as nobles exercised increasing local power, defining themselves no longer solely by military prowess but now, in a time of relative peace, by effective local administration. Military obligations were not forgotten, however; the foundations of the feudal system, with lords responsible for providing men and materiel for their overlords, were laid in Edward's lengthy reign.

By the 1050s it was clear that Edward would die childless. Many feared that the Norwegian kings would attempt another invasion to reclaim the throne that had been Cnut's. One of the four earls, Godwine of Wessex, mounted an unsuccessful coup that illustrated the problems that awaited any new king. Godwine's two sons had already inherited the earldoms of Wessex and Northumbria, together wielding tremendous power and appearing to be the logical choices as Edward's successors. The brothers fell out, however, and when Edward died in 1066 they were sworn enemies, rivals for the empty throne. The resultant battles provided the opportunity for an illegitimate descendant of the Normans, William, to muster his own forces and to invade. Some historians speculate that Godwine's son Harold had earlier been forced to swear secret allegiance to William, and that this gave William the assurance he needed to claim the throne; despite this, Harold and William met on a hill near Hastings, on English soil, as sworn rivals for the kingship of England. Harold's death gave William the impetus he needed to advance on London, and he moved troops toward the city, leaving destruction in his wake. His triumph was complete when he received the fealty of the nobles of England. The Anglo-Saxon royal dynasties were gone. The Normans, allied with the English royal family only by marriage and not by blood, were the last invaders to conquer the Isles.

3

Medieval Britain

THE NORMAN KINGS: CONFLICTED ALLEGIANCES AND COMPETING CLAIMS

William's consecration as king—secular and divine leader—took place amidst chaos. His Norman guards, alarmed by the shouts of his supporters, set fire to the houses near Westminster Abbey to deter William's enemies. The resultant disaster nearly cut short the ceremony before the holy oils could be applied. Was this a message that William's hold on England was in jeopardy?

William certainly acted to consolidate his power as quickly as possible, doing so at the expense of the Anglo-Saxon aristocracy. The first five years of his reign witnessed continual rebellion and opposition, put down by force. Lands forcibly confiscated by the new king were given to the Norman aristocracy in exchange for money, military service, and attestations of loyalty. The system of feudal relations that had begun under the Anglo-Saxon kings and the range of feudal dues paid by vassals to their overlords was strengthened and enlarged through a sophisticated bureaucratic apparatus designed to ensure that money and power remained under the new king's control. An army of educated priests—clerics—continued to fill the positions of clerks in the royal household, also acting in many instances as the king's advisors and superintending many of the bureaucratic functions of the kingdom. Perhaps the most famous artifact of William's bureaucracy is the Domesday survey, commissioned in 1086 and resulting in the Great and Little Domesday books, in which such information as acreage, titles, rents, livestock, and labor were recorded for each estate and manor in England. Not only did this survey provide a snapshot of England in 1086, it served as an important resource for generations to come for setting levels of taxation, collecting feudal dues, and settling land disputes.

Within a generation of William's accession, England had become a virtual extension of Normandy, with Norman nobility and French language and culture joined by a continental contempt for the "barbaric" Celtic cultures of the Welsh and Scots, whose lands remained outside of William's control. Even continental architecture supplanted Anglo-Saxon, in the churches and cathedrals that were built and rebuilt after the conquest. But strong ties to Normandy would ultimately cause long-term issues of conflicted allegiance for William's heirs. William himself, as both king of England (1066–1087) and duke of Normandy, owed homage only to the king of France. His Norman nobility, for their part, owed fealty to him both as duke of Normandy and as king of England. If those roles were separated, as they soon would be, the new aristocracy with ties both in England and on the Continent would face challenges to its loyalty.

This problem emerged almost immediately after William's consecration and even more strongly after his death, as the ducal title of Normandy and the conquered kingdom of England were inherited by two sons, Robert (duke of Normandy) and William Rufus (king of England 1087–1100). Tensions were temporarily resolved when in 1096 Robert gave the duchy over to the custody of William Rufus while he himself joined the Crusades, in exchange for a large payment from his brother. William Rufus now held both titles, simplifying the questions of allegiance among his aristocracy. As king of England, William Rufus was a marked contrast to the pious ruler his father had been. He tended to delay filling empty positions in the church hierarchy as long as possible—he waited years to fill the vacant archbishopric of Canterbury, for instance—preferring to enjoy these incomes for himself. At the same time, on the Continent, the pope was asserting new authority over prelates in every kingdom, and many English ecclesiasts found it simple to place loyalty to the pope well above loyalty to a worldly and licentious king who refused even to marry and fulfill his duty to secure a peaceful succession.

When William Rufus died in 1100 in a hunting accident, therefore, he left no heir. Robert, on the way back home from the Crusades, was expected to claim not only his duchy but also his brother's English holdings. But a third brother, Henry, beat him to it, claiming the English crown as Henry I (1100–1135) just before Robert's return. The renewed problem of conflicting allegiances for those with lands in both England and Normandy was once again temporarily resolved on a practical level when Robert was captured by Henry's men in 1106 and imprisoned until his death in 1134.

FAMILY QUARRELS AND CIVIL WAR

Despite Henry's efforts at forging alliances, both to secure his English throne and to protect his de facto rulership of Normandy, he was unable to arrange a peaceful succession. After the death of his son and heir in 1120, he called a meeting of his nobles to acknowledge his only remaining legitimate child, his daughter Matilda, as the rightful heir both to the English throne and to the Norman duchy. Matilda's marriage in 1128 to Geoffrey Plantagenet, the heir to the powerful duchy of Anjou, linked Normandy and Anjou to England but also set the stage for war. Henry quarreled with Matilda and Geoffrey, but stopped short of disinheriting them. However, when Henry died in 1135, those who had sided with Henry were ranged irrevocably against those who had sided with Matilda and Geoffrey. Henry's supporters transferred their allegiance to his nephew Stephen (1135–1154), who beat his cousins to London and was crowned and anointed king just before Christmas in 1135.

Stephen ruled directly until his capture by opposition forces in 1141. Now the throne was claimed both by his cousin Matilda, known as the empress, and his wife Matilda, the queen, who eventually secured Stephen's release. A low-level civil war ensued, definitively ending only when Empress Matilda's son Henry, already duke of Anjou and of Normandy, and his wife Eleanor, the divorced queen of King Louis VII of France, secured a negotiated peace with Stephen. Stephen formally adopted Henry as his heir, and upon his death in 1154 Henry II (1154–1189) succeeded to the throne of England.

Henry II's empire was enormous. He continued to owe allegiance to the king of France, but his riches far exceeded those of his overlord. England was merely one piece of a much larger pie, and it was in no way the most pressing of Henry's priorities. Within the Isles, he regained certain portions of northern England that had been taken over by the Scots king, negotiated a peace of sorts with the dynastic families of Wales, and in 1171 began his project of conquering Ireland. The Irish invasion was funded in part by the pope, who saw Henry as a necessary tool in the reform of the Irish church. By the 1290s, much of Ireland had been brought under direct English control, with English institutions of law and commerce joined to, and often swamping, those of the Irish kings.

But business on the Continent was always more immediate for Henry than business in the Isles, and he was generally content to leave the day-to-day oversight of his English kingdom to his bureaucracy. England gained his personal attention only rarely, as for instance when his friend Thomas Becket, whom he had elevated to the Archbishopric of Canterbury, defied the king in the matter of criminal behavior by priestly clerks. Henry demanded that all felons, including these clerks, be tried in the king's courts; Becket argued that such men continue to be tried in ecclesiastical courts, where they were often spared any punishment. Becket was exiled after trial on spurious charges, but returned in 1170 and was murdered by Henry's men in the sanctuary of his own cathedral, after a casual remark by an enraged king. This episode, although securing Becket's canonization, had little effect on Henry's reputation as king, and he continued to enjoy tremendous power.

Henry was not so lucky in his family of four sons, who were early at each other's throats as they sought the largest part of Henry's broad dominions. Henry parceled out the land but retained the real power for himself, and rebellion was a chronic accompaniment to the king's later years. Two of his sons died, and his preference for his youngest and least able son John led Richard, the other survivor, to seek the help of the king of France to secure his own inheritance. Richard was successful; upon Henry's death in 1189, he inherited not only England as Richard I "The Lionheart" (1189–1199), but also Anjou, Normandy, and Aquitaine. Ireland went to John and Brittany to a grandson. This enormous realm required enormous bureaucracies. The household of the king had increased dramatically under Henry, and under Richard these bureaucracies were even more necessary: Richard left on a Crusade to Jerusalem in 1190 and lay captive for months, even as his men thwarted a rebellion by his brother John. Even after his release, the years until his death in 1199 were spent mostly on the Continent.

Richard died without heirs, and both Normandy and England went to his brother John, the king of Ireland. For four years John spent most of his time on the Continent, offending almost everyone and losing many of his continental holdings through his shabby treatment of his vassal lords. By the end of 1203 he was forced to retreat across the Channel, where he focused his attention on quarreling with his English nobles and his English church and enforcing unprecedentedly high levels of taxation. Rebellion in 1214–1215 forced John to accept a statement of liberties and a clarification of the mutual obligations and duties within the feudal system that became known as the Magna Carta, or Great Charter.

John had no intention of adhering to the charter, however; it was a delaying tactic while he gathered forces to fight in the civil war that broke out in earnest in September 1215. When John died, 13 months later, the two sides were at odds over the heir to the throne: should it be John's young son, Henry, whose minority would guarantee a ruling council and could well open the doors to corruption and disaster, or should it be Louis, a princeling of France, whose ties to the country were thin at best? A series of battles led to a treaty under which Louis gave up his claims to the throne, and nine-year-old Henry was proclaimed Henry III (1216–1272). He ruled on his own only after 1232, but the council ruling in his behalf carefully avoided many of the pitfalls of minority kingships, and when Henry began to wield power independently he did so in a setting where the king's continental holdings were considered increasingly less important than his kingdom of England. For the first time, English king and lords were English first, Norman second. After 1259, Henry's French holdings were reduced by treaty to a tiny proportion of those lands once held by his grandfathers.

EDWARD I: EXPANSION, REORGANIZATION, AND THE DEVELOPMENT OF PARLIAMENT

Nevertheless, Henry's son Edward I (1272–1307) spent a great deal of time in those French lands, especially the profitable wine-making region of Gascony, after his own succession in 1272. Back on British soil, his attention was focused on Wales, where the conquest of the Welsh kings proved relatively rapid for one of Edward's wealth. Wales had been the haven of Anglo-Saxons fleeing the Norman invasion, just as it had been a retreat for the Celtic tribes menaced by Anglo-Saxons. After 1066, Welsh princes had in theory eventually acknowledged the overlordship of the English king, but in practice had continued to rule their lands as though the Norman kings were distant neighbors. In 1267 Henry III had granted Llywelyn ap Gruffydd the hereditary title of Prince of Wales, formally recognizing him as the leader of all the Welsh dynasties in the newly created principality of Wales. But his son Edward, with many fewer continental distractions consuming his time and his money, was determined to conquer Wales for his own use. Llywelyn ap Gruffydd was ambushed in 1282, and by 1284 the conquest of the principality was complete. The newly acquired territory was divided into four shires modeled after English shires. Edward allowed the continuation of some Welsh laws and customs, but only when they did not significantly clash with the common law of England. Administration of the marches was given into the hands of large lordships known as the marcher lordships.

Edward was also hungry to consolidate control over the lands to his north. But Scotland had a single and remarkably stable royal family, blessed with a series of exceptionally long-lived kings, and an independent Scottish church recognized as such by the pope. Indeed, Scotland occasionally ventured south to acquire its own new territory: Northumbria lay in Scottish hands for two decades, and the Scottish kings forged strong relationships to other kingdoms on the European continent, especially France. Despite his reputation as "the hammer of the north," therefore, Edward's hunger for northern expansion remained unsated. His efforts instead helped touch off the Scottish War of Independence (1296–1357), during which Robert Bruce gained the throne as Robert I in 1306. Edward's grandson Edward III would be forced to recognize Scottish independence in 1327, but war between the two countries continued until the 1357 Treaty of Berwick.

All of these political changes cost money, of course, and the early medieval kings proved remarkably resourceful at finding new ways to raise money from their subjects. In addition to the potentially extravagant income that could be realized through the use of patronage and the manipulation of feudal dues, these kings also began to experiment with direct taxes based upon moveable goods as well as land. Customs duties also became a fixed part of the Crown income during this period. The English church was also supported through a new body of taxes, many of which were first levied to pay for the Crusades but which were quickly made a regular part of church finance. Papal authority demanded these taxes, but the pope also clearly saw that the judicious assignment of this income directly to the English church would strengthen the ties between Rome and England.

All of these new taxes had to be collected. Collection of land and property taxes required the direct cooperation of the landowning nobility, the magnates; collection of customs duties required the cooperation of the merchants of the towns. Thus it was that kings began to summon the men of the shires, chosen by their peers to represent them in these important matters, to parlay or discuss the nature of taxes and the reasons for new levies. These discussions, or parliaments, inaugurated the necessary relationship between consultation with the substantial men of the kingdom, on the one hand, and the collection of taxes, on the other. The great nobility had always had access to the king's ear. It was the need to include lesser men in this conversation that began the move to an established and formal parliament with two separate houses. Thus the knights who had formerly been completely attached to their overlord's households were given new responsibilities, beyond their traditional military function. By the 1100s, knights were becoming landed gentry, beginning the transformation into a class that would bear the responsibility for ensuring that the king's laws were enforced even far away from the king himself. The dispensation of justice in turn more and more relied on jury trials presided over by traveling circuit judges, rather than on the traditional trial by sword, for nobility, and trial by ordeal of fire or water, for others less fortunate.

The medieval English church remained firmly tied to the church at Rome, even with the development of church taxes raised almost completely for the use of the English church. In 1066, there were approximately 50 religious houses in England; 150 years later, there were 700. Joining the traditional orders of monks and nuns were mendicant friars, who crossed parish boundaries to minister to men and women across the land, performing sacraments especially in the new towns that sprang up as population pressures increased. England's few Jews were formally expelled in 1290, not to return until the 1650s. They had already been subject to increasing persecution: herded into Jewries and forced to wear identifying badges, accused of ritual murder of children, and slaughtered in large numbers in York and London.

WAR, PLAGUE, AND UPRISINGS 1307–1399

Edward II (1307–1327) inherited a kingdom that was English, not French; that had subjugated Wales but not Scotland; and that had begun an extraordinarily difficult program of conquest in Ireland, which remained maddeningly elusive. The Scottish leader Edward Bruce, brother of Robert, staged an invasion in 1315 and was declared High King of Ireland in 1316. This signaled a renewed struggle for power both amongst the Irish lords and against the English conquerors, a struggle that permanently weakened the hold of the medieval English kings. The expense of wars at home and with France turned the attentions of Edward II and Edward III eastward, not westward. English influence in Ireland had contracted by the 1400s to a narrow area around Dublin, known as the Pale.

The wars with France began in 1337 under Edward III (1327–1377), motivated both by the chronic issues of overlordship in Gascony and also France's extension of shelter and military help to the Scots in their wars against the English. Edward declared himself not overlord of Gascony but the king of all France, setting off the episodes that became known, erroneously, as the 100 Years' War. It was war in the plural, punctuated with short intervals of peace, lasting until 1453. England at first held the upper hand—Henry VI would be crowned king of France in Paris in 1431—but by 1453 had been shorn of all of its French holdings except the port city of Calais. The wars themselves were fought not simply on French soil but throughout the western regions of the Continent and at sea. These wars, like the ongoing battles against the Scots beginning in 1296, were paid for through new and heavy taxes across the kingdom, including unprecedented levels of taxation on the clergy. These taxes were met with widespread resistance. In the case of Edward II, the ill will of his subjects was so intense that it led to his forced abdication in 1326–1327 in favor of his young son. Edward III was better able to win his subjects' support, in part by managing to make his magnates and his parliament feel that they were crucial to the good governance of the kingdom. It was in Edward III's final parliament, the "Good Parliament" of 1376, that impeachment was introduced as a tool of parliamentary and therefore public control over bad advisors.

Edward's death in the following year placed his 10-year-old grandson Richard II on the throne, introducing all the problems of a minority rule. Richard's ruling council had to address serious uprisings that were a response not only to the ongoing and escalating expenses of war but also to the economic and social dislocations still being played out after the Black Death robbed the land of more than a third of its inhabitants. The first terrible wave of plague hit in 1348 with subsequent waves between 1360 and 1375. A century after the first wave, the population of the British Isles had dropped from approximately 4 million to around 2.5 million. Ironically, many survivors found their lives considerably improved after the plague: many peasants were able to increase the acreage they leased and worked; wages for artisans and other laborers increased; rents decreased. Landlords, on the other hand, found their income significantly contracting because there were so many fewer renters, and many of the agricultural innovations introduced in the early 1300s were abandoned owing to expense and lack of labor. Despite parliamentary statutes as early as the 1350s designed to keep labor on the land, the system of unfree labor known as serfdom was fatally injured (although not immediately destroyed) by the plague, and the reactions by landlords were varied. Some landowners sought to retain their previous ways of life at any cost, and used draconian pressures to reinforce their economic and social powers. Others began to adopt the new, more rational land use practices that would become much more common in the fifteenth and sixteenth centuries. All of these pressures helped contribute to the social unrest that under Richard II exploded into rebellion and threatened to become revolution.

The most serious of these rebellions was the episode known as the Peasants' Revolt in 1381. The changes in rural life involved in the shift from grain to sheep farming, the apparently endless tax increases to fund war with France, the increased assertiveness of peasants and artisans no longer so closely bound to traditional social and economic structures, and dissatisfaction with a church no longer seeming to fulfill its duties to the people—all of these contributed to the revolt led by Wat Tyler and John Ball. The rebels moved from the countryside into London to appeal to the new king, Richard II, and attacked many of the traditional symbols of a repressive old monarchy, throwing open prison doors, sacking the homes of royal ministers, and kidnapping and killing the Archbishop of Canterbury. The rebellion was put down with force, its leaders killed; none of the demands of the rebels were met, although the hated poll, or head, tax (at a uniform 1s. per head, this was a particularly difficult burden for the poor) that had sparked the uprising was abandoned for many years.

Richard himself, at the age of 14, met the appeal of the rebels without sympathy. For several years his uncle, John of Gaunt, duke of Lancaster, had led the ruling council. Now Richard began to assert his own authority. Unfortunately, despite his intelligence, he alienated many of his supporters through his arrogance and his open promotion of royal favorites. Parliament responded by resorting to the still novel tool of impeachment, infuriating Richard but ridding the government of incompetent ministers. Richard delayed his revenge for several years, concentrating instead on the continuing war with France, but in 1397 the king made his move against several of his magnates. Several nobles were killed or exiled, including the man who would eventually depose the king, his cousin Henry Bolingbroke, and Richard confiscated their estates. The king's visit to Ireland provided his enemies with the opportunity they needed to arrange his forced abdication, which took place in 1399.

CLAIMS TO FRANCE AND THE WARS OF THE ROSES (1399–1485)

When Henry Bolingbroke became Henry IV (1399–1413), his accession was based more on raw power than on his relatively weak blood claims. Not surprisingly, the early years of Henry IV's reign were punctuated by rebellion, including an uprising by Owain Glyndwr that liberated Wales temporarily from English control in 1405. War with France was renewed despite a truce entered into by Richard II in 1396, and war with Scotland continued unabated until the Scottish king James I entered an 18-year period of captivity in England in 1406. Peace between Scotland and England was only reached with a 1475 treaty, after the conclusion of war with France and the end to immediate fears that Scotland and France were allies against the English. And in Ireland, the other drains on the English treasury resulted in a de facto period of freedom from direct English control; the great magnates enjoyed increasing powers, undeterred either by directives from the Crown or by rebellion by the Irish themselves.

Within England, once the immediate period of resistance to Henry's coup had passed, the kingdom entered a period of relative stability, as the great magnates threw their support behind the new king in return for increased influence and unfettered local power. The cooperation of families such as the Nevilles and the Percies, enshrined later on in the plays of William Shakespeare, was crucial to Henry's success, as it would be to his heirs. By this time the feudal system had developed into a hybrid often referred to by historians as "bastard feudalism," with direct military obligation replaced almost entirely by money dues, but even under this hybrid the great magnates especially of the north and west could muster formidable levels of men and materiel. The magnates for their own part had developed strong relationships with their own dependents, their client gentry, and would be able to assert ever-increasing levels of local control as disputes over succession kept Crown attention focused on Westminster and London.

When Henry IV died in 1413, his son's claims to the throne as Henry V (1413–1423) were not seriously challenged. Henry V was not content to be king of England, however, and he inaugurated a new push to regain control of France. An astonishing and impressive victory at Agincourt resulted in Henry's elevation as heir to the French throne in place of the Dauphin of France, and although Henry V himself died in 1422, before he could wear the French crown, his infant son Henry VI (1422–1461) became a dual monarch. It was an elusive and costly victory; under the inspired leadership of Joan of Arc the French regained much of the land claimed by the English kings. Henry VI's marriage to Margaret of Anjou, the niece of the French king, was an abortive attempt to iron out a settlement between the kingdoms, but to Henry's great distress the French continued their campaign to reconquer their lands, and by the end of 1450 all of Normandy was once again out of English control. Three years later, Gascony also was transferred to France, and English holdings on the Continent were limited to Calais. This was a symbolic defeat but also a very costly blow to English trade, as it completely disrupted the wine and cloth trades so crucial to the English economy.

Henry reacted to this set of defeats with a complete breakdown, ushering in a protectorate and the intense struggle known as the Wars of the Roses, in which the York and Lancaster branches of the family battled for control of the kingdom. After years of intrigue and costly bloodshed, Edward of York solidified his claims to the crown as Edward IV (1461–1483). Edward's claims to the throne rested on the notion that Henry was a weak and bad king, as well as on his own blood claims through Edmund Mortimer, but his successes after 1471 were due to a careful extermination of his Lancaster rivals and their supporters (including his own brother the duke of Clarence) and generous rewards to his friends and allies.

However, even that was not enough to cement the Yorkist hold on the throne. Edward died in April 1483, leaving two young sons. Rivalries within the factions of Yorkist supporters emerged with such force that they threatened to plunge the country into civil war. Edward's only surviving brother, Richard of Gloucester, secured the throne for himself and placed his two nephews in the Tower of London, where they mysteriously disappeared. Historians and amateurs alike have for centuries debated the personality and behavior of Richard III, some claiming that he was personally responsible for the deaths of the boys and others arguing that his reputation for very bad behavior was a result of the propaganda so skillfully promulgated by Henry Tudor, the man who would defeat him on the battlefield at Bosworth in 1485, just two years after Richard's own usurpation.

Henry Tudor's victory over Richard ushered in a new dynasty and a new era, bringing to an end the period of instability that had characterized England in the late Middle Ages. He inherited a kingdom that was almost wholly English, in two senses: first, the claims to Scotland, Wales, and Ireland were still so shaky as to be nearly or completely insupportable, and second, the severing of ties to France meant that the noble families of the kingdom no longer were buffeted by the pressures of competing loyalties.

England by the accession of the Tudors was not yet part of a "Great Britain," but it was almost a nation. Its people were bound together by a common language, a strong church that despite membership in the Roman Catholic community was characterized by peculiarly English laws and customs, and a confidence that England itself was no longer an easy prize for waves of foreign invaders.

4

Britain under the Early Tudors

SECURING THE CROWN

When Henry Tudor defeated Richard III at Bosworth Field and claimed the throne as Henry VII (1485–1509), he immediately had several major issues to contend with. First, his claims to the throne based upon bloodline were dubious at best, traced through illegitimacy on his mother's side. (On his father's side, he was descended from Owen Tudor, the Clerk of the Wardrobe.) At least half a dozen direct descendants of the Yorkist line had more impressive blood claims to the throne in 1485.

Second, he took the throne at a time when no king had held power for more than a dozen years at a time. In fact, England had had eight kings in 86 years, and Henry Tudor himself certainly appeared to be no more capable than his predecessors of taming the lawlessness and violence associated with the Wars of the Roses since 1399. The monarchy itself had little inherent power over Britain's magnates, the great feudal families whose noble leaders were crucial to the successes and failures of the Yorks and Lancasters as they plotted, bargained, and killed one another. Henry's success at Bosworth was due in large part to the deliberate neutrality of two of these magnates, and many would have confidently argued that

Henry's future hinged upon the power of his nobility rather than vice versa.

Third, and related to these problems of rival claimants and powerful magnates, the administrative, legal, and fiscal structures of the country were in significant disarray. Henry VII took the throne as a feudal monarch, but at a time when feudal structures were in flux; power, allegiance, and order were nowhere near so clearly defined as they had been previously, and independent nobles had been able to exploit this situation to an extent that belied any notion of a single law or a single administrative system for the entire kingdom.

Thus, the new king faced a menu of difficult but crucial tasks: he would have to justify his kingship without relying too heavily on his obviously weak blood claims; he would have to eliminate other contenders for the throne through judicial murder and lavish rewards for service; and he would have to establish his ascendancy *as king*, giver of law and preserver of peace, who was clearly more powerful than the magnates who had exploited the chaos of constant warfare for their own ends.

Few would have bet on Henry. And yet, through a combination of luck, skill, cunning, and hard work—and a very long life—he established a monarchy that was no longer feudal even as it was not yet completely "modern."

His first problem, convincing his new subjects as well as neighboring rulers that his own claims to the throne were legitimate, he addressed in several ways. First, he claimed that God had chosen him to rule and had expressed this choice on the battlefield: Richard III was defeated despite an army many times greater than Henry's, simply because God had determined who would be the victor. Second, he married Elizabeth of York, one of the clutch of Yorkist descendants who could argue against Henry's claims of blood inheritance, who produced for Henry four surviving children. Other Yorkists were unluckier: by 1525, most rivals were dead or exiled. And third, he effectively dispatched with two serious attempts to place imposters on the throne. In 1487 the French and Irish invaded under the banner of a boy named Lambert Simnel, who claimed to be the missing earl of Warwick. Four years later, Perkin Warbeck appeared and claimed to be Richard IV, one of the vanished "Princes in the Tower." Henry dealt with this in part by turning his public relations machine loose with the injunction to implicate Richard III, the "wicked uncle," a task carried out with expedience by Sir Thomas More, William Shakespeare, and others.

Thus, through a series of military victories, political executions, marriages, alliances, and exiles, Henry was able to resolve the most vexing of the challenges to his claims of kingship. This did not, however, make for

clear sailing. Henry's biggest problem lay in the strength and independence of the magnates, who had filled the power vacuum formed in previous reigns and had accrued so much autonomy as to be an ongoing
threat to the stability of the throne. By 1485, when Henry took the throne,
nearly a century had elapsed since a single ruler was able to keep the
various factions of English nobility in check and relatively happy. The
Wars of the Roses had cost the country heavily in terms of blood and
stability: five kings had been toppled through military defeat at the hands
of one or the other of these magnates and their powerful private armies.

Further, the lack of a strong central ruler with staying power meant that
magnates not only had developed private armies, they had also developed
their own codes of law and governance, especially in the areas farthest
from London. The feudal system that had traded military service and
fealty for land and protection, with rights and duties appertaining to both
overlord and vassal, had by now completely given way to bastard feudalism, in which money payments for military support both supple-
mented and helped erode and corrupt the former system of bonds based
upon loyalty and homage. By 1485, when Henry VII took the throne, bastard feudalism had begun to destroy old systems of social structure, with
one very problematic example of this in the increasing assertion of autonomy and independence by the greater nobles in the kingdom.

Henry came to power, therefore, at a time when the social structures of
the Middle Ages had significantly decayed. This was a boon on the one
hand, because it meant there were opportunities for innovation; it was a
problem on the other, because it meant that the Crown would have to
work vigorously to reassert itself and to begin to rein in the most powerful
of the rival magnates.

CHANGES IN LAW AND ADMINISTRATION

Over the course of his lengthy reign, Henry and his ministers presided
over the beginnings of what many historians contend was a veritable revolution in government—the implementation of new and more efficient
bureaucracies, combined with a renewed emphasis on the central authority of the Crown and its offices. At the same time, many of Henry's "innovations" were simply revivals of feudal law and custom that enriched
the Crown's coffers. The constant upheavals of the Wars of the Roses had
resulted in an overall tendency of the Crown to allow these feudal dues
to go uncollected, in part because loyalty on the part of the magnates often
rested on some sort of financial incentive. Henry and his administrators
began to systematically review all of the Crown's feudal relationships and

to begin to collect the dues owed by nobles. More efficient administration of these feudal relationships helped double the royal income during Henry's reign. His son Henry VIII (1509–1547) would continue to tighten up the collection of feudal dues, although by 1540 landowners were protesting so insistently that the Crown had to compromise and formally exempt certain lands from these obligations.

Over the two decades of his reign, Henry also steadily and carefully brought into his power the magnates—especially in the north—who had been so dangerously autonomous for so many years, forcing them to recognize that the king's law was the highest law of the land. One tool was financial: Henry levied enormous fines for retaining private standing armies, then replaced these impossible terms with stringent but manageable debt payments that kept the magnate under Crown control. The Crown was also lavish with rewards for service, which attracted the lesser nobility to Henry's side.

A more effective tool was the Crown's renewed emphasis on law and justice. During the Wars of the Roses, noble autonomy had included local control of legal machinery, and local control in turn often rested on bribery and forceful coercion of judges and juries. Henry's solution was to pour new strength into the existing system of king's or prerogative courts, reorganizing the Court of Chancery for civil cases and establishing what would become under Henry VIII a separate Court of Star Chamber for criminal cases. These courts were based on the notion of "equity law," law dispensed directly by the Crown and guided by common sense rather than the often cumbersome machinery of judge-made precedent that was the common law. Under the Stuarts, and after the jury system had been resuscitated and reinvigorated, the Star Chamber would gain notoriety as a place of secret and unjust justice; but during the Tudor period it was a welcome alternative to local courts, a place where justice was dispensed according to the king's law, not the noble's own self-interest, and where decisions were quick, affordable, and accessible.

The Tudors were equally effective in reinvigorating offices of government. Statecraft under the two Henrys was devoted not simply and exclusively to war but also issues of national health and prosperity and to diplomatic alliances. Both kings were particularly successful in choosing able and effective councilors who were devoted not only to the person of the king but also to the office of the Crown. Henry VII in particular was, as king, also an energetic administrator, taking an unusual interest in the day-to-day affairs of his kingdom. His son was less focused on these details, but was an astute judge of his officers and chose both wisely and well, balking only when his heirless marriage to Catherine of Aragon provoked differences between himself and his advisors. On the whole, the first Tudors greased anew the wheels of Crown administration, taking old offices and renewing them with men dedicated to the arts of governance.

HENRY VIII AND THOMAS WOLSEY

One reason that the Henrys were successful rulers was their longevity—a gift of fortune that had been, and would be, denied to others. Henry VII ruled for 24 years, a period sufficient to cement into place many of the administrative and judicial changes he had introduced. It was also a period more than sufficient to get the Crown out of debt. When he died in 1509, the crown passed to his second son, who became Henry VIII at the age of 18. Bluff King Hal, as he was fondly called, had not initially been schooled for kingship, but his older brother Arthur, the Crown Prince, had died childless seven years earlier. In one of his father's diplomatic successes, Arthur had been married to Catherine of Aragon, the eldest daughter of Isabella of Castile and Ferdinand of Aragon, but within months of the wedding the groom was dead. Henry VII had toyed with the idea of sending Catherine back to Spain, but, loathe to send her dowry home with her, had eventually decided to betroth her to his second son. Catherine, age 24, and Prince Henry were married a scant two weeks before his coronation as Henry VIII.

Henry inherited a full, although not brimming, treasury and a land in which the magnates that had so troubled his father had been relatively tamed through liberal distribution of both reward and punishment. His undisputed position as heir prevented any outbreak of civil war or disobedience, and his dashing manner and handsome looks inspired artists and writers, on the one hand, and ordinary men and women, on the other, with optimism and a sense of excitement. Here was a king who was also a warrior, built like a lion and dedicated to hunting and chivalry and the old glories of England. Indeed, Henry was virtually uninterested in the tedium of governance, and relied instead upon skillful ministers, especially the man who would become his chief minister, Thomas Wolsey.

Thomas Wolsey was at Henry's accession one of the royal chaplains. Son of an Ipswich butcher, he had risen to his position by dint of hard work and a daunting intelligence; these same two characteristics would lead him upward through several bishoprics and the archbishopric of York to appointments as cardinal in 1515 and papal legate in 1524, signals of the pope's favor and positions of immense power within the church. He was equally successful in gaining secular power, becoming Lord Chancellor in 1513 and eventually uniting the highest positions of church responsibility with the role of chief minister of the land. Wolsey's humble birth and significant arrogance irritated the nobility, but his shrewd exercise of power forced his enemies to mask their hatred. As cardinal and papal legate, he oversaw every inch of church business within the country; as Lord Chancellor, he controlled among other things the courts of Chancery and Star Chamber, thus exercising judicial authority in matters of canon, criminal, and civil law. He also dominated the king's privy chamber, that inner sanctum where influence was exercised, as well as the King's Council, where the business of the realm was crafted. Indeed, Wolsey's combination of both church and secular authority paved the way for Henry's own assumption of dual authority over his subjects.

Wolsey was particularly interested in diplomacy and international relations—his position as papal legate capitalized on these two areas—and under his tutelage the young Henry VIII entered into a set of alliances that appeared to protect England's relative weakness as a country small in wealth and manpower. Henry's initial attempts in this regard were shaped by his friendly rivalries with the two other young princes of Europe, Francis of France and Charles of Spain, the latter of whom was the nephew of Catherine of Aragon. Henry and Wolsey had to tread carefully in any attempt to strengthen England's position: Scotland, to the north, was allied through marriage and blood ties to France; the Low Countries, the conduit for English trade with the Continent, belonged to Spain; and disagreements with either of the other two legs of the "diplomatic triangle" could result in disaster through trade embargoes or military engagements, neither of which England could afford. Early efforts to weaken France, England's traditional enemy, through membership in the pope's Holy League were less than positive, but the English racked up victories in 1513 and 1514 and temporarily suspended war with France upon the marriage of Henry's 18-year-old sister Mary to the 60-year-old king of France, the father of Henry's rival and friend, the prince who would become Francis I. Three months later, in 1514, Mary was a widow and Francis I was king.

In 1516, the third prince of the triangle ascended to the throne as Charles V of Spain and also as Holy Roman Emperor, prompting Wolsey to negotiate a quick alliance between the powerful Spain and the relatively weak England. This alliance was paired with continued assurances of affection for France, affection demonstrated in 1520 in a contest of chivalry on the Field of Cloth of Gold in Flanders, but both Wolsey and Henry would choose Spain over France, and Charles over Francis, when expedient. "Expediency" translated to a string of victories for the Holy Roman Empire beginning in 1525, whereby England's relative weakness as an international player became glaringly apparent. All of this was complicated by two related issues: first, Wolsey coveted the papacy, and met Spanish promises of support for his candidacy in 1523 with renewed declarations of war against France; second, Charles V was Catherine's nephew, and when Henry began in 1527 to seek an annulment of his marriage, Wolsey once again began to court French support against the Spanish, who had in the end chosen not to champion him as the new pope. Some historians argue that this constant waxing and waning of alliances was due more to Henry's personal love of combat and victory than to Wolsey's own ardor for diplomacy, but certainly Wolsey was the key figure in these often confusing negotiations.

THE KING'S GREAT MATTER

Wolsey failed, however, in the one issue where failure meant personal disaster: in Henry's "Great Matter," his desire to be off with his first wife in order to wed a second, the younger, prettier, and presumably more fertile Anne Boleyn. His marriage to Catherine of Aragon had initially been a happy one, but only one child out of many pregnancies had lived beyond infancy, and that child was a girl. Henry became convinced that Catherine's failure—certainly not his own—to produce a healthy son was a sign of God's disapproval of the marriage. Examining his conscience, he concluded that he and Catherine had married against God's will, and indeed that they had foolishly courted divine wrath by disobeying injunctions against marrying one's brother's widow. Catherine had always maintained that her earlier marriage to young Prince Arthur had never been consummated; Henry now chose to believe that she had lied, arguing further that even the pope could not override God's law. As one pope had granted dispensation to marry, another would be able to annul the marriage and free Henry to contract a legal union that would be blessed with sons. Wolsey was the obvious choice as messenger to Rome, and Henry dispatched him with no fears that Wolsey would fail in his request that the Holy Father allow him, Wolsey, to decide the annulment case as papal legate.

However, the pope, Clement VII, was in no position to grant Henry's wish for local jurisdiction over the matter. He had been captured in early 1527 by the invading armies of the Holy Roman Emperor, and was now the prisoner of Catherine's nephew Charles V. He procrastinated and proposed other alternatives, but Henry wanted an annulment to ensure an uncomplicated succession. And Wolsey, no matter how articulate and coaxing, could not persuade Clement to grant him legatine jurisdiction.

When Clement finally formally denied Henry's request for an annulment and sent Wolsey home, a furious Henry turned to a little-used law to destroy his former friend and minister. Three separate so-called Statutes of Praemunire had been passed between 1353 and 1391, barring legal communication with Rome on ecclesiastical cases involving English subjects. The statutes had been designed to keep Rome out of England's backyard. Now they were invoked against Wolsey, charging the archbishop and papal legate with illegally transferring an English case from the English church courts to the Vatican. Of course, Wolsey had done this at Henry's bidding, but it was no real surprise to find that Henry was now invoking these dusty laws to destroy him. Wolsey only escaped trial and execution because he died on the journey back to London.

Henry's immediate rage might be satisfied, but he was still no closer to shedding his infertile, unhappy, but very loyal wife. She had steadfastly refused to change her version of events—or non-events—in her first marriage, and had just as steadfastly refused Clement's informal pleas to retire to a convent and thereby free Henry to marry again. Henry knew even constant intimidation would be insufficient to change Catherine's mind, so he turned next to Parliament and began the train of events that would lead to the formal break with the Roman church.

THE ENGLISH REFORMATION

The men who carried out Henry's will—personally shaping many of the subsequent events—were Sir Thomas More, who had replaced Cardinal Wolsey as Henry's Lord Chancellor, and Thomas Cromwell, who filled Wolsey's shoes as Henry's prime councilor, or minister. Cromwell, a lawyer and a member of Parliament, had been one of Wolsey's clerks and was both fascinated by and skilled in the legal machinery of the country. It was Cromwell who orchestrated the break with Rome, using Parliament as a tool to do so. As a government man, he was devoted to administrative reforms that would strengthen the systems and structures around the Crown, and he attacked the problem of Henry's marital woes with the idea that any reforms necessary to achieve a divorce and remarriage should be placed on such a footing that no future politicians or nobility or churchmen could possibly undo it. Such reforms would have to be hardy, practical, and conservative enough to satisfy Henry's own innate religious conservatism, and yet sufficiently far-reaching that the Church in Rome would acknowledge—peacefully if possible—a shift in power.

Cromwell began his work in an atmosphere of widespread anticlericalism. The 1528 pamphlet by Simon Fish called *Supplication for the Beggars*, for example, was typical in criticizing the church for the immorality of its clergy, the corruption of its ecclesiastical structure, and the very practical related problems of non-residency and pluralism, which resulted in a large number of parishes without an active priest. Fish's pamphlet, like other anticlerical works, was read eagerly by the growing number of Lutherans who were living relatively hidden lives in London and Cambridge, but who were eager for public discussions of both theological and ecclesiastical reform. Even staunch Catholics—at this point, of course, still by far the majority of the English—began to feel that reform from within was both necessary and preferable to reform from without.

The parliament called in 1529 and convened in 1530—the Reformation Parliament—held the express mandate of reforming the church from within. Henry wanted a way to pressure the pope into annulling his marriage—highly preferable to a divorce, and soothing to Henry's troubled conscience. Cromwell wanted the opportunity to reform and refresh the structures of the English church so that Rome got a clear message of non-interference. Both of these agendas—Henry's marriage and Cromwell's desire to strengthen the administrative structures of the English church—were compatible with membership in the Roman church. Theologically, Henry was appalled by the changes inherent in Lutheranism. Even after the formal break, he would continue to regard himself as more theologically Catholic than anything else. And the eventual break with Rome was most definitely an ecclesiastical reform, rather than a theological reform. It would be Henry's children whose actions would focus on the doctrines of religion rather than its outward structures. Thus, the measures passed by the Reformation Parliament focused upon the worst abuses of the church—forbidding plural holdings and non-residencies, limiting the fees that could be charged for burials and wills, imposing strict standards upon the church court judges known as ordinaries, and in general cleaning house from the inside.

But Parliament was not the only institutional weapon at Henry's disposal. He wanted to make sure that the pope and the cardinals, bishops, and other church officers of England acknowledged the king's own and superior jurisdiction over the church in England. So he summoned Convocation, that "other" parliament of archbishops, bishops, and high-ranking clergy whose mandate was to oversee the smooth running of the church within England and Wales, and dangled the example of Cardinal Wolsey before them. Convocation members had clearly violated the Statute of Praemunire, said Henry, by communicating with Rome on matters of English church courts. They would be outlawed and further punished—unless they did two things. First, they must come up with nearly £120,000 in order to soothe Henry's feelings and earn a royal pardon. Second, they would have to formally agree that Henry was the supreme head of the English church and clergy.

Convocation finally agreed, acknowledging that Henry was the church's "singular protector, only and supreme lord, and as far as the law of Christ allows, even supreme head." In exchange, the clergy received a formal "pardon" from Parliament in 1531. Next, under Henry's pressure and Cromwell's guidance, Parliament passed a series of acts placing certain church monies under the Crown's control and removing all English church court cases from Rome's jurisdiction. This latter act cleared the way to hear Henry's petition for annulment in England, without any chance that Catherine might successfully appeal to the Pope. Henry's new Archbishop of Canterbury, Thomas Cranmer, moved rapidly to declare that Henry's marriage to Catherine had never been valid, and that he was free to marry Anne. Since Anne had finally succumbed to Henry's demands and was expecting a child that Henry was sure would be a son, this annulment came in the nick of time. Anne was crowned queen on June 1, 1533, and gave birth three months later to a daughter, Elizabeth.

Henry was furious that all of this work had been undertaken for a girl, and his fury pushed him further. Up until this point the changes wrought in the English church had been ecclesiastical, not theological, and relatively minor at that. Some historians go so far as to argue that Henry's church merely replaced the pope with the Crown, leaving the rest of the ecclesiastical structure virtually intact. But Elizabeth's birth moved her father to undertake more far-reaching reforms. He and Cranmer had been excommunicated by the pope for the annulment decree; now Henry retaliated by declaring that the pope was merely the "bishop of Rome." In 1534 his parliament passed the Act of Supremacy, according to which "the King's Majesty justly and rightfully is the supreme head of the Church of England." A further act named all children of the marriage with Anne Boleyn as legal heirs to the throne, formally bypassing the now illegitimate Mary.

In 1536, at Henry's behest, Parliament passed an act requiring all clergy and government officials to formally approve of the break with Rome and the declaration of royal supremacy. Henry wished to gain open approval of men like Sir Thomas More, who had replaced Wolsey as Lord Chancellor, but his act had the opposite effect. More strongly disapproved of the break with Rome but had been willing to keep this disapproval relatively private, and when Henry demanded public support he refused. He and others who also refused to swear were imprisoned, tried, and executed, and Henry responded to those forced losses as he had to the birth of a daughter—with a renewed fervor for more radical demonstrations of his power. Much of this energy was directed toward the monastic houses, whose members were also required to pledge allegiance to the new head of the church. The result was a series of actions dissolving the monasteries and transferring much of the extensive landholdings of the church— nearly 25 percent of all land in England—to the Crown. The confiscation of monastic property prompted several uprisings, especially in the north where the so-called Pilgrimage of Grace encompassed five separate pro- tests in 1536–1537, but these were efficiently and brutally put down. Cromwell was the practical author of the parliamentary acts effecting this huge land transfer, and he hoped thereby to provide a large and perma- nent source of income to his relatively impoverished king; but the land would be given away or sold off to satisfy debts and to pay for continued military expenditures on the Continent. The beneficiaries would include the lesser gentry, who bought up land with great enthusiasm to increase their own social power in the countryside.

While the monetary benefits of such a huge real estate transfer were fleeting—the Crown's worth increased by nearly two-thirds, but much of the gains were dissipated within a few short years—the dissolution itself demonstrated clearly that the Henrician church would not be cowed by fears of papal revenge. However, further than this Henry was unwilling to go. He wanted a full acknowledgement of his powers over church struc- ture, but was reluctant to use that power over church doctrine. He was no Lutheran, despite pressures in this direction from both Anne Boleyn and, especially, Thomas Cromwell. Most theological changes were rela- tively minor—the Ten Articles of 1536 reduced the number of sacraments from seven to three, eliminated the tradition of praying for souls in pur- gatory, and introduced other reforms—and Henry resisted any further shift to truly Protestant doctrine. What he wanted, and what he got, was a power structure under his own command. Changes in theology and in tradition were largely deferred to the reigns of his children.

As for the woman who acted as catalyst to this ecclesiastical shift, she was soon gone. Henry blamed Anne for the daughter he did not want, and although she became pregnant again she delivered a deformed fetus rather than the male heir he thought he deserved. As he had done with Catherine's failure in this regard, Henry soon discovered that this was an expression of divine wrath, and he accused Anne of sorcery, bestiality, and incest. She was executed in 1536 along with several of her accused para- mours, and Henry turned for comfort to Jane Seymour. This marriage, he was sure, would be blessed with a son; there were no annoyances in the form of previous wives to haunt it, for Catherine had died of old age and grief in the same year that Anne was executed. And Jane Seymour performed her duty appropriately, giving birth to Henry's only legitimate son, Edward, in 1537 and dying quietly within a few days.

Henry's subsequent wives were less satisfactory. Anne of Cleves, his fourth wife, was chosen for her ties with the Lutheran princes on the Continent, at a time when England needed allies to avoid becoming the next casualty in the ongoing power struggles between France and Spain. The marriage, arranged by Thomas Cromwell, appalled Henry, who called his bride "the Flanders Mare." An annulment was quickly arranged and Cromwell was executed. On the day of his execution, Henry married the young Catherine Howard, whose penchant for extramarital affairs led her to the scaffold. Henry's final choice, Catherine Parr, was the comforting wife of his advancing age: she nursed him through a series of illnesses until his death in 1547. None of these women swayed him from an increasingly conservative theology. It would be the actions of his heirs—first Edward, then Mary, then Elizabeth—to make any significant changes in the doctrines and ceremonies of his independent church. Henry himself remained emotionally tied to the habits of his Catholic faith, even as he stoutly denied the authority of the pope and the Roman hierarchy.

5

Political and Religious Change under the Later Tudors

EDWARD VI AND THE EARLY REGENCY

Henry's son succeeded him in 1547 as Edward VI (1547–1553), the first king in 60 years to be crowned as a minor. Only nine years old, he was unprepared to assume the full duties and responsibilities of the Crown, and his maternal uncles, led by Edward Seymour, duke of Somerset, formed the heart of his Council of Regency. Somerset acted as Lord Protector and, in this capacity of power and influence, encouraged his nephew to introduce theological reforms that were gradualist but also unequivocally "Protestant." Somerset was supported in this gradualist approach by Thomas Cranmer, who remained Archbishop of Canterbury under Edward and who was determined to make sure that the ecclesiastical reforms instituted under Henry would be cemented so firmly into place that any return to Rome would be practically impossible.

This gradualism took several forms. "Hot" Protestants, inspired by the Calvinist theocracy in Geneva, pressed unsuccessfully to get conservative bishops replaced, to implement harsh heresy laws, to use execution as a tool to root out Roman Catholicism. They were only moderately placated by Somerset's decision to open up England to Protestant refugees from the Continent; by the newly commissioned and Lutheran-influenced *Book of Common Prayer* that appeared in English in 1549; and by the dissolution of private chapels or chantries, where rich men and women had traditionally endowed continuous prayers for their souls in purgatory. Somerset and his successor, John Dudley (first earl of Warwick and later duke of Northumberland), also provided their young king with a resolutely Calvinist education, ensuring that Edward too was a hot Protestant by the time he began to take an active interest in his duties as king.

Somerset's tenure as regent was marked by popular riots and rebellions, many of them prompted not by religious dissent but by the ongoing shift to agricultural capitalism in the countryside. This slow but steady rationalization of large-scale land ownership, begun in the wake of the Black Death, is often known simply as the "enclosure movement," but it encompassed a much broader set of reforms than merely hedging or enclosing fields. Crop rotation, new technologies of plowing and fertilization, consolidation of tenant farms ("engrossment"), and the reclamation of wastelands traditionally used for forage and fuel all increased land productivity and profitability, but they often squeezed small tenant farmers into landlessness in the process and almost universally pushed the already landless laborer into destitution. Even more damaging was the conversion of cropland into sheep pasture; whole villages could be swallowed up overnight by these conversions, as large numbers of farm laborers were replaced by single shepherds tending flocks of extremely profitable sheep. Sir Thomas More had lamented the incursion of what he called these "man-eating sheep" in his 1516 *Utopia*, although he himself was hauled into court on charges of illegal enclosure under Thomas Wolsey's administration. Laws had been passed in 1489 and in 1514 limiting the ability of landlords to convert arable land into sheep pasture, but this had not stopped the process, and by Edward's reign there were continual protests against both sheep farming and the widespread practices of engrossment and enclosure.

WARWICK AND RELIGIOUS CHANGE

In 1549, one such uprising in the north—Ket's Rebellion—provided the impetus for Somerset's ouster. He was replaced by Warwick, who found his ward Edward moving into adolescence and gaining greater confidence in his own powers as king. Under Warwick's guidance, Edward continued to embrace Calvinist Protestantism, and the period between 1549 and 1553 was characterized by the rapid introduction of radical theological reforms that reflected Warwick's own rejection of "lukewarm" moderation. Cranmer remained in his position as archbishop but was relatively open to these reforms. All remaining papists were banished from the land; any deviation from Edward's 1549 *Book of Common Prayer* was severely punished, as was absence from church itself; and all clergy were expected to take on heavy preaching responsibilities in addition to traditional sacramental duties.

This latter requirement made many clergy terribly unhappy. Ecclesiastical reforms had been difficult to swallow but Henry's church had remained essentially Catholic in its theology. Now, however, Edward was mandating a new and radically different role for men of the cloth. Further, an even more radical prayer book was introduced in 1552, and this prayer book made it impossible to intellectually reconcile the new church with the old theology, especially over the matter of the Eucharist: did the sacrament involve a miraculous change in the bread and wine, or was it instead a nonmiraculous commemoration of Christ's sacrifice?

These developments signaled a period of attack on the physical trappings of "popery," attacks that saw local churches looted, stained glass windows destroyed, and the confiscation of elaborate plate and tapestries used during services. Violence in and of itself was distasteful to the Crown, but Edward and Warwick both felt that the reminders of Rome should be eliminated in any way necessary, and so the government tended to look the other way. Edward's fervent Calvinism meant that even when the reforms originated outside of the Crown, his own behavior legitimated the shift toward a more radical Protestantism.

But fate was unkind to Edward and his reforms. He died in 1553, before the innovations in theology had time to be fully absorbed outside of the cities. Protestants in London, Cambridge, and a handful of other urban areas were fully convinced that Calvinist theology should and would take root throughout England, but in the countryside many men and women remained emotionally attached to the Catholic Church, willing to accept the ecclesiastical innovations of Henry's reign but dismayed and appalled at the theological reforms introduced by his son. And at Edward's death, the religious fate of England seemed up in the air.

Warwick—now Northumberland—scrambled to preserve "his" religious changes as Edward lay dying, persuading Edward to circumvent the royal succession and name his cousin, Jane Grey, as the heir in place of Mary Tudor. Jane was Northumberland's 15-year-old daughter-in-law and an unwilling participant, but Edward's fondness for her was as genuine as his desire to protect his church from Mary's Catholicism. However, Jane reigned only nine days. Mary and her supporters rapidly rallied the countryside, appealing to those whose fears of a civil war outweighed their suspicions of Mary's plans for the English church, and were able to remove both Jane and her father-in-law from power. Mary took the throne in triumph to begin a reign that would, to many, seem infinitely longer than the five years it occupied in reality.

MARY I

Mary's sufferings as a child and young woman had not diminished her personal charm. By all accounts she was both kind and good, but her own alternating experiences of neglect and persecution had hardened her faith and solidified her conviction that she must, at all costs, turn her country back to the true faith. All other political issues would be subsumed to this one overriding goal; and it was this single-mindedness that would lead her into the intolerance and cruelty that would earn her the nickname "Bloody Mary."

Initially, however, she exercised lenience. Northumberland was beheaded, but Jane and Dudley were merely imprisoned (they would be executed later), as was Archbishop Cranmer, whom she held personally responsible for the Protestantization of her beloved church. He was replaced by Reginald Pole, Mary's spiritual advisor, as the new Archbishop of Canterbury. Another bishop, Stephen Gardiner, who had spent years in prison for resisting the break with Rome, became her closest advisor and Lord Chancellor. The three of them together—Mary, Gardiner, and Pole—began to engineer the return to Rome, a move that like the initial break would need to be cemented into place through various acts of Parliament. The first step was the 1553 Statute of Repeal, which at one stroke turned the clock back to the time of Henry VIII. Once again the English church was liturgically and theologically Catholic but independent from the direct control of Rome.

Any attempt to reinstate the old ecclesiastical forms of the church would be very difficult, for a number of reasons. The most important of these was, perhaps, the fact that the men in the House of Commons who would be required to pass the necessary laws for such a transformation were the same men who had benefited most materially from the dissolution of the monasteries. They enjoyed the perquisites of expanded land ownership and were not about to surrender their enlarged incomes to the control of the church. Further, there were a number of rather warm, if not exactly hot, Protestants among the M.P.s summoned in 1553, and they resisted Mary out of religious scruple. Finally, any changes that would increase the relative international power of the pope were bound to be viewed with suspicion.

None of these objections swayed the queen. She strongly encouraged

English Protestants to leave the country, although at this early stage verbal persuasion was the only tool used to convince some 800 of the country's wealthier citizens that they would be more comfortable in the Protestant Low Countries. In 1554, after privately guaranteeing the Henrician land transfers, she had the Lord Chancellor read a petition before a joint session of both houses of Parliament in which England penitently and formally asked for reconciliation with the Catholic Church. In 1555 she revived the heresy laws and began to persecute Protestants in the wave of burnings that earned her her unfortunate reputation. These so-called "Smithfield Fires" consumed several hundred men and women, most of whom enjoyed little social power and were thus safe targets. Only a handful of these victims were men of standing, including the former archbishop Thomas Cranmer, who had initially recanted and then took back his recantation, thrusting first into the fire the hand with which he had signed his original confession of error.

Protestantism itself, especially of the hotter sort favored by Edward, was rooted only shallowly in English soil by the time Mary took the throne. Mary felt this would work to her advantage, easing the way to a reconciliation with Rome. But in her revival of attacks on heretics she made a grave miscalculation. It was the Smithfield fires, almost more than anything else, that turned England into a Protestant nation. The attacks on Protestants evoked a deep hatred for Mary and for the Roman church, a hatred rooted in social and political resentment at least as much as in theological belief. Mary's victims were vulnerable and easy to attack; further, their deaths at the hands of incompetent executioners were agonizingly slow and torturous. They were celebrated as martyrs almost immediately, and enshrined by the Protestant divine John Foxe in his famous *The Acts and Monuments of the Church,* a book that would eventually be chained to every cathedral pulpit under the Protestant Elizabeth.

Mary's program of reconciliation with the church included marriage to the devoutly Catholic Philip of Spain, her cousin. Philip was made king of England and co-ruler with his wife, but a suspicious Parliament insisted that Philip be denied any powers of appointment in his new kingdom. All offices in the English government and in the English church had to be filled by Mary, and they had to be filled with Englishmen. Even these strictures were almost not enough; a revolt nearly derailed the Spanish marriage and led to a spate of executions, and threatened to place the princess Elizabeth under suspicion of treason as well.

Despite the uprising, Philip and Mary were wed in July 1555, and almost immediately afterward Philip began a pattern of spending as little time in England as possible, returning to Spain to live for long periods alone. The marriage was unsuccessful from the very start, and Mary's failure to conceive a child filled her with grief. Her increasingly poor health, her personal loneliness, and the growing resentment of her subjects toward her religious and ecclesiastical policies distressed her immeasurably.

In 1557 her beloved Philip involved England in a war between Spain and France, during which France reclaimed the last English outpost on the Continent, the city of Calais, symbol of former glory. This humiliation was compounded by actions by the Vatican: during the course of the war the new pope excommunicated Philip and declared Reginald Pole a heretic. Spain, still commanding English assistance, invaded Rome. Mary, a devout Catholic whose only wish was to return her kingdom to the embrace of the true church, found herself at the age of 41 ill and barren, wed to an excommunicant who did not love her, with a declared heretic as her spiritual advisor, in a war against her Holy Father, and facing the hard truth that her successor had only outwardly conformed to the Catholic faith. Her death in 1558 ended a reign short in days but interminable to many of her subjects. On November 17, the crown passed to her sister Elizabeth.

ELIZABETH I AND THE RELIGIOUS SETTLEMENT

Elizabeth's accession as Elizabeth I (1558–1603) was welcomed by many who had found Mary's reign wearying indeed. She was young, attractive, well educated, and undeniably Protestant. And while she had no sympathy for a Catholic church which had declared her a bastard and a heretic, she was determined to pursue a moderate course in religion. Her model was, initially, a modified version of the church of her father: moderately Catholic in ritual and tradition, but Protestant in its rejection of papal influence, and flexible enough to accommodate the hotter Protestants who were returning from the Continent after years among the Calvinists. Her famous "middle way," her via media, would be a state church that was under the direction of the Crown: no independent congregations along the Calvinist lines, no dispensing with bishops and other offices, but no loyalties to the pope nor any other foreign authority. She wanted outward conformity with a church structure that upheld and supported the Crown and its authority, but personal theological belief was another matter: "I do not want to make windows into men's souls." So long as her subjects attended a church recognized as an arm of the state, and so long as certain basic liturgical forms were followed, she was content to allow flexibility in many of the details of observance.

The 1558 Act of Supremacy and Act of Uniformity laid the ground rules, stating once again that England was a kingdom under one church, and that church was under the leadership of one Crown. All office holders had to take an oath of allegiance to support the royal supremacy. All subjects were required to attend their parish church—no alternate service would be allowed—every Sunday and Holy Day. The 1552 prayer book was reinstated, although Elizabeth ordered certain changes moderating the tone of certain ceremonies. In particular, the language of the Eucharist was deliberately reworked so that the sacrament could be interpreted either as a commemorative act, remembering and honoring the Last Supper, or as the miraculous transformation of bread and wine into body and blood. Clergy were also required to wear vestments to administer communion. These and other minor changes were too papist for the hotter Protestants, now known as the Puritans, and not nearly papist enough for the Catholics, but Elizabeth was determined to carve out a compromise that would allow as many of her subjects as possible to participate comfortably in mandatory religious observance.

There was, of course, resistance, especially on the part of those who had applauded Mary's return to Rome. Most parish priests took the oath of allegiance without objection—only about 300 out of 7,000 lost their livings over their refusal to swear—but none of the bishops would accept the Act of Supremacy and so were replaced. Catholics generally were not rigorously persecuted—Elizabeth was fully aware that the persecution of Protestants had solidified the country's rejection of Rome, and she did not want the persecution of Catholics to have a similar effect—but they were subject to fines of a shilling a day for nonattendance. Within a month or two, most English Catholics had established a pattern of general attendance except on communion Sundays, paying fines about once a month while preserving their consciences. However, no Catholic priests were legally permitted in England, and for the first decade of Elizabeth's reign, a number of Catholics gradually transferred their allegiance to the Church of England, whose rituals and traditions were so similar to those of Rome. Elizabeth and her advisors, especially William Cecil (later Lord Burghley), deliberately chose this policy of careful leniency, hoping that in this way Catholicism in England would die a natural death.

Initially, Elizabeth's more Protestant subjects found this objectionable in the extreme. Puritans returning from the Continent found the via media too mushy, too full of compromise, too accommodating to what they regarded as heresy. But political reality, and the careful appointment of Puritans to positions of power within the state, helped persuade most of them to accept the Elizabethan church. The Act of Uniformity established

a system that allowed individual congregations a certain amount of lee-
way in the general temperature of their services; vestments might be popish, but the language of the Eucharist was deliberately constructed to
accommodate both Calvinist and Catholic interpretations of the sacrament, and the Calvinist emphasis on a preaching ministry could be satisfied in congregations who wanted to invite visiting divines to speak. It
was clear to returning Puritans that Elizabeth was not going to jeopardize
her church to satisfy either extreme of Calvinist or Catholic, and most
Protestants eventually acquiesced.

THREATS TO THE ENGLISH THRONE: FRANCE, SCOTLAND, AND SPAIN

Thus, for a decade, Elizabeth's via media allowed for relative peace and
stability. By the end of the 1560s, however, two factors converged to drive
the Crown into antagonism against England's Catholics and to give the
Puritans an apparent edge. First, a revitalized Catholic Church had two
new weapons against the heresies of the Protestants. The Jesuits, who were
a rapidly growing evangelical force, eventually crossed the English Channel, and a new Catholic college at Douai, in the Spanish Netherlands, was
established to train new priests specifically for England. Between 1568
and 1585, approximately 300 newly trained priests crossed surreptitiously
into England to take up their responsibilities to the country's Catholics,
many of whom found renewed meaning in their faith once priests were
available to administer sacraments and guidance. Second, in 1568 Elizabeth found herself saddled with an unwanted houseguest: her cousin
Mary, Queen of Scots, who became the focal point for a number of plots
against Elizabeth.

Mary (1542–1587; r. 1542–1566) was a Catholic with strong blood ties to
the English throne: her paternal grandmother had been Margaret Tudor,
the sister of Henry VIII. She inherited the throne of Scotland from her
father, James V (1513–1542), just a week after her birth, and was raised by
her mother, the French Mary of Guise, who arranged her marriage to the
heir to the French throne in 1548. Mary became the child bride of the much
older prince, who ascended to the throne in 1559 as Francis II.

Scotland's ties to France had been strong since the death of King James
IV (1488–1513) at the hands of the English on Flodden Field. His widow
was Henry VIII's sister Margaret, and thus his infant son James V was
half English, but the actions of the English armies pushed the Scottish
government closer to the French. In 1542 relations further soured, when
the Duke of Norfolk invaded Scotland, killing James V and some 10,000

Scots troops at Solway Moss and leaving James's infant daughter Mary as ruler under the regency of her French mother. Henry VIII viewed the action at Solway Moss as justifiable in order to secure his own backyard against possible incursions by the French or Spanish; obviously, the Scots did not agree. Henry was able to force through the Treaty of Greenwich, proposing the formal union of the two Crowns through the marriage of his son Edward to the infant Mary Stewart (or Stuart, as the name was spelled by the English), but the Scots were never willing partners in the treaty and the betrothal was never formalized. Further depredations at the hands of the English in 1545, including the sack of Edinburgh, intensified the Scottish hatred of their neighbor to the south.

At the same time that England's actions appeared to move Scotland politically closer to France, with Mary of Guise as the Scottish Queen Regent exercising increasing power within the kingdom, the Scottish Reformation provided a rallying point for the many who found de facto French rule abhorrent. Thus, Protestants within Scotland increasingly linked religious reformation with political independence from France and looked to co-religionists, even those in hated England, for support. In 1557 the Protestant nobility pledged themselves to establish a Protestant Scotland, a move that gained strength with the return of Protestant divine John Knox from exile. The 1559 accession of Francis II and Mary, and the potential formal union of Scotland and France, compelled the Protestant nobles and their supporters to appeal to England and Elizabeth for help. The battles that ensued after English troops crossed the northern border were ended by the convenient death of Mary of Guise and the 1560 Treaty of Edinburgh, which expelled both French and English troops from Scotland. At the same time the Scottish parliament voted to formally adopt Calvinist Protestantism—or Presbyterianism, as it would become known —as the state religion. Late that year, Mary returned to Scotland a 17-year-old widow and was compelled by Parliament to swear to preserve the new Presbyterian kirk.

In 1565 Mary—Queen of Scotland in her own right since her mother's death in 1560, and now also heir apparent to the English throne—married for the second time. Her choice was her cousin Henry Stewart, the earl of Darnley, who shortly afterward murdered the man he suspected of being Mary's lover. In 1566, after the birth of their only child, Darnley himself was murdered by James Hepburn, the earl of Bothwell, who then eloped with the new widow. Mary was forced to abdicate the Scottish throne in favor of her baby son, who became James VI of Scotland and was raised as a Presbyterian despite a lavish ceremony baptizing him in the Catholic faith. Mary continued to claim that her rights had been illegally taken from her, and after a failed attempt to reclaim her throne she fled to England in 1568 to seek refuge with her cousin.

Elizabeth was an unwilling hostess. Mary was still young, beautiful, once again marriageable, and devoutly Catholic, and as such was a magnet for any number of high-ranking English Catholics who saw her as the natural focus of any attempts to return the English church back to Rome. Elizabeth was well aware of the lightning rod Mary represented for Catholic plotters, but she also supported Mary's arguments that she had been forced against her will to give up her crown. Only after a series of plots between 1569 and 1586 did Elizabeth finally acknowledge that Mary's continued existence would always endanger the English Crown. Mary was beheaded in 1587 after the fourth and final of these intrigues, which like earlier conspiracies had involved Spanish and papal efforts to place her on the English throne in place of her cousin.

Without Mary as a rallying point, Spanish attempts to subdue England took another turn. Philip began openly to build up his naval fleet, setting ships into place along the English Channel and preparing for invasion. The actual launch took place in May of 1588, when a mass of large and cumbersome Spanish ships—well-equipped and loaded with armaments —began to sail up the Channel. To the surprise of both Spanish and English, however, and with the help of the weather, the smaller and lighter English ships were able to force the Spanish Armada to retreat. The medals struck in honor of the victory read, "God blew, and they were scattered," and all across the country and well into the Continent Protestants took the victory as a sign that their faith was the true faith.

This defeat was not the end of Philip's attempts to subdue his former sister-in-law. Spain's subsequent efforts to wage war against England focused heavily on the conquest of Ireland as a natural portal to Elizabeth's realm, persuading Elizabeth in turn to pour money and men into a renewed attempt to establish English control over her Catholic neighbor. The conquest of Ireland, completed by 1603, was of necessity a violent one, and attempts to impose Protestant culture upon a Catholic and in many ways very foreign country were universally a failure.

The war with Spain—no matter where that war was fought—was a significant burden for England, in part because England lacked the money and men that Spain could command. Elizabeth was forced to conclude treaties with various Protestant forces on the Continent as war engulfed much of western Europe, treaties that cost the Crown over £1 million in the six years after the Armada. These costs were met by heavy borrowing and serious depletion of the royal coffers rather than any significant reworking of the tax rolls. The income from taxes had become increasingly insufficient as inflation proceeded apace and tax rates themselves remained stagnant. Elizabeth preferred to turn a blind eye to her wealthier tax evaders, even as local tax levels increased in order to cover rising military expenditures. At the same time, Elizabeth looked with favor upon those like Sir Francis Drake who could bring her gifts of gold and silver gained through privateering and outright piracy, especially at the expense of Spain. Many of the voyages to North America that punctuated the reign of Elizabeth were the result of private investment marked with royal favor, as was the case with Drake's expedition to the coast of the Americas and Sir Walter Ralegh's attempts to establish permanent settlements in the new colony of Virginia. Disaster often ensued owing to lack of Crown funding, exacerbated by the need to keep the English fleet as close to home and to Spain as possible. More successful was the gradual expansion of English trade throughout the Mediterranean and eastern Europe, as well as the establishment in 1600 of the East India Company with the goal of displacing the Dutch as the prime players in the spice trade.

AFTER THE ARMADA: RELIGION AND POLITICS

The defeat of the Armada, because it appeared to signal divine sanction of a Protestant nation, had important repercussions both in the popular imagination and within Elizabeth's government. Her relations with her Puritan M.P.s had grown increasingly strained as they called for Mary's execution and punitive measures against all of the kingdom's Catholics. But many Puritans had actually been disgruntled for years, for although they accepted as a practical compromise Elizabeth's via media, they had never stopped seeking ways in which to warm up the Calvinist aspects of the state church. Among their concerns were certain traditions that were extra-biblical in nature and therefore not only unnecessary but positively distasteful: the infrequent mentions of predestination within the prayer book; the use of vestments; and the church's structure of archbishops and bishops, which robbed individual congregations of autonomy.

Elizabeth relied on her archbishop, John Whitgift, to break the back of what she saw as a radical Puritan movement that threatened the very stability of the church she had worked so hard to establish. Whitgift cleaned up a number of internal abuses that had angered many besides the most radical of the Puritans, but also reiterated that the state church was founded equally upon the prayer book and the episcopal structure of bishoprics and parishes. Conflict between Puritan M.P.s and the Crown continued, however, until the defeat of the Armada, which ironically served to diminish the Puritan voice within Parliament because it seemed to show that God had smiled upon Elizabeth's "middle way" rather than smiting those with moderate views. Puritans thereafter slowly began to represent themselves as voices of social and moral change rather than as agitators for political and ecclesiastical change.

This shift did not mean Elizabeth's government ran without opposition. Her reign was marked by increasingly vocal parliaments that had gained confidence through a confluence of factors. First, Henry's break from Rome had occurred through the careful use of parliamentary legislation, giving M.P.s in the House of Commons a strong sense that they were true if still unequal partners with the Crown. Second, as a group the M.P.s of the 1500s were highly educated, much more so than their predecessors. Many of them were well versed in the complexities of English law in a way that was new to the character of the House of Commons. Third, most members of the House of Commons, while still dependent upon good relations with their local nobles, were much less tightly bound economically and politically to the old aristocracy; this relative independence was translated into assertive debates within the chambers of Parliament. Fourth, a growing number of Puritan M.P.s translated their general sense of anticlericalism into a broader skepticism about authoritarianism generally. Elizabeth was correct in assuming that those who attacked the episcopal structure of the English church were implicitly attacking the royal supremacy and thus the full range of Crown authority. And finally, a deeply rooted period of inflation, economic depression, and pressures from local constituents persuaded many M.P.s to discuss, if not to reform, all manner of Crown economic policies.

These factors were not enough to encourage any kind of revolt or even organized opposition among M.P.s, but Elizabeth's parliaments were increasingly vocal about the rights and privileges they enjoyed within the chambers of Parliament. The House of Commons persisted in discussing matters that the queen felt were her prerogative alone, including the vexed question of her marriage, the royal succession, the royal supremacy of the church, foreign policy, and trade. Over the years the House of Commons established its right to debate these issues even while conceding that they had no power to directly influence them. Elizabeth herself continued to brook no interference in her refusal to wed or in her leadership of the church, and contented herself generally with managing her ministers through courtship, concessions, and oppression. One historian has compared her handling of her privy council in particular to that of a nanny managing her recalcitrant charges. Such a style depended upon a forceful and engaging personality, and Elizabeth inadvertently set the stage for some very difficult times for her less charismatic successor by relying so heavily on personal relationships with M.P.s, courtiers, and councilors. When Elizabeth died in 1603, that successor was James VI of Scotland, the son of her cousin Mary, Queen of Scots. Elizabeth had resisted almost to the last naming James as her heir, but finally agreed to the inevitable.

6

Stuart Britain, the Republic, and Restoration

THE EARLY STUARTS

James VI of Scotland became James I of England at the age of 35, having ruled Scotland since his infancy. Initially England welcomed the new king, but personal and political conflicts soon developed. James was shy, awkward, and fond of lecturing his ministers and subjects. His appointment of Scots to positions of power and influence alienated many Englishmen, and his open and ardent pursuit of a formal union of the two countries that would include a common church and a common Parliament alarmed observers on both sides of the border. Certain personal traits, including his sexual preferences, further alienated many of his courtiers, and his tendency to find and elevate beautiful young men as his personal favorites, showering them with positions of wealth and power no matter what their antecedents or abilities, provided a continuous source of friction between king and subjects.

Within the first year of his kingship, James had so alarmed his Parliament that the House of Commons drafted a document reiterating the important responsibilities and privileges enjoyed by this partner of the Crown. Although the document remained undelivered to the king, it indicated early on the Commons' sense that the new monarch lacked appropriate respect for the skills and duties of Parliament. Thus, the issue of power that would eventually lead to outright civil war began to emerge before the new reign was a year old. And although the vexed question of power and authority remained veiled during James's reign, it never fully disappeared. James consistently sought and used occasions to reinforce the powers of the Royal Prerogative in matters of trade, religion, and foreign policy—all of which Parliament itself increasingly regarded as matters for negotiation and discussion. Parliament issued several formal protests over the next several years attempting to force the Crown to recognize the rights of elected representatives to help shape policy. James also used his powers of patronage to enrich the Crown, creating the new title of baronet and selling baronetcies to commoners eager to buy their way onto the lowest rung of the aristocratic ladder. After James put much of the control of royal patronage into the hands of his favorite, George Villiers, the duke of Buckingham, other titles—including peerages that carried membership in the House of Lords—were also placed on the market. While this put money in the depleted royal coffers, it also angered many members of the traditional aristocracy and taught them to regard the new king as antagonistic to the blood and honor of the elite.

Despite these constant tensions, James ruled a stable kingdom, and one in which the first outposts of the empire crystallized through colonies in Virginia and expanded trade in the East Indies. His death in 1625 meant the crown passed to his younger son, Charles, who like Henry VIII had not been groomed to be king but had become the heir after the early death of an older brother. Charles I (1625–1649) shared with his father a complete and unshakeable belief in Divine Right kingship, and joined with this belief several unfortunate character traits, including a profound level of untrustworthiness. Even his wife, the French Catholic princess Henrietta Maria, admitted that her beloved husband was an inveterate liar.

This fundamental flaw made relations between king and Parliament much more tense than had been the case with the first Stuart. James had been the recipient of several formal attempts to force the Crown to recognize the rights and duties of Parliament in such things as trade duties and the negotiation of foreign policy. These issues, argued Parliament, concerned the Commonwealth and as such they should at least be matters for discussion within the House of Commons. James tended to ignore such arguments, reiterating the extensive powers of the Royal Prerogative and claiming that Parliament's rights of free speech within the chambers of the House of Commons were in reality extremely limited. Parliament's hands were relatively tied because James had been voted a life income at his succession and was theoretically free of money woes unless special circumstances arose, such as war, that required additional expenditures approved by Parliament. Because the Royal Prerogative covered trade, James could and did manipulate such things as excise taxes to supplement his treasury without having to go through Parliament.

When Charles came to power, however, Parliament refused to follow normal practice and instead voted the king an annual income that would have to be renewed, forcing Charles—at least in theory—to use his parliaments as true partners. Charles was enraged; and, far from bowing to this pressure, he began to look for ways to stretch the power of the prerogative to avoid what he felt was deliberate humiliation. But his early reign was marked by two wars, one with Spain and another with France, and the money required for armies and armaments forced him to ask for extra money bills to be passed.

In 1628 Parliament took the unusual step of presenting Charles with the Petition of Right, which sought to limit the powers of the prerogative, especially in regards to extra-parliamentary taxation such as excise duties, and to guarantee civil liberties at all times, including during times of war. Since England was still embroiled in wars with both Spain and France, this was a direct attack on Charles's actions. Charles signed it under duress, hoping that his acquiescence here would move Parliament to vote the extra taxes, called subsidies, that he needed to continue his wars on the Continent. But Parliament refused to do so until Charles had agreed to certain changes in the church, in particular a move away from the more ceremonial aspects of the church that had been introduced by Charles's archbishop, William Laud. Charles in his fury dissolved the House of Commons, whose members in their own fury refused to disband until they had passed resolutions regarding the church and certain financial matters. Charles was within his rights to do this; the House was absolutely out of bounds to continue to meet after being dissolved by the Crown; and this impasse was indicative of the growing hostility between king and Parliament.

THE PERSONAL RULE AND CIVIL WAR

Charles vowed to rule without Parliament, and did so for the 11 years known as the Personal Rule. In 1640, under pressure of another war, he finally reconvened this very same Parliament, with men who had been waiting at home, stewing, for over a decade. This does not mean that these M.P.s were already planning revolution, but they were generally incensed by the king's actions. Had not the two Henry Tudors placed great emphasis on the necessity of Parliament as a partner in government? Had not the complexities of religious settlements under the Tudor children required constant parliamentary action? How could this Stuart king simply ignore the precedents set during the previous 150 years? James had contributed to this situation of sullen resentment inadvertently, because his sale of honors had allowed many members of the House of Commons to buy their way up into the House of Lords, leaving the Commons without older leaders who might be able to dampen the independent spirit of this generation of M.P.s.

At the same time, there was no recognizable parliamentary "opposition," merely groups of men within the House who felt strongly about any number of issues, including religion and the protection of "ancient liberties" that appeared to be under attack by an innovative king. They would claim that they were protecting and conserving tradition, even as Charles would claim that they themselves were the radical innovators, trying to gain new powers for the legislature. Essentially, the tensions that would erupt into war came down to claims by each side that they were the conservers of ancient tradition, with Charles claiming primacy for the long history of the Royal Prerogative and his opponents arguing just as vehemently that his personal rule deliberately trampled over the rights and liberties of the freeborn Englishman that had been enshrined in the Magna Carta. These rights and liberties appeared to be under direct attack through the king's use of the prerogative courts (such as the Court of Star Chamber), the creative expansion of prerogative taxation (including levies such as Ship Money), and a renewed emphasis within the English church on a strong priesthood organized through an episcopal structure that bound church and state tightly together.

Charles would undoubtedly have continued to rule without Parliament except that arguments over religion eventually sparked a war within the kingdom. In 1636, Charles ordered the introduction of a new prayer book into Scotland, doing so via royal proclamation to bypass the inevitable protest of both the official Presbyterian Church and the General Assembly. In this, however, he gravely miscalculated; the imposition of the prayer book simply further alarmed many Scots who already worried that the informal union that existed between the two countries would soon be replaced by a formal union that would subjugate Scotland to full English rule.

In response, the Scots drafted a document called the National Covenant, which outlined Scottish opposition to Charles's policies. The Covenant went on a tour of the country before it was presented to Charles in 1638 with signatures from vast numbers of commoners, Presbyterian and Episcopalian alike. Charles suspended the mandatory use of the prayer book, but at the same time sent a small and ill-equipped army north to suppress dissent. The result was the First Bishops' War of 1639, a minor skirmish with the Scots as winners that set the stage for what was to come. Charles called his close advisor, the earl of Strafford, back from his administrative duties in Ireland in order to oversee the deployment of a new army. At the same time, he called upon both the English and the Irish parliaments to vote funds for a war against Scotland. The Irish parliament voted to raise the money; the English parliament, made up of men who had cooled their heels for nearly a dozen years, did not.

Instead, the English parliament prepared a list of grievances to present to Charles before they would even consider voting money for a war against another part of the kingdom. Charles in his turn dissolved Parliament—the so-called Short Parliament—a mere three weeks after it had been called, and sent another army north. The Second Bishops' War ended, like the first, with defeat at the hands of the Scots. The terms of the truce left Scots troops quartered in the north of England, and to pay for this expensive billeting, Charles once again called his M.P.s to Westminster, convening what would be known as the Long Parliament because it would formally sit from 1640 to 1653.

No M.P. seriously considered any kind of direct attack on Charles himself in 1640, instead impeaching his "evil councilors," Laud and Strafford. Once it had rid the country of these men, the House of Commons under the leadership of John Pym moved quickly to dismantle many of the instruments of Charles's personal rule. The prerogative courts were dissolved, extra-parliamentary taxes were ended, and laws were passed guaranteeing that Parliament could not be dissolved without its own consent and also that it would automatically be summoned every three years whether or not the Crown wished it to meet. Charles signed these and other acts legally preventing the monarch from ever again ruling without Parliament. Yet despite these important concessions, England found itself embroiled in civil war by 1642.

The spark to this war was another war within the kingdom, this time in Ireland. An uprising against the Protestant Crown, calling for toleration for the Catholic faith and an end to the political and economic disabilities imposed on Irish Catholics, posed a new set of problems for the government. Protestant M.P.s had little or no sympathy for the Irish Catholic resistance, viewing this uprising from a radically different perspective than that informing the Bishops' Wars in Scotland. The rebels should be quashed. But—and here was the key—if Parliament sanctioned the funds for an army to fight the Irish, what was to prevent the king from using this very army against the House of Commons?

Pym and his followers tried to get around this problem by drafting a bill that granted the money for an army but retained the appointment of army officers as a right of the Parliament, not the Crown. This was the first time anyone had even suggested that the defense of the realm should be taken away from the king and placed into the hands of the Commons. The narrow passage of the bill split Parliament into two recognizable camps. Pym's faction became strongly identified with the rights of Parliament, not only the ancient rights recognized by Charles in his assent to recent acts, but also new rights that gave Parliament the power of an equal in the government of the realm. The opposing faction argued that the Militia Bill robbed the Crown of its traditional powers of appointment, essentially turning the king into a figurehead. These men, soon to rally as royalists, did not defend Charles personally, and in fact were as suspicious as Pym's parliamentarians of Charles's motives and secret actions. But they saw this issue as a constitutional one, and strongly asserted the rights of the monarch to conduct the kingdom's defense and to appoint his own ministers and advisors. They wanted Parliament and king to rule as equal partners; the parliamentarians, according to this group, were seeking to eliminate the powers of the Crown altogether. The parliamentarians themselves codified their concerns in a November 1641 document called the Grand Remonstrance, which not only rehearsed the grievances against the king but also proposed major reductions in the powers of the Crown. On August 22, Charles raised his royal standard in Nottingham and civil war in England officially began.

The civil war was both political and religious, and split the country in a variety of ways. In 1642, when the war began, Charles commanded the loyalty of about 70 percent of his aristocracy and a slight majority of the gentry. Within the House of Commons, the split was 316 in support of Pym and 226 opposed. A number of royalists continued to mistrust the king, but chose to oppose the parliamentarians because they wanted to preserve the tradition of Crown and Parliament and the powers of a state church with its episcopal hierarchy. Most of the parliamentarians, in contrast, were of an older generation than the royalists, sharing a common experience of university education and law training in the 1630s that had grounded them in theories of governance emphasizing the traditions of shared power between Crown and Parliament. They argued vociferously that they were conserving the true government of the realm, and that the royalists were the radical innovators. Parliamentarians also tended to identify themselves as Puritan, many of whom were receptive to proposals to replace the episcopacy with a Presbyterian or even an independent Congregationalist structure of religion. Among these parliamentarians was Oliver Cromwell, who would soon emerge as the military commander of Parliament's New Model Army, and his son-in-law Henry Ireton.

At all times changes in both politics and religion were driven more by practical necessity than by pure ideological conviction. This was true from the very beginning, when the need for a military alliance between parliamentarians and Scots pushed even the most reluctant and moderate Puritans to vote to dismantle the episcopal hierarchy. In 1643 they passed the Solemn League and Covenant, a document that placated the Presbyterian Scots with its pledge to establish a new and "reformed" state church but also was deliberately vague in what that "reform" might be. Not until 1646, pushed again by necessity, was the episcopal structure of the English church formally destroyed and church property confiscated and sold to finance the ongoing war. Instead of a Presbyterian system, however, in 1648 England adopted an Established Congregational Church that was formally the state religion but that guaranteed toleration for other forms of religious worship, including, for the first time since 1290, the Jews.

In 1646 Charles surrendered to the Scots, who turned him over to the New Model Army after Charles agreed to certain changes in government and religion. During a failed attempt within the army to push for more radical social and political reforms, Charles escaped to the Isle of Wight and war resumed. This time, when Charles was defeated, Parliament was in the hands of independent Congregationalists, purged of all moderate and royalist influences in the episode known as Pride's Purge, which signified the transfer of power to one small group of the Long Parliament. This group, known as the Rump Parliament, was under the military leadership of Cromwell and Ireton.

The Rump Parliament very quickly began implementing radical policies and immediately placed the king on trial for treason. The arguments against Charles were novel: he was accused of treason against the land, of having taken up arms against the people, and of having violated the political trust through which he governed. His accusers argued further that Charles's life must be forfeit in order to cleanse the nation of his sins. Charles's defense responded that every action Charles had taken could be justified through precedent and through a full understanding of the Royal Prerogative. Further, they argued vehemently that the very court in which he was tried had no jurisdiction and was in fact illegal. The result was a foregone conclusion, although the votes both to convict and to execute were very narrow. Charles was sentenced to be beheaded for treason against the people, a sentence carried out on January 30, 1649. Only after his death was his office, the monarchy, abolished; Charles died as a king, tried and executed by his subjects. The House of Lords was abolished after the monarchy, leaving only the Rump of the Commons as a holdover from the traditional government of the realm.

THE PROTECTORATE AND MILITARY RULE

The Rump moved quickly to dismantle the monarchy, not only to legally eliminate Charles's two sons as heirs but also to take over Crown lands and replenish war-drained coffers. Oliver Cromwell, who already commanded great respect within his army, became the dominant member of the Council of State erected to govern the newly proclaimed republic. This Council worked with the Rump, still the sitting Parliament, to eliminate all vestiges of divine right monarchy and Episcopalian hierarchy and theology. At the same time, however, more radical groups were barred from power. New laws against blasphemy were joined to a new and extensive program of government censorship. Radical and even moderate groups, such as the Leveller faction within the New Model Army, were ruthlessly suppressed.

Cromwell and his army were kept extraordinarily busy during the first years of the Republic, quelling uprisings not only at home but also, more bloodily, in Ireland and in Scotland. Ireland had been a simmering cauldron for years, erupting in 1641 and then temporarily quieted, but the Puritan Cromwell and his fellow Council members were sure that a Catholic and royalist country was by its very nature a source of sin and sedition. By the summer of 1649 troops had moved across the Irish Sea to put down rebellion, killing hundreds of thousands in the process. Within three years Ireland had been emasculated, as Cromwell "awarded" appropriated Irish lands to his officers and fellows and imposed draconian measures upon Catholic peasants, setting the stage for centuries of trouble to come. Scotland too posed a serious threat; the Scots had already crowned Charles II as the King of Scotland and Cromwell's armies killed nearly 60,000 Scots before that country was subdued. By 1653, Scotland and Ireland were under English military control.

In 1654, after a failed attempt at a more godly administration via Cromwell's handpicked Parliament of Saints, a new constitution known as the Instrument of Government remodeled the executive branch of government once again. The Council of State would henceforth assist Cromwell, now Lord Protector; an elected single-chamber parliament would convene triennially; and England would be administered by 12 major-generals from Cromwell's army. This new government would be supported by a new property tax on all royalists. Money was desperately needed, for the proceeds from the sale of church lands had long since been spent, and England was now at war with both Catholic Spain and the Protestant Netherlands. England was moving into a new phase as a military regime—still a republic, still far from a democracy, holding control over Scotland and Ireland only through brutal military occupation, and with England itself now under the control of a standing army.

In 1657 the Council gave Cromwell the right to choose his successor. In September 1658, Cromwell died and his third son Richard became Protector. Richard, however, lacked even the backing of the military and within seven months had been forced by his father's armies to dissolve the government and reconvene the Rump Parliament, which had never been formally dissolved. The reconvened Rump, however, immediately locked horns with the army, and the army forced it to disband. The country toppled on the brink of anarchy: no parliament, no leader, no constitution, no tax collection, no judicial machinery, no faith in the law, no trade. Chaos reigned.

At this juncture the commander of the army in Scotland, General George Monck, gathered his troops and marched south to London, where he and his compatriots summoned the old Long Parliament—not the Rump, but the entire body of elected M.P.s who were still technically undismissed. Many had died and many were failing; of the 547 elected in 1640, only about half were able to come to Westminster. But when they convened, the first thing they did was to officially dissolve themselves, as they were bound to do under the act passed by Charles and before any new parliament could be called. New elections followed, under the supervision of the army to prevent fraud and coercion, and a strongly royalist group of men was elected to the new parliament.

Technically, since no king had called the body together, it was a convention rather than a parliament, and thus was known as the Convention Parliament. And this group of men, not only royalist but devoted as well to the former established church with its episcopal hierarchy, began the delicate process of negotiations with Charles's son, Charles II, who had been crowned King of Scotland before his exile on the Continent. They asked Charles II to make certain promises—they wanted him to settle the army's back pay, which was significant, to confirm all the land sales made during the protectorate, and to call new elections. Charles refused to make any promises; given the state of his kingdom, he held all the trump cards, and the Convention Parliament wearily agreed to restore him without conditions. And on May 25, 1660, he entered London amidst great cheering, without a drop of blood having been shed in the long 18 months since Cromwell's death.

THE RESTORATION

What would a restored monarchy do to reestablish stability and peace, and to secure the legitimacy of the throne? How much of the king's reign would be marked by a quest for vengeance? Charles was young, handsome, marked by years of exile; as a result of his difficult early life, he developed a deep streak of cynicism that left him canny, practical, flexible, and determined to enjoy his life as king. Known as "the Merry Monarch," he almost immediately set about to eradicate the Puritanism that he held responsible for his father's defeat. He had before his exile already pledged to support the Presbyterian state church in Scotland; now he moved to restore the church hierarchy in England. Puritans became known as Dissenters, signifying not a purer form of religious belief and piety but rather potentially dangerous disagreement with the state religion and thus with the state itself. And dissent was contained and punished through a number of laws. The Corporation Act of 1661 excluded Dissenters from local political office; the Act of Uniformity of 1662 penalized ministers unwilling to swear an oath to uphold the entire contents of the *Book of Common Prayer;* the Conventicle Act of 1664 imposed harsh punishments—including but not limited to stiff fines—upon those who attended dissenting meetings. Much of the early force of the Conventicle Act was turned upon Quakers, who suffered terribly in the 1660s, but all forms of religious Puritanism were vulnerable.

Charles also used other, extralegal means to ostracize Dissenters, setting a tone of decadence within his court and encouraging extravagant behavior among his aristocracy in a clear message to Puritans that the days of self-denial were over—at least among the wealthy. Charles himself became notorious for his many mistresses and the veritable stable of illegitimate children he sired, even as his pious and reserved wife, Catherine of Braganza, failed to produce any royal heirs. He also rescinded laws against theaters and other public entertainment, ushering in a period marked by wit, eroticism, and excess. Necklines plunged, condoms were available on the open market, Sundays became days of enjoyment and self-indulgence rather than strict observance of the Sabbath. Much of this remained within the capital, but even outside London many formerly Puritan parishes began to relax their Sabbatarianism as new parish priests came to fill their pulpits. Even the 1665–1666 outbreak of plague and the Great Fire of London in 1666 did not restore the harsh piety of Cromwell's Rule of the Saints.

While many of his subjects welcomed or at least tolerated the relaxing of Puritan standards, and were happy to see the reintroduction of an episcopal hierarchy, Charles's apparent toleration for Catholicism was not so easily swallowed. Charles had been raised in France by a Catholic mother and her Catholic family, and he had married a Catholic wife. The unshakeable belief in the minds of many in his kingdom, that Catholicism was inextricably linked to political absolutism, was underscored by Charles's clear affection for the French royal family. And although certain aspects of the Royal Prerogative had been abolished by his father, Charles still enjoyed broad powers of independent action, especially regarding foreign policy.

In 1670 Charles negotiated the Treaty of Dover, which pledged England and France to come to one another's aid in time of war. In 1672 France and the Netherlands entered into the Third Dutch War and England, honoring the Treaty of Dover, joined France. Charles immediately put into effect secret clauses of the treaty, using his prerogative powers to suspend penal laws against Catholics. A furious Parliament was powerless until 1673, when Charles was forced to ask for more war funds. Parliament responded by passing the Test Act of 1673, requiring that all M.P.s and government officers be observant Anglicans and swear an oath of allegiance to the king as the supreme head of the Church of England. The act, which extended the clauses of the 1661 Corporation Act that had targeted local government officials in a similar way, forced out of office several of Charles's closest advisors, including his own brother James, who was Lord Admiral of the British Navy. Despite this concession, by 1674 Charles was forced to withdraw from the war.

Shortly thereafter, to placate his Protestant subjects, he arranged the betrothal of his niece Mary, the daughter of his brother James, to the Protestant William of Orange. This did not signify any lessening of Charles's affection for Catholic France, but was instead a practical, if only partially successful, move to help alleviate some of the pressures of anti-Catholicism already gripping the country. Much of this pressure was directed at Charles's younger brother and heir, James, who had converted to Catholicism years before. In the Popish Plot of 1678 he was named—along with a number of high-ranking men, his wife, and Charles's own wife, Catherine of Braganza—as the centerpiece of a purported plot by the Jesuits and the French to kill the sitting king and elevate James in his stead.

In the midst of this fever of anti-Catholicism, Anthony Cooper, the earl of Shaftesbury and a longtime member of Charles' government, introduced a bill in 1679 to formally exclude James from inheriting the throne. Shaftesbury had spent a number of years shaping a group of men who would eventually become the formal Whig party. Anti-Catholic and anti-French, they tended to vote together in the House of Commons as a block, although true party organization was still far away. Beginning in 1679, this group pushed for a formal Exclusion Bill that would remove the threat of a Catholic king. The so-called Exclusion Crisis resulted in Charles simply proroguing Parliament. The Long Parliament had passed laws mandating that it be called triennially, but had not anticipated that a king would call a parliament but then refuse to allow members to assemble.

Charles had calculated correctly that even the most energetic of the Whigs did not want civil war. At the same time, he began to use the ancient powers of quo warranto—literally, "by what warrant"—to oust Whigs from local power and to place royalists—now the Tory party—in their place. By 1685, when Charles lay on his deathbed, he could rest assured that he had done all within his power to hand to his brother a realm securely in the control of Tories.

Despite this careful staging, James was forced to abdicate within four years of his ascendancy. Much of this was due to personality. Whereas Charles had been intelligent, witty, and lazy, his brother was slow, hardworking, and dour; further, he viewed any divergence of opinion as outright rebellion and selected his advisors accordingly. And whereas Charles had waited until the moments before his death to openly convert to Catholicism, James had embraced the faith years earlier, and had taken as his second wife a devout Catholic, Mary of Modena.

Initially, however, his subjects welcomed him. An abortive uprising to replace James with Charles's illegitimate son, the duke of Monmouth, was viciously put down, and James's first parliament was overwhelmingly Tory, ready to support their king in anything so long as it was not pro-France or pro-Vatican. But James moved quickly to bring his fellow Catholics back into the mainstream of British life through a widespread program of "romanization." This program included suspending the Test Act, establishing a new church court aimed at Protestants, founding the Catholic Magdalen College at Oxford University, and replacing Tories with Whigs and Dissenters, whom he calculated would be more receptive to changes in the state church.

In all of this James seriously miscalculated. Even as he acted to antagonize the Tories, who should have been his natural supporters, his son-in-law was being courted as a potential "invader" who could save the country from its king. William of Orange regarded the British Crown as a tool for his greater project of containing a hungry France, which had been at war with the Dutch intermittently for decades. But it was not a serious part of his military plans until James and his wife, Mary of Modena, did the unthinkable and produced a male, and Catholic, heir.

The baby's birth galvanized both Whigs and Tories, many of whom agreed that invasion by an invited Protestant leader was a much more attractive option than an apparently inevitable civil war. They extended their invitation to William on the same day that James lost an important court case against seven Anglican bishops who had refused to acquiesce in his romanization campaign. Many of these men used the work of John Locke to justify their decision, arguing that James had failed to fulfill his obligations as ruler and had forced them, the sovereign people, to form a new government. Locke's works would be published in the following year as the *Two Treatises of Government,* but they had been circulating among Shaftesbury's supporters since the early 1680s and the Exclusion Crisis.

William answered the call and invaded on November 1, 1688, under a banner that read, "For the restoration of the constitution and the true religion in England, Scotland, and Ireland." James was appalled, unable to rally his own troops, and faced with a series of bloodless coups as one city after another joined the rebels. By mid-December he was forced to open negotiations, but William's proposals were so purposely outrageous that James was both disgusted and defeated. He bundled his wife and son off to France and followed soon after, tossing the Great Seal of the government into the river Thames as he went.

This nearly bloodless revolution, almost immediately called the Glorious Revolution, was not concluded until William and Mary had actually accepted the crown. William refused to act as consort or, as he put it, "gentleman usher," demanding instead that he and his wife rule jointly as equals. Further, he demanded new elections before the coronation, so that he could receive the crown from a duly elected body—another convention parliament, since it had not been summoned by a sitting king. This convention drafted a Declaration of Rights, presenting it along with the crown to William and Mary as co-monarchs. William and Mary, in accepting the crown, took a coronation oath that differed significantly from the oath used before 1689; previous rulers had sworn to confirm the laws and customs granted by the crown, but beginning in 1689 all rulers had to swear to govern by the laws of Parliament. It was an important shift in the location of power, and the mutual relationships of Crown, Parliament, and law: the model of king-in-parliament was now firmly and irrevocably established. Infrequent attempts by James's son and grandson to regain the throne would fail to gather much support within Britain.

The Declaration of Rights became the Bill of Rights, and among the provisions guaranteeing the ancient rights and liberties of the subject were clauses preventing any future monarch from adhering to the Roman Catholic faith or from taking a Catholic spouse. Other provisions outlawed the prerogative powers of dispensing and suspending laws; outlawed a standing army in peacetime; reaffirmed the Triennial Act and added clauses that made it impossible for the Crown to manipulate the process of calling and dismissing Parliament; and confirmed the rights that had by now come to be regarded as "ancient liberties." The Act of Settlement in 1701 further cemented the idea that Parliament was a true partner in governance, when Parliament itself determined that the crown would pass from the childless and widowed William (Mary died in 1694) to Mary's sister Anne, and through Anne's heirs to the House of Hanover, a distant branch of the family, bypassing altogether the exiled Stuarts. William agreed to this act and to others that reiterated the need for a parliament that met almost continuously in the period of constant war that ran well into the eighteenth century.

7

Hanoverian Britain: War and Industry

A FOUR-MEMBER KINGDOM

Eighteenth-century Britain—indeed, the entire period beginning with the end of the Glorious Revolution and lasting through the Napoleonic Wars—was a time of chronic warfare, imperial expansion and loss, technological and economic innovation, and a shift in the basic structures of society. From William III and Mary, through Mary's sister Anne and on through the four Hanoverian Georges and William IV, rulers after the Glorious Revolution presided over a kingdom made up of four distinct entities. In addition to England there was Wales, which had been conquered in 1283 and which under two Acts of Parliament in 1536 and 1542/43 had been formally "incorporated, united and annexed" to England and empowered to send M.P.s to Westminster. English was made the formal language of the land and the law. Scotland was united to England in a 1707 Act of Union that formally established the United Kingdom of Great Britain (the United Kingdom of Great Britain and Ireland would not be established until 1801). The act dissolved a separate Scottish parliament—45 Scottish M.P.s were instead elected to the Parliament in Westminster—but preserved the Scottish Presbyterian Church as the state church and retained the separate Scottish legal system. Ireland retained its anomalous

position, enhanced under Cromwell and the Restoration Stuarts, acknowledging the English Crown as the highest ruling authority but only held
as part of the English kingdom through force and under duress. Irish
Catholics were prevented from bearing arms, holding public office, or
sitting in the separate Irish parliament that met until 1801; they were also
forced to support the Protestant Church of Ireland and could not inherit
property from Protestants.

WAR AND INTERNATIONAL COMPETITION

This multi-part Britain was the heart of an international empire increasing in size and importance. The North American colonies that would
break away in 1776 were well established by William III's reign, as were
settlements in other parts of the globe: colonies in the West Indies by 1700
included Antigua, Barbados, and the Bahamas, while the first settlers arrived in Australia in 1788 and settlements had begun in parts of coastal
Africa nearly a century earlier. Where settlements did not yet exist, economic temptations attracted English privateers, especially in Central and
South America. The British Empire was nowhere near its pinnacle, but
those portions of the map shaded red were already increasing in number
and they brought with them new responsibilities and worries for the
Crown.

William also brought with him as king a deep concern about his continental holdings, and his various ministers and parliaments were forced
to consider political issues from a European, rather than a strictly British,
point of view. Much of this involved chronic wars on the Continent with
both Spain and France. These wars had begun before 1688 and continued
for decades, punctuated by brief intervals of peace, until 1815. The War
of the League of Augsburg (1689–1697) concluded with an indecisive
treaty. The War of the Spanish Succession (1702–1713) ended with the
Peace of Utrecht, in which Britain gained Gibraltar and Minorca from
Spain and Nova Scotia, the remainder of Newfoundland, and Hudson's
Bay from France, deepening claims to control over large parts of North
America. This war also cemented British claims as the major sea power
in Europe. The subsequent peace was tense, however, because lack of
declared war simply masked chronic rivalries, particularly in India where
the British East India Company deliberately intervened in the local political struggles of the native states in a successful effort to maintain control over an increasingly lucrative source of trade. War in India was
averted but imperial hunger became a driving force as France and England struggled to claim and maintain international supremacy.

War broke out again formally in 1739, this time with Spain. In 1731 a Captain Robert Jenkins reported atrocities committed by the Spanish Coast Guard on himself and his crew, including the severing of one of his ears, touching off popular agitation against Spain. Parliament eventually pressured for war to prevent Spain from forming an alliance with France. Prime Minister Robert Walpole finally capitulated in 1739, and war was declared against Spain. In the context of complex rivalries on the Continent, however, this war too became a war against France, and this war too became a war for control across the ocean. The War of Jenkins's Ear shaded into the War of the Austrian Succession (1740–1748), involving every major power in Europe, costing England alone 80 million pounds, and ending with almost no significant changes in the world map. Britain itself gained nothing new.

This peace was also brief. For nine years outright warfare was avoided, but 1757 saw the outbreak of the Seven Years' War (1757–1762). For Britain, the main opponent was France once again; this time, the main theater of war was in North America, although the trade rivalry on the Indian subcontinent continued to resemble outright political struggle as both the East India Company and French traders seized control of local ruling families and demanded increasing levels of men and weapons from home. Over the course of the war, the British vanquished the French in India where the British presence, although still technically devoted solely to commerce, had developed into a full-scale ruling presence. In North America, British troops were also successful in wresting control from the French, and in the West Indies a series of battles gained the French islands of Dominica, Martinique, Guadeloupe, and St. Lucia for the British Crown. The Peace of Paris, signed in 1763, awarded to Britain the entirety of French holdings in North America except for Louisiana and a portion of Newfoundland, while France regained control of its former West Indies holdings and returned to India in a diminished presence. Britain gained recognition as the largest imperial power in Europe, commanding superior sea forces and controlling vast trading relationships.

CROWN AND GOVERNMENT

The year 1763 thus signaled the end to nearly a century of war, much of it pitting Britain against France. It was an expensive century, and as such it required almost constant parliamentary action to vote extra taxes and to levy new forms of taxation. This in itself required a close relationship between Crown and legislature, a relationship cemented by the constant drift of royal attention to the Continent. William III focused on his

Dutch holdings, while the Hanoverian kings who succeeded after the death of Queen Anne (1702–1714), the last of the Stuarts, were at least as preoccupied with their Hanoverian interests as they were with their new, and to them foreign, British kingdoms. Indeed, the first two Hanoverian kings, George I (1714–1727) and George II (1727–1760) regarded themselves as German first and English a far second, never even bothering to consider the other portions of their British kingdom as forming a part of their own national character. Indeed, George I did not bother to learn the language of his English subjects. Not surprisingly, the result in Britain was the strengthening of ministerial power as the two rival political parties, Tory and Whig, vied for royal favor and strove to control the riches of patronage and the perquisites of power. Ministerial success rested on managing the Crown but also upon managing Parliament, while Parliament in its turn was indispensable in a century of war through its powers of the purse.

Under this system of increased royal dependence upon ministers and Parliament, oligarchic government became a fact of political life. And for much of the century, that oligarchy was controlled by the Whig party, although Anne herself favored the Tories. Indeed, George I took the throne with the full knowledge that he owed his position to the support of both the Whigs and the small number of Tories who had acquiesced in the Act of Settlement of 1701. Despite the virtual lock on power enjoyed by the Whigs, however, which by the end of William's reign was led by a group of ministers known as the Junto, the reality of eighteenth-century politics forced the Whigs not only to work with the Tories but also to operate under the knowledge that very significant power continued to reside in the Crown. Certain royal powers fell into disuse; Anne, for instance, was the last ruler to use the royal veto. But while the Crown might have to swear a coronation oath to uphold the laws of the country and of Parliament rather than to rule as he or she saw fit, the monarch still maintained crucial control over the ministry through the powers of appointment and dismissal.

Oligarchic government was itself dependent upon the leadership of shrewd men in these appointed offices, and so the balance between Crown, ministers, and Parliament endured. The most powerful of these appointed ministers under the Hanovers were Henry Pelham, the two William Pitts—father and son—and, above all, Robert Walpole. Walpole came to power during the economic crisis known as the South Sea Bubble, an episode in 1720 that involved the private South Sea Company's plan to finance a majority of the country's debts. Massive stock speculation and the consequent collapse of the company led Walpole, untainted by any personal relationship to the directors, to transfer much of the stock to the Bank of England and the East India Company, thus averting a national economic disaster. Walpole became Chancellor of the Exchequer and First Lord of the Treasury in 1721, in which latter capacity he introduced new excise taxes to finance the wars with France.

Walpole's excise taxes served another purpose as well: they brought more men into the government to collect these taxes. And the use of these so-called placemen, who owed their positions to the patronage of the various members of the government, was an important characteristic of Hanoverian society. Walpole, like many others, believed that patronage created men with a vested interest in the prosperity of the nation, contributing to the public good and also, not unimportantly, casting appropriate votes when it came time to elect members of Parliament. Patronage was the glue that held the system together, and Walpole's use of patronage even in such areas as devising new schemes of taxation was part of his ministerial genius. Those who paid these taxes were less impressed than the tax collectors who lined their own pockets. Indeed, Walpole and his fellow ministers were transformed into patriarchs of the criminal underclasses in John Gay's *The Beggar's Opera* (1728), as corruption and influence were portrayed as theft and deceit. But the system of finance served the government well, even as it provided grounds for grousing and annoyance that would eventually swell into outright antagonism.

The machinery of government was in place to serve the king, protect the nation, maintain order, and raise money to carry out these tasks effectively and efficiently. Stability, not change, was the goal; war abroad might be a fact of life, and so it was, but rebellion at home was not to be tolerated. Thus, for example, the Jacobite risings of 1715 and 1745, to restore the heirs of James II to the British throne, were put down with rapid and brutal force. One result of these episodes was a tradition of hatred and resentment for the English among the Scottish Highlanders who had been the Stuarts' strongest supporters.

By the accession of George III (1760–1820), the threat of Jacobitism had faded. George himself both represented a new type of king and stimulated certain changes in the monarchy. He was the first of the Hanover line to be born in England, and he took a lively and intelligent interest in questions of constitution, law, and foreign policy. Further, his attitude toward the duties of the Crown and the dignity of the throne were characterized by a profound sense of duty. In this he differed widely from his grandfather, George II.

Despite his personal convictions, however, George's reign was subject to critical public scrutiny, which often took the form of attacks on the king's character and ability. For example, the radical John Wilkes, elected to Parliament in 1757, published scurrilous reports of government mismanagement in his paper, *The North Briton,* and went so far as to call the 1763 Treaty of Paris a dishonorable end to the war with France. Wilkes was a stirring orator despite his personal misbehaviors, which were legion; his continuous critiques of the government were enshrined in the slogan, "Wilkes and Liberty," which echoed throughout London during Wilkes's various trials for libel. Another, similar thorn in George's side was the Yorkshire clergyman Christopher Wyvill, who focused on the corruption endemic in the system of political patronage and organized a strong campaign for parliamentary and ministerial reforms that won the support of the landed gentry.

George's constant attempts to micromanage his parliaments were equally distasteful to Whigs and Tories alike, coming to a head in 1783 when he made it known that anyone who supported the India Bill, designed to reconfigure the East India Company, would be regarded as a personal enemy of the Crown. Not until his later years did he enjoy good relations with his parliaments, largely owing to the skills of William Pitt the Elder (later the earl of Chatham). Pitt came to power after the loss of the North American colonies in a protracted war from 1776 to 1781, serving after 1783 as prime minister. The loss of this large portion of the British Empire was a terrible blow to George, who had taken the throne determined to uphold and extend imperial domination.

George's unfortunate illnesses, interpreted as "madness" although almost certainly caused by the metabolic disorder porphyria, formed the main portion of his legacy in popular memory. An initial attack in 1788 prompted the Regency Crisis, in which the Prince Regent prepared to assume control. He was widely expected to dismiss Pitt and others of his father's ministry, but George recovered after four months of illness and continued to wield power until he became completely incapacitated in 1810. It was at this juncture that the Prince Regent came to power, bringing with him a history of dissolute behavior and chronic debt. A weakness for women and alcohol were matched by a love of luxury and personal indiscretion, all of which were extremely distasteful to his morally upright parents. In 1795 the king forced his son—whose earlier marriage to a Catholic widow was valid in the eyes of the church but illegal under law—to marry Princess Caroline of Brunswick in exchange for the payment of massive debts. The marriage was a private disaster and became a public relations debacle when the Prince Regent took the throne as George IV in 1820. Caroline, who had remained on the Continent for much of her marriage, arrived at Westminster for the coronation only to have the doors shut in her face. Her cause was championed both by the popular press and by the king's opponents. Even after her sudden death in 1821, the damage to the personal reputation of the king lived on. George's inability to negotiate with his ministers, as well as his lack of political finesse, further strengthened ministries and parliaments at the expense of the Crown, and his personal life provided no counterbalance. Only his love of pageantry and the arts could be regarded as positive royal attributes, and these were not enough to win widespread affection.

Many blamed the king for allowing the repeal of the Test and Corporation Acts in 1828, permitting non-Anglican Christians for the first time to hold political office, as well as for the passage of the 1829 Catholic Emancipation Act. George himself vociferously opposed especially the latter, but the successes of Irish lawyer Daniel O'Connell and his primarily middle-class Catholic Association convinced Tories Wellington and Peel to force this measure through a Tory-controlled House of Commons. Many traditional Tories regarded this as the end of the world as they knew it, and the success of the Whigs the following year cemented their conviction that church and king were no longer two necessary halves of a whole.

George himself was deeply distressed at this evidence that the Crown had apparently lost any power to influence parliamentary action. His brother and heir, William IV (1830–1837), did nothing to stop the current of power that was moving very slowly away from the Crown and toward the House of Commons. Instead, he reinforced the royal family's reputation for unorthodox living, celebrating his coronation by conferring titles on all 10 of his illegitimate children. It would be years before the Commons could justifiably argue that it was the primary source of governmental power, but under the Hanoverian kings the circumstances that would lead to this argument began to take shape. William's primary and self-proclaimed goal in his waning years was to live long enough to prevent his hated sister-in-law, Princess Victoria of Leiningen, from gaining control when his niece, the young Princess Victoria, inherited the throne. In this he was successful, dying a month after Victoria reached her eighteenth birthday.

SOCIETY AND RELIGION

Despite this slow shift in the location of political power, Georgian society as a whole remained relatively stable. Just as the wheels of government moved smoothly only through the linked notions of patronage and place, everyday life was also dependent on mutual relationships. In this case, a society of many "orders" of men and women was glued together through the twin notions of deference to those above and obligation to those below. Ideally, this hierarchy was multilayered enough to accommodate growth and the changes inherent in a world of expanding imperial responsibilities, but flexible enough to absorb such changes without recourse to bloodshed. The civil and religious wars of the 1640s were still an acute and painful memory to many, and as a result there was a deliberate lowering of the temperature of both politics and religion as leaders sought to avoid the conflagrations of the previous century. In politics, this was manifested in oligarchic government and the system of patronage, as well as in an almost ridiculous toleration for the abuses they encouraged; corruption in and of itself, if it did not endanger the Crown or the ministry, flourished.

In religion, this focus on stability was reflected in a church that emphasized "reasonableness" but inadvertently cultivated religious indifference. Officially, this approach to religion was known as latitudinarianism, a descriptor designed to signal that the eighteenth-century church was self-consciously more accommodating than its seventeenth-century predecessor. Theologically, the Anglican Church continued to hold to the 39 Articles of the Prayer Book, including the article on predestination, but practically the church began to emphasize the importance of man's own reason and common sense to salvation. Toleration within this broader view was considered a key to the stability of the realm. And this latitudinarian church also pulled back from its former emphasis on the theological errors of Dissenters, purposely trying to create an atmosphere that did not create willing martyrs. It was an approach that worked: the number of Dissenters as a proportion of the overall population shrank very rapidly, due in part to what one dissenting minister called "the lenity of the government, the want of a persecution to keep us together."[1] Those Dissenters who remained were eventually renamed Nonconformists, a less pejorative label that covered a variety of religious beliefs.

This emphasis on stability and peace rather than theological certitude meant in practice that religious enthusiasm of any kind was discouraged. But the resulting moral sleepiness led to a search for more personal forms of religious expression and meaningful piety, a search that was met within the Anglican Church by the development of Wesleyanism among the lower orders and Evangelicalism among the higher. John Wesley's emphasis on a personal sense of conversion and salvation, communicated through open-air meetings throughout the kingdom, combined an emotional faith with a conservative emphasis on social stability. His followers were exhorted to live a godly life in the station to which God had called them, no matter how lowly and full of suffering.

For their part the Evangelicals, whose numbers included Hannah More and William Wilberforce of the Clapham Sect, focused their personal and rigorous piety upon the ungodly behavior of those in the higher stations, from the "middling orders" up through the kingdom's aristocracy. They had plenty to work with, as a growing commercial class embraced conspicuous consumption and spent enormous amounts on luxury goods. The complacency of the well-to-do, especially when matched with the corruption of public officials, had already provided fodder for writers and artists from William Hogarth (1697–1764)—most famous for such engravings as *Marriage a la Mode* and *Rake's Progress*—to John Gay (1685–1732; *The Beggar's Opera* appeared in 1728) and Alexander Pope (1688–1744; *The Rape of the Lock* was published in 1712). The Evangelicals were more sober but just as vigorous in their critiques. Further, they tended to cast their nets widely; among other successes, they persuaded Parliament to end the slave trade in 1807, nearly a century after England had won the sole right to supply slaves to Spanish South America. Further efforts ended slavery itself in the British Empire in 1833.

Like the Wesleyan movement, which broke away to form a separate denomination of Methodists only after Wesley's death, the Evangelical movement emphasized personal faith and the necessity of moral behavior in every aspect of life, including work and business where fair dealing was taken as an indicator of good stewardship. Both movements remained socially conservative despite the potentially democratic tendencies of the faith: a focus on the world to come helped defuse the dangerously subversive possibilities entwined in the twin emphases on individual morality and the equality of all believers—male and female, rich and poor— before God.

INDUSTRY AND URBANIZATION

The hierarchical nature of eighteenth-century society worked so long as there were many layered orders. With the advent of the Industrial Revolution, however, Britain began the painful shift to a society organized around three classes. Historian E. P. Thompson famously defined a class society as one in which interests of a given class were both "different from and opposed to" the interests of any other class, thus injecting an inescapable note of conflict into society.[2] And although social conflict had not been absent from the hierarchical society of the pre-industrial period—

laws protecting the rights of the aristocracy and gentry to hunt, for example, were outrageously punitive toward both poachers and the small farmers whose crops might be trampled by horses and hounds, while the aristocracy and broadening middle classes of the Georgian period were both mocked and aped by their social inferiors, by novelists and dramatists, and by observers on the Continent—the transition to an industrial urban society introduced new sources of antagonism that periodically erupted into new types of conflict.

This transition would also form the basis of Britain's status as an industrial leader. England was the first country to industrialize—Wales and Ireland and much of Scotland remained rural long beyond the growth of England's industrial urban centers—and as such both reaped significant rewards and paid tremendous costs. England in the middle of the 1700s enjoyed conditions that would favor a move to industry: peace at home and a consequent climate of confidence that encouraged both inventors and investors; an infrastructure of canals and roads that made movement within England relatively easy; and surplus labor in the countryside that was not tied to the land and could thus migrate to new cities. King Cotton propelled England into the industrial era, with raw cotton coming in from the colonies in the West Indies, India, and the southern colonies of North America, and finished goods going back out to the same captive markets. Cotton transformed towns in the north of England into industrial centers. During the same period, roughly the last third of the eighteenth century, there were equally transformative innovations in steam power and in cheaper, stronger iron products. (For some, these innovations were too transformative: former Board of Trade president William Huskisson, posthumously dubbed the unluckiest man in the world, stepped in front of the inaugural Liverpool-to-Manchester train at the opening ceremony in 1830 and was run over.)

Industrialization and the growth of urban areas changed the English world in immediate and often very negative ways, just as they also wrought larger and more subtle changes on Britain as a whole. In the decades between 1760 and 1830, huge numbers of workers migrated into new cities that were unable to provide adequate housing and hygiene. Between 1801 and 1831, London grew from under 100,000 persons to 1,656,000; Manchester from 89,000 to 223,000; Liverpool and Birmingham in similar ways. Further north, the population of Edinburgh nearly doubled and that of Glasgow nearly tripled. And these new urban dwellers swelled the ranks of industry; the percent of the population in "manufacture, mining, and industry" grew from 29.7 percent in 1801 to 40.8 percent 30 years later. Attempts to regulate the movement of this new labor pool, and to reduce the costs of supporting the unemployed, led to the New Poor Law of 1834, which tied poor relief to the workhouse through a system designed to repel all but the truly desperate.

Although there were multiple gradations of skill and expectation within this new population, many observers collapsed them into a single, unitary, and incendiary working class. Friedrich Engels (1820–1895), more famous perhaps for his later collaboration with Karl Marx, wrote a scathing exposé of Manchester in his *Condition of the Working Classes in England* (1844); his descriptions of slum housing, working families made up of emasculated husbands and unwomanly wives, factory discipline, and incipient revolution frightened the new middle class, that vast portion of men and women who were themselves working without a road map. They looked in turn to political economists like Adam Smith (1723–1790), Thomas Malthus (1766–1834), and David Ricardo (1772–1823) for "natural" and thus unchangeable laws governing industrial organization, population, and wages; they found in philosophers like Jeremy Bentham (1748–1832) and other Utilitarians justifications for change that would recognize their economic powers and reward their collective virtues of thrift, duty, and hard work. By mid-century, they would find in Charles Dickens (1812–1870), Elizabeth Gaskell (1810–1865), and other authors of "social problem" novels expressions of deep concern about the difficulty of reconciling economic gain with human suffering.

POLITICAL ACTIVISM: MIDDLE-CLASS AND WORKING-CLASS RADICALISM

Like the working class, the middle class contained widely divergent interests and incomes, but a common sense of anxiety, as well as a deeply held belief in progress, bound this vast middle together into a lengthy struggle for social respect and political recognition. Political recognition came through several movements that initially linked the interests of the industrious and virtuous working and middle classes against the interests of an effete and idle landed class. Such propaganda was most vituperative in the work of the Anti-Corn Law League, which worked to return M.P.s who supported free trade and who would labor to eliminate the tariffs on grain. Such tariffs, they argued, protected the great aristocratic landholders by keeping prices for domestic grain artificially high and harmed the rest of the population by inflating the price of bread. The League was formed in Manchester in 1838 and became a national force in 1839, but success in abolishing the Corn Laws didn't come until 1846, after the Irish potato famine made the importation of cheap grain imperative.

A similar conjunction of class interests propelled the agitation for the Whig-sponsored Reform Act of 1832, which enfranchised large numbers of the middle classes who had spent so much time and energy establishing their worthiness and indispensability to the nation. The vote was given to those adult male tenants who paid annual property taxes of at least £10 in urban areas and, in rural areas, annual property taxes of at least 40s. or annual rent of £50. The franchise expanded dramatically in Scotland (from 4,500 to 65,000 eligible voters); nearly doubled in Ireland (from 49,000 to 90,000); and included an estimated 400,000 to 600,000 new voters in England and Wales.[3] Towns like Birmingham and Manchester, whose populations had skyrocketed in the previous decades, were finally allocated parliamentary representatives, and attempts were made to eliminate the worst abuses of so-called "pocket boroughs" (boroughs in the "back pocket" of a single family who chose the representative to be elected) and "rotten boroughs" (districts with no qualifying voters but which still returned members; the most notorious of these, Old Sarum, had been empty since 1220). While these reforms alarmed many conservatives who feared that leaseholders could not possibly have the same kind of abiding interest in proper government as actual landowners, and satisfied the moderates who had lobbied for a relatively limited set of changes, they enraged many in the working classes who had joined with middle-class radicals to work for reform. As we will see in the following chapter, many of the political reforms they had sought were enshrined in the Chartist movement of the late 1830s and 1840s.

Working-class radicalism prior to the Chartist movement took a number of forms, both social and political. For example, the decades after trade unions were outlawed by the Combination Acts of 1799 and 1800 witnessed machine-breaking by the elusive Luddites, who used violence to try to coerce employers to address economic and social grievances in a period of trade depression. Similarly, radical agitation drove much of the popular support for George's ill-fated Queen Caroline, as well as such extreme episodes as the Cato Street Conspiracy (in which a former army officer led an 1820 attempt to assassinate many of the ministers in Lord Liverpool's Cabinet) and the Peterloo massacres (where a huge open-air meeting outside of Manchester in 1819 to hear orator Henry Hunt was broken up by force, resulting in 11 deaths and hundreds of injuries). The government's response to such agitation included the Six Acts of 1819, which outlawed large meetings, increased the government's powers of repression, and tightened up regulations on newspapers and pamphlets. Despite these acts, a radical press flourished in the early nineteenth century, pressing for an end to censorship and the so-called "Taxes on Knowledge" and providing constant if illegal critiques of governmental policies.

Political radicalism provided one focus for the formation of working-class identity. Various clubs and societies, including friendly societies, self-improvement societies, and sick and burial clubs, provided another. The Combination Acts had not banned these mutual aid organizations, and in the years after 1799, these clubs and societies evolved into a significant feature of working-class culture. After 1824, when the Combination Acts were struck down, trade unions began to legally reemerge and to reclaim their importance in the lives of skilled workingmen. These unions tended to be localized, well-organized, and often—like the friendly societies that continued to exist alongside them—centered around the pub as a meeting place where business and conviviality could co-exist. Most of these early unions avoided the strike as far as possible, instead using collective bargaining to secure wage and hour guarantees. And most of these early unions refused entry to the unskilled, instead limiting membership to the educated and skilled artisans referred to collectively by historians as the "labor aristocracy." In 1834 to 1835, the Grand National Consolidated Trade Union emerged as the first attempt to coordinate unions across the country, but failed within a year owing to lack of funding.

Trade unions could not, however, speak to the broad working-class experience outside the factory or workshop. Like the middle class, the "working class" was neither unitary nor cohesive. Differences in education, skill, work experience, and family structure merely heightened the already profound separations dividing urban and rural workers. Women and children were necessary to both agricultural and factory life, but the problems specific to their work experiences tended to be overwhelmed by the more articulate agendas of male workers. Domestic service employed the vast majority of women, and this segment of the workforce—especially those servants in small households where back-breaking overwork was the norm—remained particularly underrepresented and in fact ignored by those seeking legal protection for other workers. Most early laws protecting children in the workplace lacked teeth, and horror stories surfaced whenever Parliament was considering new regulations in the face of opposition by factory or mine owners. The problems of working women, especially working mothers, and of working children whose parents depended on their meager wages to help pay for food and rent, would remain part of working life for much of the next 100 years.

In many ways these problems of class and industry, of urbanization and protest, would be inseparable from the enormous changes that would characterize the Victorian Age. Yet the long eighteenth century, from William III to William IV, was itself host to very significant changes both domestically and internationally. The commercial society that would underwrite industrialization solidified during these years, becoming wealthier with the steady expansion of a British Empire still based primarily upon trade rather than the more elusive notions of "civilization" that would trail in the wake of commerce under Victoria. Peace at home was disturbed but not fatally disrupted in 1789 by the outbreak of revolution in France, and many in the ruling and "middling" orders remained complacent about their influence over the lower orders, despite the criticisms leveled at the aristocracy and the commercial classes in an expanding press, relatively free by continental standards, and a thriving culture of theater, arts, and literature. Intellectual life flourished, not only in the coffeehouse culture of the towns but throughout the kingdom, as witnessed by the prolific output of scientists, economists, philosophers, and novelists. The chronic wars with France, interrupted by brief intervals of peace, were costly but only distantly bloody for much of the time. Britain as a whole, and England in particular, regarded itself as both particularly deserving of and distinctly blessed by domestic stability and increasing commercial success. The nineteenth century would change much of that attitude, replacing complacency with anxiety and certainty with doubt.

NOTES

1. Strickland Gough, *An enquiry into the causes of the decay of the dissenting interest* (London, 1730), quoted in W. A. Speck, *Stability and Strife: England, 1714–1760* (Cambridge, Mass: Harvard University Press, 1978), p. 102.

2. E. P. Thompson, *The Making of the English Working Class* (New York: Vintage Books, 1966).

3. JAC [John A. Cannon], "Reform Acts," in John A. Cannon, ed., *The Oxford Companion to British History* (Oxford and New York: Oxford University Press, 1997), pp. 793–94.

8

Britain in the Victorian Age

A NEW QUEEN AND POLITICAL CHANGE

Although the entire nineteenth century is often referred to as "Victorian," Victoria did not take the throne until 1837, ruling until her death in 1901. As queen for 64 years she presided over first a kingdom, and then an empire, that commanded respect if not obedience around the globe. The changes during her reign—economic, political, social, imperial—were so profound that the world of 1837 bore almost no resemblance to that of 1901. Her strength was her ability to represent the broad middle classes of her kingdom throughout these changes, both to themselves and to outside observers. She embraced domesticity even as she claimed political dominions that stretched around the globe. She ruled as a wife even as her kingdom only reluctantly began to recognize the injustice of laws that ignored the autonomous legal existence of the married woman. She weathered significant dips in her popularity and reputation, inspiring passionate loyalty among her subjects that culminated in an unprecedented display of grief and mourning at her funeral. Most significantly, in a period where the direct political power of the crown was considerably diminished, she imbued the monarchy with a sense of honest worth that had been seriously absent during the reigns of her predecessors.

Victoria began almost immediately to restore a sense of morality and stability to the crown. Her marriage in February 1840 to her cousin Albert of Saxe-Coburg produced nine children—Victoria herself considered babies "nasty creatures" but she and Albert were close and loving parents to their large brood—and the two of them provided a model of domestic tranquility and mutual love to the kingdom. No hint of scandal attached to Victoria's private life, although her subjects never took to her intellectual husband; he was not awarded the title of prince consort until 1857, and throughout his life he was regarded with suspicion as to his intentions for his adopted country.

Despite this antagonism, Albert was an energetic patron of developments in science and industry, helping enable the 1851 Great Exhibition of the Industries of All Nations at the famous Crystal Palace built specifically for the event, and also providing important support to music and the arts. His death in 1861 of typhoid fever left Victoria bereft, so grief-stricken that she refused to undertake any of her accustomed duties for months and even years. And while that withdrawal struck many of her subjects and ministers, and many onlookers, as tending toward the extreme, her eccentricities in this regard were interpreted as merely an excess of womanly feeling, of a different kind altogether than the misbehaviors of her predecessors.

Victoria retained important symbolic and political functions as head of state even as her reign witnessed the increasing powers of Parliament, particularly within the House of Commons. The enfranchisement of the solid middle classes in 1832 inevitably altered the ways in which the two major political parties—first Whig and Tory, then Liberal and Conservative—conducted electoral business, and the parties were forced to redefine themselves at intervals as new interests and demands pressed upon M.P.s and ministers. Despite her desire for affectionate personal relationships with her ministers, Victoria's own preferences—most famously for Conservative leader Benjamin Disraeli (1804–1881, created the earl of Beaconsfield in 1876) over Liberal leader William Ewart Gladstone (1809–1898)—could not influence the outcome of elections or policy. Disraeli and Gladstone themselves appeared to be opposites in many ways, with the personally charming and politically opportunistic Disraeli—who famously compared the slog to the prime ministership as a climb to "the top of the greasy pole"—providing an often suspect counterpoint to the occasionally wearisome moral rectitude of Gladstone.

The men, like their parties, were in uneasy partnership. The Liberals were the majority and the Conservative party was in opposition almost continually from 1830–1886, until the Liberals split in 1886 over the question of Home Rule for Ireland. Broadly speaking, the Liberal party was for many years the party of reform, offering a platform for proposals for increased state intervention despite the party's formal adherence to individualism and free trade. The Conservative party supported the established institutions of Crown and church, a limited franchise, and the interests of agriculture and a landed society against the incursions of industry and manufacturing.

The inevitable expansion of the franchise in 1867 (to include most urban and some rural adult males) and in 1884 (almost all adult males) forced both parties to rethink their platforms. The Conservatives had to attract working-class voters even as they retained supporters who regarded the enfranchisement of the great unwashed with open mistrust and disapproval. They did so by focusing most heavily on the issues of empire, using crises like the 1878 Suez Canal incident to rally voters to the party. The Liberals focused not on empire but primarily upon domestic reform, redefining the ideal of personal liberty to include a complex set of interlocking individual and state responsibilities. In this they drew upon the arguments of John Stuart Mill's 1859 *On Liberty*, which had argued that individual freedoms must be accompanied by opportunities for achievement, and that neglecting to remove such impediments to progress as poor housing or lack of education could be as dangerous and wrong as placing unnecessary restraints upon business activity or personal liberty. In the process, the Liberal party developed a highly effective political machine that would eventually become the National Liberal Federation. In 1886, however, the Liberals split when former Birmingham mayor and current M.P. Joseph Chamberlain formed the Liberal Unionists with the primary objective of preserving the British Empire. Chamberlain argued that Home Rule for Ireland, the issue under consideration, was merely the thin edge of the wedge that would dismantle the overall empire upon which British superiority rested. It would take decades for the Liberals to patch themselves back together after Chamberlain's defection.

Working-class voters continued to disappoint expectations that they would vote en bloc, and while many chose Liberal or Conservative as appropriate representatives of their interests, still others in increasing numbers found neither party entirely satisfactory. They turned instead to varieties of socialism, most of them rooted in the "cooperative socialism" of Scottish textile magnate Robert Owen (1771–1858), who had successfully and profitably reorganized his cotton factories to replace capitalist competition with mutual cooperation. Owenite socialism, especially its emphasis on mutual self-help, retained a strong hold on British working class loyalty, even as it faced competition from the more politically strident Chartist movement of Feargus O'Connor, which emerged in the late 1830s.

The Six Points of the People's Charter included universal manhood suffrage, annual parliaments, introduction of the secret ballot, an end to property qualifications for M.P.s, salaries for M.P.s, and equal electoral districts. After a decade of political, social, and economic activism, Chartists gathered thousands of signatures for these reforms on a series of petitions that were presented to Parliament in 1848 to no avail. The movement itself fractured over the ways in which to work for change, with groups advocating "moral force" and "physical force." Many in the moral force category split into smaller groups focusing on temperance, education, and land reform. Chartism as a political movement achieved none of its immediate goals, although all of the six points except annual parliaments were eventually made into law, but it offered a means by which a common working-class identity could be forged, at least among the skilled urban workers of England and Scotland.

Socialism, in any form, was generally absent from the political landscape in the 1850s and 1860s. After the Great Depression of 1873–1876, the renewed energy of the socialists split into such varieties as F. D. Maurice's Christian Socialism, the Settlement House movement of Arnold Toynbee and Samuel Barnett, H. M. Hyndman's Marxist Socialist League, and William Morris's "aesthetic socialism." These varieties of socialism never completely settled into a monolithic political force. However, they did help shape the Fabian movement (established 1884) of Sydney and Beatrice Webb, George Bernard Shaw, and—for a short while—H. G. Wells. The Fabians believed in a gradual shift to inevitable state control and public ownership, achieved peacefully rather than through revolution—a commitment that, like the earlier offspring of Robert Owen's utopian socialism, tended to draw sneers from the more traditional socialist parties on the Continent. But the Fabians were instrumental in introducing important social reforms, including revisions to the Poor Law (1905), Old Age Pensions (1908), and National Insurance (1911).

The growth of political parties responsive to the issues of the working classes was the result in part of a shift in the nature of industrial organization. In the 1850s and '60s industrywide unions—sometimes called "New Model Unionism"—began to replace completely autonomous local unions, primarily among the skilled trades of engineering and carpentry. Local unions remained important, however, and presided over a number of extremely bitter strikes that pitted low-wage workers primarily in the coal and cotton industries against their employers. Several of these strikes were immortalized by novelists like Charles Dickens (*Hard Times*, 1854) and Elizabeth Gaskell (*Mary Barton*, 1848, and *North and South*, 1854–1855). Many mid-Victorian novels about the problem of labor fixed sympathetic attention upon the workers while pinning blame upon greedy employers rather than upon the industrial system itself or the commitment to free trade that underpinned the British economy.

In 1868 another attempt to consolidate across industry resulted in the formation of the Trades Union Congress (TUC), which began in the 1870s to lobby Parliament for pro-labor legislation. Only now were semi-skilled and unskilled workers, including women, slowly brought into the larger fold of unionized workers. The TUC and its counterpart, the 1897 Scottish TUC, laid the foundation for the eventual establishment in 1903 of the formal Labour Party to harness the considerable voting power of its membership: the TUC had over 1 million members in 1893 and 6 million by 1920.

THE EXPANSION OF EMPIRE

By the 1860s, the British Empire had become not only more vast but exponentially more complex than its counterpart in the early modern period. The empire of the high Victorian period continued to be driven by economics, with Britain importing most of its raw materials (including food) and exporting the majority of its finished goods, especially in metals and textiles. But the relatively simple equation of supply and demand was complicated by moral and cultural imperatives, so that both colonies and areas of "influence" became venues of commerce and a particular type of evangelical Christianity. Salvation included soap as well as Scripture. Countless missionaries were determined to assist native peoples in the growth from savagery to civilization that anthropologists and other scientists had "proven" was inevitable.

British colonies and spheres of influence spanned the globe, and just as they had been added haphazardly to the red-shaded portions of the world map, so also they were administered through a patchwork of systems. Generally speaking, the so-called colonies of settlement included those areas of a white, British majority: Canada, Australia, South Africa. These were groomed for varying degrees of self-rule, with the British parliament and Whitehall making decisions about foreign policy but leaving much domestic decision-making to the colonists themselves. The example of the American colonies had already shown that a formal break between colony and colonizer did not mean an end to shared economic interests. Further, in the case of these colonies of self-rule, the strong ties of kinship and culture with the home country meant that any commitment to eventual independence was always ambivalent.

For colonies of direct rule, the second category of empire, no such ambivalence existed. Although many British leaders at home claimed that the settlements in Africa and Southeast Asia might eventually evolve into self-governing regions, the small British minorities in these settlements always wielded direct political, social, and economic power over the non-white majorities.

In the third category of empire, the so-called "informal empire" where Britain chose not to impose direct rule, economic and cultural influence existed without being embodied in formal political structures. This meant that areas of China, the east and west African coasts, and parts of the East Indies were subject to trading agreements that often included non-economic pressures and sanctions. India, long the lynchpin of British holdings abroad, combined degrees of all three types of administrative systems, beginning as a trade partner with the British East India Company but eventually becoming a colony of direct rule. All types of colonies and settlements were expected to be self-sufficient, which translated not only into membership in the British free-trade system but also into heavy local taxation that was used to pay for administrators and infrastructure.

The nineteenth century saw a series of protests and uprisings in the broad sphere of British influence, from the Opium Wars in China (1839–1842, 1856–1858) to the uprisings in Jamaica and in India. The Opium Wars stemmed from the Chinese government's actions against British merchants bringing Indian opium illegally into the country to sell. The British government ignored Chinese law and instead claimed the privileges of free trade, demanding the right to protect its citizens. Over the course of the conflict the 1842 Treaty of Nanking ceded Hong Kong to the British government. War broke out again over charges of piracy by the Chinese government, and a victorious Britain formally established many of the trading rights that British merchants had claimed as a practical matter for decades.

In Jamaica, governor Edward Eyre brutally suppressed a rebellion by the descendents of former slaves in 1865. The episode resulted in a formal investigation into Eyre's actions, particularly in his suspension of the rule of law against Jamaican blacks. The investigation itself polarized public opinion into pro- and anti-Eyre forces. The pro-Eyre forces included many of the kingdom's most famous essayists and writers, among them Thomas Carlyle, Charles Dickens, and Alfred Tennyson; anti-Eyre forces included men associated with economics and the sciences, like Charles Darwin, Thomas Huxley, Herbert Spencer, and John Stuart Mill. The anti-Eyre forces tried without success for five years to bring the governor, now retired, to trial. The entire episode renewed discussions about colonial policy, the problems of post-slave economies, social and legal attitudes toward blacks, and the government's use of often brutal force against nonwhites.

In India, the Indian Rebellion (called the Sepoy Mutiny by British officers in India, who regarded the uprising primarily as a military mutiny) crystallized years of dissatisfaction and unrest. The British East India Company ruled its holdings on the subcontinent until 1857, when the uprising focused serious attention on the patchwork of policies and administrative structures that had sprung up haphazardly over the two centuries since the East India Company had established its first "factory," or merchant warehouse, in India. The constant return of very rich merchants to England sparked public interest in the subcontinent, and the missionary impulse of many readers was heightened by newspaper stories detailing the exotically repellant practices of thuggery (gang murders by secret societies) and suttee or sati (the ritual self-immolation of Hindu widows). Vigorous attempts to eliminate these cultural practices followed.

Native princes were tied to the East India Company by a variety of client relationships, in all of which the East India administrators increasingly tried to maximize their control, and by mid-century outright annexation was becoming common, sometimes preceded by forcible deposition of the hereditary or elected prince. In 1857 these and other issues ignited in Bengal when soldiers in the Indian Army protested the use of animal fat to grease bullet cartridges. The uprising spread throughout the Ganges Valley with savage massacres on both sides, with one of the most notorious being the slaughter of 200 British women and children at Cawnpore.

In an age where the telegraph allowed immediate newspaper coverage of international events—the Crimean War of 1854 had seen the first major international use of the telegraph and of what today would be called "embedded" journalists—news of these disasters animated the British public and worsened Whitehall's problems in dealing with the uprising. British troops were sent in great numbers to quell the revolts and in 1858 control of the subcontinent was formally taken out of the hands of the East India Company and placed under the newly formed India Board, destroying any hope of a prompt transition to self-rule. Victoria added "Empress of India" to her titles in 1877.

Perhaps the most expensive and difficult of the attempts to maintain an international empire came in South Africa. South Africa was a key part of the British presence in Africa, due first to its strategic location on the route to India and later to the discovery of diamonds and gold. Attempts to control the Zulu natives culminated in their massacre in 1879; the difficulties with the Boers (descendants of the original Dutch settlers in South Africa) led to wars in 1880 and again in 1899. The 1899 war lasted for three years, much longer than anticipated. On the one hand, it tapped anew the strident patriotism—"jingoism"—that had first emerged in the 1870s. On the other hand, it was terribly costly in terms of both men and international reputation. More than 28,000 Britons were injured or killed. The death toll for the Boers was much higher, because Boer civilians—men, women, and children—were herded into unsanitary and uninhabitable concentration camps by the military command. Public opinion turned against the British military, even at home, as journalists and social investigators showed just how brutal the camp facilities were. Perhaps unintentionally, the war also focused attention on problems of public health in Britain's cities, where countless potential conscripts were turned away after failing the army physical.

REFORM AT HOME

Municipal reforms occupied an increasing portion of public attention throughout the nineteenth century, as problems in health, hygiene, and education proved too overwhelming to be fully tamed by individual effort. The rapid growth in urban areas that had begun in the late 1700s continued throughout the period. However, population pressures were only one factor in the shift to a mixed economy of aid that harnessed with varying degrees of success both public and private projects of improvement. Reformer Edwin Chadwick's (1800–1890) monumental and conspicuously tactless efforts in introducing sanitary reform in the 1850s were only slightly less contentious than his earlier work on the Poor Law of 1834, but by the end of the century the work of men like Charles Booth (1840–1916) and Seebohm Rowntree (1871–1954) in demonstrating the endemic problems of chronic urban poverty found more receptive ears. Booth's 1899 study of London and Rowntree's study of York two years later showed that what Rowntree called "primary poverty" was due not to immorality and vice but rather to low wages and other institutional impediments to success. Intervening voices had called for municipal reforms as a form of Christian service—Birmingham's so-called "civic gospel" was perhaps the most successful in this regard—or as a necessary domestic adjunct to the civilizing mission of empire.

Certain reforms directed toward the working classes met with strong resistance: the introduction of mandatory smallpox vaccines in 1853 sparked fears of deliberate infection, while missions like Dr. Thomas Barnardo's for the care of slum children, often through their relocation to Canada, had to contend with suspicions that the rights of working-class families were being destroyed. Other programs were more obviously beneficial, especially those aimed at providing police protection, piping in safe water, establishing local medical officers, removing the "nuisances" of human and animal excrement from town and city streets, and replacing unventilated back-to-back housing units with more and healthier dwellings.

Even these acts were often met with cries of undue governmental interference or excessive increases in the rates (taxes paid by the occupiers of property, whether business or home, for the purpose of providing relief for the poor), and a great deal of the burden of daily charity remained in the hands of private groups or individuals. Similar problems dogged the eventual creation of a program of national elementary education in 1870: some reformers warned that an uneducated working-class electorate would be overwhelmingly dangerous, while others lamented the passing of educational responsibilities from church and family into the hands of an unfeeling bureaucracy. Over the course of the Victorian age, however, the focus of responsibility shifted more and more into the public sphere, as the energies of volunteers were augmented and eventually overwhelmed by governmental programs.

SOCIAL CHANGES AND THE EXPANDING ROLES OF WOMEN

This shift in the nature of municipal responsibility had widespread effects, many of them initially unforeseen. Perhaps one of the most far-reaching results of increased governmental responsibility was to place more power in the hands of middle- and upper-class women. Single women ratepayers gained the municipal vote in 1869, including the right to vote for and eventually stand for school board, vestry, and poor law board. (The first woman Poor Law Guardian was elected in 1875.) This limited extension of the franchise to women was controversial; it appeared a first step toward an inevitable extension of the parliamentary franchise, even as many observers argued that women's "natural" nurturing capabilities made them ideal participants in charity and education.

Yet despite involvement first in acts of personal and institutional charity and then in political activity within municipal government, other rights for women were slow to come. For most of the century, married women in England were viewed as having no separate legal existence apart from their husbands (in contrast to Scotland, where married women enjoyed significantly greater legal independence). This led inevitably to grievous personal disasters that were only partially remedied by such changes as the Custody of Infants Act of 1839, which gave mothers the right to request custody of children up to age seven, and the Married Women's Property Acts of 1870, 1882, and 1893, which expanded the control married women retained over any property they brought to marriage and allowed wives access to the money they earned while married.

Professional gains were as difficult. The establishment of teachers' training colleges for women, as well as schools and institutions to educate governesses and nurses, sparked only minor public debate. However, while women could attend classes at colleges and universities, they were not permitted to sit for matriculation examinations until 1863; they were not admitted into medical schools until 1869. (Sophia Jex-Blake founded the London School of Medicine for Women in 1874 and a medical school for women in Edinburgh in 1886.) Half a dozen years later, women were hired as bank clerks for the first time, a major step into what would become white-collar work. Not until 1881 were women admitted as clerks in the Civil Service, which had undergone a major reorganization at mid-century when examinations replaced patronage as the primary criterion for admission.

The question of the national franchise continued to surface at regular intervals after John Stuart Mill's failed attempt to extend the vote to all adults, male and female, in the debates leading up to the Reform Act of 1867. By the last decades of the century, arguments had become noticeably shrill. The anti-suffrage camp included men who claimed women were simply incapable of appreciating the complex issues involved in governing an empire that stretched around the world. Some, like Herbert Spencer, argued that women's intellectual development would always come at the expense of their ability to nurture children and that women's public involvement would inevitably lead to the decline of the race, a fear shared by many in an age of imperial expansion.

Many women also took an anti-suffrage position, rejecting what they depicted as the violent, chaotic, and ugly world of international politics. Other women, less dismissive, argued that "influence" within the family and the social circle was much more powerful than a direct political voice, and that they would lose more than they would gain with suffrage. Pro-suffrage adherents dismissed both of these positions, but split into groups of variously radical positions. In 1897 Millicent Fawcett founded the National Union of Women's Suffrage Societies to amalgamate the efforts of the various smaller organizations working for the parliamentary vote for women. The emergence of pro-suffrage groups advocating the use of violence, such as the 1903 Women's Social and Political Union led by Emmeline Pankhurst and her daughter Christabel, received more press than less militant organizations, but arguably delayed the adoption of female suffrage by a number of years. This violence endured for over a decade: one young suffragette gained notoriety in 1913 by throwing herself under the king's horse at the annual derby, killing herself. Supporters of Fawcett's organization argued that the rival Pankhurst organization hurt rather than helped the cause, but no one could deny that it kept the issue of women's suffrage in the public eye.

Other "women's issues" dividing educated society in the late Victorian period included the cause of social and sexual purity, represented in various ways by the campaigns to repeal the 1860s Contagious Diseases Acts (requiring the registration and forcible physical examination of prostitutes as a way to control the spread of venereal disease) and to raise the age of sexual consent from 13 to 16. Anxieties about prostitution and sexual predators were linked specifically to poverty during the Jack the Ripper murders in 1888, even as charges of vice and sexual immorality against men of the upper classes continued to resonate throughout the debates over marriage and women's independence. As always, the wars of the sexes and of the generations provided material for novelists and essayists: Eliza Lynn Linton satirized the undutiful mid-Victorian girl as "The Girl of The Period" in 1868, while Sarah Grande painted a sympathetic portrait of her descendant, the "New Woman," in her 1893 novel *The Heavenly Twins*.

CHANGES IN SCIENCE AND RELIGION

The Victorian age has been called the age of improvement, but it was also an age of tremendous anxiety. One major source of this anxiety focused on the place not of women in British society but of "man" in the universe at large. The shift in the relationship between religion and science began decades before the 1859 publication of Charles Darwin's *Origin of Species*. Anglicanism in England and Wales had cooled again after the warmth of evangelicalism, even as the movement toward disestablishment—breaking the formal ties of church and state—had fueled some attempts to reinvigorate the church as a state institution. The Tractarian or Oxford Movement of the 1830s, for example, emphasized the importance of ritual and the role of the church as the conduit for Christ's truth. Many viewed the movement as an underhanded way to return the church to Roman Catholicism, and the formal conversion in 1845 of John Henry Newman, one of the movement's leaders, only underscored those fears. By the 1840s the expressive spirituality of the Tractarians had begun to give way to a more careful emphasis on intellectual components of faith. The Victorians called this "earnestness," by which they meant, in the context of religion, an intellectual understanding of the objects of belief. An emotional response was important but insufficient; an intellectual appreciation of sacred duty was crucial to the full moral development of the individual.

Earnestness in religion might symbolize progress to those who felt scientific inquiry could only amplify the message of God, but earnest believers had several very difficult problems to address by mid-century. First was the nagging issue of nonattendance. A religious census in 1851 revealed that only some 35 percent of those in England, for instance, attended a church or Nonconformist chapel, and barely half of those were Anglican. Further, of the 7 million who stayed away on Census Sunday, at least 5 million of those were from the working classes. Equally problematic were intellectual challenges to religious belief. The 1860 publication of *Essays and Reviews* was predicated upon what one essayist, Benjamin Jowett, called a reasoned reaction against the "abominable system of terrorism" that forbade the earnest discussion of the texts of the Christian religion. In 1862, such discussion became more heated with the publication of Anglican Bishop J. W. Colenso's *Pentateuch*, in which Colenso publicly disavowed a literal belief in the Scriptures. (Colenso was excommunicated in 1866.)

For many the biggest challenge to the nature of religious authority came from the scientific community. Charles Darwin's work riveted the public's attention, forcing most educated men and women to address the questions raised by the theory of evolution by natural selection even if they ultimately rejected the idea. Evolution as a mechanism to explain the extinction of species had been a part of scientific discussion for decades, fueled by work by Jean Baptiste Lamarck, Robert Chambers, and others. Darwin himself was strongly influenced by the school of geological inquiry called uniformitarianism, which emphasized that changes in the earth were slow, gradual, and still perceptible in the contemporary world of the Victorians. He also placed strong emphasis on environmental pressures, using pigeon breeding to show how certain traits could be bred into or out of groups of individuals. Finally, his reading of Thomas Malthus's work on population and food supply suggested the mechanism by which such changes might occur.

Evolution, he argued, was driven by natural selection. Species themselves, just like individuals within a species, competed for food and space. Individuals within a species that were better at such competition because of some random variation would reproduce at a higher rate. The offspring of these individuals that inherited these variations would themselves survive to reproduce in higher numbers, and so on. The mechanism here was not the divine, but rather nature; in nature, certain variations worked and others did not, and those that did work were selected by nature to continue. Species would thus evolve very slowly but in direct response to the pressures of the natural world.

Darwin himself anticipated many of the objections—both scientific and religious—his work would provoke, and refrained from publication until the younger naturalist Alfred Russell Wallace began to publicize his own very similar theories about the mechanism of evolution.

In *The Origin of Species* Darwin limited himself to discussions of change rather than addressing the issue of initial creation itself. He deferred entirely the question of man's own evolution until the 1871 *Descent of Man*, despite the clear implications of his theories. Reaction was swift and intense. From a religious perspective, it was feared that "our moral sense will turn out to be a mere developed instinct . . . and the revelation of God to us, and the hope of a future life [will be revealed as] pleasurable daydreams invented for the good of society."[1] At the 1860 meeting of the British Association for the Advancement of Science, Bishop Samuel Wilberforce tried to kill the Darwinians with satire, asking whether it was through his grandfather or his grandmother that Darwin's representative Thomas Huxley claimed to be descended from a monkey.

Scientific objections focused upon the problems of "intermediate" characteristics—what good was half a wing, and how would natural selection favor the precursor of an eye or another similarly complex organ?—as well as the great span of years necessary for the evolution of one species into another entirely different species. Since the age of the earth was still estimated to be 6,000 years, this was a serious problem. So also was the lack of any clear understanding about the mechanisms of heredity itself. Despite these and other problems, however, young and ardent scientists like Huxley took up the cudgels for this new theory, and even those who found Darwin's theories troubling on moral or theological grounds had to grapple with the scientific questions raised by the quiet man from Down.

Darwin's theory of natural selection was immediately appropriated by other fields, most noticeably the infant field of sociology, where Herbert Spencer coined the phrase "survival of the fittest" and applied it to competition among the societies of Europe and the non-European world, as well as to individuals within society. His followers would claim that the government provision of assistance to the poor or poorly educated stood in the way of this "survival of the fittest," and that the fitting of a society to survive and to conquer was best accomplished by a strictly hands-off government. Others would take the opposite tack, arguing that "survival of the fittest" meant that the government had an obligation to remove impediments to success and perhaps even to provide some assistance in the form of education, child health care, municipal services, and the like. In this latter capacity, the rhetoric of reformers borrowed not only from Darwin and Spencer but also from the vast literature of empire, as the slums of the inner cities were increasingly compared to the outposts of Asia and Africa and, alas, to the problematic next-door neighbors, the Irish, who were invariably consigned to subhuman status in discussions of culture and improvement. (The first gorilla brought back for the London Zoo was named "Paddy," and contemporary political cartoons frequently portrayed the Irish with ape-like features.)

VICTORIAN ART AND LITERATURE

The controversies over religion and science were widely read in an era of cheap periodicals. The nineteenth century saw the expansion of the reading public—perhaps better characterized as several reading publics, because by the end of Victoria's reign there were many groups of readers, all demanding inexpensive and accessible newspapers and books. Many of the "men of letters" of the early and middle parts of the century occupied a particularly powerful position in society, providing an important set of guidelines for the moral and intellectual development of the middle classes. Essayists like John Ruskin and Thomas Carlyle, novelists like Charles Dickens and Elizabeth Gaskell, poets like Alfred Tennyson and Robert Browning used their skills to preach and teach. And to entertain: the serialized novel, made famous by men like Dickens, reached unprecedented numbers of readers, many of whom waited breathlessly for the next month's installment to find out if Little Nell really did die. Women became the primary novel readers of the period, but men also consumed fiction along with the more serious essays and political writings that filled the pages of countless newspapers. There was, for the middle part of the century, truly a unified reading public, with smaller groups of readers on either end of the middle classes providing limited but important audiences for iconoclastic writers.

By the last third of the century, however, this position of power had eroded, as more and different groups of readers demanded a wider range of materials. The growth of the popular Sunday and daily papers was a response to these demands. So was the growth of periodicals aimed at working women, or middle-class wives and daughters, or members of the kingdom's many self-improvement societies. All of these groups were expected to partake of "culture," but they demanded their culture in specific and particular forms. This meant that the unified voice of the mid-Victorian "preachers and teachers" was no longer able to reach these many different consumers of culture who now flocked to art museums, libraries, local parks, and lecture halls. The poet and the man of letters lost their status as heroes of society and representatives of a higher and morally more worthy calling.

In the visual arts, the nineteenth century witnessed a variety of responses to the often confusing developments of industry and society. Many public buildings, such as train stations and city halls, were often elaborately beautiful, designed to provide the common man and woman with an uplifting visual point on an otherwise bleak and monotonously redbrick urban landscape. Men such as William Morris took this a step further, arguing that the design of furniture, wallpaper, and other household objects should reflect a soul-nourishing beauty that was lacking in mass-produced goods but that could be reclaimed through a return to handicrafts and a certain kind of taste in decorative objects.

Morris was associated with the Pre-Raphaelite movement of the 1850s, a loose collection of painters and other artists who wanted to return to the style of art of the early religious painters and of Raphael himself. They tended to focus on medieval subjects and a scrupulous realism in the representation of the natural world, using models whose loose clothing, brooding faces, and wild red hair were in direct contrast to the dimpled roundness of the women in more traditional mid-century paintings. The Pre-Raphaelites looked at art as art rather than as a necessarily "improving" moral message, and in this way they injected a breath of fresh air into the visual arts. The Aesthetic movement of the 1870s and '80s followed this same path, representing arts and literature as a higher kind of reality and a more intense kind of pleasure than any offered by the daily life of a new industrial and urban Britain. The Aesthetics, from Walter Pater to Oscar Wilde, reviled middle-class morality and art as vulgar, boring, and bourgeois, and tended to treat the Artist as an individual destined to be misunderstood by the rest of society. In this they were borrowing from the Romantics of the late eighteenth century, but they resisted the Romantic impulse to worship a chaotic and wild nature and instead turned their literary and artistic guns on what they perceived as the wearisome hypocrisy of the Victorian age. The Aesthetics gave way to the Decadents of the so-called "Naughty Nineties" or "Yellow Nineties," a group of artists and writers who courted excess in their personal lives and who conveyed their own experiences of absinthe, sexual misbehavior, and ennui through works that were designed to deliberately shock their audiences at the fin de siècle.

NOTES

1. *Edinburgh Review* 134 (1871), pp. 195–96, quoted in Alvar Ellegård, *Darwin and the General Reader: The Reception of Darwin's Theory of Evolution in the British Periodical Press, 1859–1872*, 2d ed. (Chicago: University of Chicago Press, 1990), p. 100.

9

A New Century: Britain under Edward VII and George V

A FRESH START?

When Victoria died in 1901, her son Bertie came to the throne as Edward VII (b. 1841; r. 1901–1910). Many welcomed the change. As with Elizabeth I, Victoria's reign had grown old and stale and her death appeared to signal a fresh start in a fresh century. Edward, known facetiously as "Edward the Caresser" for his notorious love life and equally well known for his smoking, gambling, and horse racing, represented a clear departure from the earnest and eventually rather stodgy reign of his mother, but he was not the disastrous monarch that some had feared. He presided over an empire that, like his mother's, took on his name. The Edwardian era appears in retrospect as an interlude of peace and prosperity, an Indian summer before the outbreak of the Great War in 1914. In truth, however, there were crises aplenty. Many of these crises did not fully erupt until after Edward's son George took the throne in 1910, but their roots can be firmly traced back to the first decade of the new century.

POLITICAL AND ECONOMIC CRISES

The Conservative victory in 1900—in the so-called Khaki election, where the primary campaign issue was the Boer War and where Liberals were divided from Liberal Unionists—ushered in the first set of serious domestic crises, both of which reopened religious wounds that had been presumably healed. The Education Act of 1902 had the practical effect of reducing the power of local Nonconformist school boards and placing elementary schools under the control of county councils, many of which worked to reintroduce a more Anglican religious instruction. The Licensing Act of 1904 similarly outraged Nonconformists, who had expected the Conservative government to limit the number of public houses and who were deeply troubled that the act instead increased taxes on drink licenses. It appeared that the government preferred to increase its income from the drink trade rather than to try to curb the abuses of alcohol.

Other divisive battles followed. The Unionists, a coalition of Liberal Unionists and some Tories, remained committed to free trade, as did the Liberals. But a growing faction within the Conservative party began to argue that protectionist tariffs were the only way to conserve the empire and to protect the British economy against the industrial wizardry of both Germany and the United States, neither of which was saddled with the expensive burden of an aging manufacturing base. They suggested a customs union that would link the raw materials of the colonies with the manufactured goods of the home country. They also argued for tariffs on imported goods, including food. These pro-tariff forces claimed that the increasing burden of "civilizing" natives in Asia and Africa required new sources of income, as did the level of economic planning that was Britain's only hope in the renewed race for industrial supremacy. The anti-tariff Liberals and Unionists countered that such tariffs would simply reimpose the burden upon the common man that had been lifted when the Corn Laws had been repealed at mid-century, and in a series of by-elections the proposed Tariff Reform program was defeated. This defeat was repeated on a national scale in the 1906 general elections when the Conservatives lost their hold on office.

The economic challenges of the new century were visible as well in the growing gulf between labor and management, a gulf that had significantly increased as industry had reorganized in the wake of the depression of the 1870s. By the 1890s industrywide unions had emerged to protect all workers, not just the skilled, in a development known as New Unionism. Inevitably, these larger and more powerful unions had turned to political activism, reflected in the development of independent political parties. The Scottish Labour Party (founded 1892), for instance, sent Keir Hardie to Parliament in 1892 before it became part of the larger Independent Labour Party (founded 1893), which remained independent of the larger Labour Party formed a decade later. Hardie presided over the establishment in 1900 of the Labour Representation Committee (LRC), which after negotiations with the Liberals helped in 1900 to elect two Labour M.P.s to Parliament.

Within a year, however, the LRC was embroiled in a political battle over trade union liability, in the Taff-Vale crisis of 1901–1902. Taff-Vale, a large Welsh railway concern, had sued the railway union for losses suffered during a legal strike, and the courts in 1902 awarded the company £23,000 in damages. Although this court decision did not eliminate the legal right of unions to strike, in its practical effects it did just that; with legal costs, the union paid £42,000, a sum not even the largest unions could afford to risk. Workers and union leaders were outraged, in part because the company had appealed lower-court decisions against them up to the House of Lords, and the Lords reversed these decisions in actions that appeared to be completely motivated by a bias against the working man.

The immediate result of this action was increased support by many unions for the LRC, which was rechristened the modern Labour Party in 1903. In 1906, 30 Labour M.P.s were returned to Parliament. This support survived the 1909 Osborne Case, where unions were legally barred from using membership dues to fund the political activities of the growing Labour Party. Because M.P.s worked without salaries, this in effect crippled the ability of the party to support its candidates both during and after elections. Not until 1911 were M.P.s paid, and not until 1913 did unions gain the legal right to use voluntary contributions by members to support political activities.

THE CONSTITUTIONAL CRISIS OF 1909–1911

When the Conservatives lost power in 1906 to the Liberals, the new prime minister David Lloyd George immediately introduced a wide program of social reforms. These included not only the Fabians' Old Age Pensions and National Insurance, but also school meals for poor children, eight-hour workdays, and the Trade Disputes Act of 1906, which protected union funds against claims for damages like those awarded in Taff-Vale. However, the Liberals ran up against a brick wall in many cases, as the House of Lords exercised its traditional veto powers for the first time in two decades. The Lords were struggling to preserve aristocratic privilege in the face of what was perceived as a blatant attempt to turn the country over to workers and socialists. And although these veto powers were completely legal, they were portrayed by the Liberals as arbitrary measures taken against the common man.

In 1909 prolonged antagonism came to a head over a particularly radical budget proposed by Lloyd George, who wished to fund the Liberals' various new social welfare programs as well as new military battleships—the dreadnoughts—through a combination of sources: a supertax on incomes over £5,000, a duty on undeveloped land, and a capital gains tax on all land transactions. The Lords saw this as a renewed and fatal attack on the landowning gentry and aristocracy, and blocked the budget bill. Lloyd George went on the offensive, arguing that no country could "permanently afford to have quartered upon its revenue a class which declines to do the duty which it was called upon to perform," and also that "a fully-equipped duke costs as much to keep up as two [battleships], and dukes are just as great a terror and they last longer."[1]

King Edward died in the midst of this battle and his son, George V (1910–1936), came to power in a crisis that appeared to threaten the stability of the nation and in which the major political parties and both houses of Parliament appeared to be acting solely out of entrenched self-interest. The new monarch eventually threatened to end the stalemate by using his own prerogative to create new peers in order to ensure that the Lords would indeed pass the budget bill, but in 1911 a compromise was reached. The Commons could pass any money bill without the formal assent of the Lords, so there would be no future risk of a veto. The Commons could also override any veto by the House of Lords after two years. In return, there was a pledge that no new Lords would be created and that the existing powers of the aristocracy would remain intact. The Liberal social welfare programs, many of them badly needed, were funded.

GROWING ANTAGONISM BETWEEN LABOR AND INDUSTRY

Yet there were losses for the common man as well, as real wages steadily declined in the decade before the Great War. Despite the punitive effects of both the Taff-Vale and the Osborne decisions, union activity increased apace as wages fell. Union membership itself more than doubled, from 2 million in 1901 to 4.1 million in 1913. Industrywide strikes became the norm after the 1906 Trades Disputes Act guaranteed unions the right to strike. In 1908, for instance, more time was lost from strikes than had been lost in the previous 10 years combined, and in 1911 the entire railway union went on strike. The government had given the Board of Trade the powers and responsibilities of mediating trade disputes, and these efforts were relatively successful during the first decade of the century. After 1911, however, the government increasingly resorted to military force as one of its negotiating tools. Unions themselves responded by renewing the idea of a national union of all workers as the obvious way to maximize the power of the workingman. The first attempt at this was the so-called "triple alliance" of miners, railway workers, and transport workers proposed in 1914 and eventually ratified in 1915. The railway contract was to expire in December 1914 and many feared that the new alliance would take this opportunity to flex its muscle, effectively shutting down the country. Only the outbreak of war averted this disaster.

THE CONTINUING PROBLEM OF FEMALE SUFFRAGE

The Great War tabled another potentially disastrous crisis as well: the women's suffrage movement, which by the 1910s had fractured into several smaller groups that together polarized the nation. By the turn of the century most women and many men in the middle classes had come to support higher education and increased responsibilities for women. However, the issue of the parliamentary vote continued to be virtually unresolvable. Generally speaking, the Conservative party opposed the issue with one voice. Labour largely ignored the issue by arguing that the problem of women's suffrage was less pressing than the terribly troubling relations between labor and industry. Liberals tended to be painfully divided, and it was under the auspices of a Liberal government that the so-called Cat and Mouse Act was passed in 1913.

Formally the Prisoners' Temporary Discharge for Ill-Health Act, the Cat and Mouse Act was clearly aimed at the militant suffragettes, whose use of the hunger strike while in prison continued to draw attention to their cause. Forced feeding of these prisoners made prison officials look deliberately cruel, since inflexible feeding tubes caused internal injuries. The insertion of such tubes also clearly violated the personal integrity of the individual, a cause held dear by Liberals and Conservatives alike. The Liberal government, hoping to divert the public's attention to less emotional matters, used the Cat and Mouse Act to release prisoners and then re-arrest them after they had regained their health. Predictably, however, the act was a public relations disaster, and by the eve of the Great War many felt that this issue, like the problems of trade and industry, would bring the nation to revolution.

IRELAND AND HOME RULE

A final deeply divisive issue colored the last years of the Edwardian period, and that was the recurring question of Home Rule for Ireland. The problems of Irish land ownership had been particularly acute in the period since the Great Famine of 1845–1848. By 1900, however, Irish independence had become the main focus of reformers and agitators. Nationalist movements had come and gone since the early 1800s, including Daniel O'Connell's 1840s movement to repeal the 1801 Act of Union and the 1842 movement called Young Ireland, which was suppressed after a failed rising in 1848. The Fenians (founded in 1858 in both Ireland and the United States, and known also as the Irish Republican Brotherhood and the Irish Revolutionary Brotherhood or IRB) staged a rising in 1867, attracting a mere 10,000 men despite widespread support—probably 50,000–60,000 by the 1860s—for the nationalist sentiments of the movement. But the Fenians' devotion to so-called "physical force" nationalism alienated many, who instead were drawn to the "moral force" nationalism of the Home Government Association (HGA, founded in 1870 by Isaac Butt).

The HGA emerged as the symbol of Home Rule, working through the existing British Parliament to win acceptance of an independent Irish government. Charles Stewart Parnell assumed the leadership of the association in 1881, and for the next decade he presided over an increasingly disciplined parliamentary force of Irish M.P.s. He also helped direct pressures for land reform through the Irish Land League (1878–1882), encouraging rural agitation that ranged from withholding rents to more traditional displays of local violence.

In 1881, British Prime Minister William Gladstone, viewing the support of the Irish Parliamentary Party (founded 1870) as crucial to the continued success of the Liberal Party, successfully introduced a Land Act that formalized many of the demands of the Land League. But Gladstone's attempts to push through bills for Home Rule were less successful. The limited Home Rule Bill of 1886 failed to pass the House of Commons, where both Conservatives and Unionists opposed it on grounds that ranged from religion ("Home rule is Rome rule") to empire. The distress over the bill prompted the founding of parties devoted to blocking any modification of the 1801 Act of Union. In 1890, Parnell's star dimmed considerably when he was named as co-respondent in a nasty divorce case involving his long-term mistress and her husband, and the Home Rule cause temporarily faltered. Gladstone's 1893 Home Rule Bill died in the House of Lords.

A third Home Rule bill was introduced by the Liberals in 1912, supported by both the IRB (the former Fenians) as well as a new nationalist organization called Sinn Féin ("we ourselves"). Sinn Féin was founded in 1905 by journalist Arthur Griffith, dedicated to nonviolent change and the establishment of a dual Irish monarchy with one ruler in Ulster and another in Dublin. It focused on both political transformation and the preservation of an autonomous Irish culture. This latter goal was shared by the Gaelic League (founded 1893), which had been formed to preserve the Gaelic language. But these nationalist movements faced increasingly militant opposition in Ulster, which in 1913 spawned the Ulster Volunteer Force dedicated to the use of violence "if necessary" to preserve the union with Great Britain.

Perhaps inevitably, pro-repeal forces formed their own militia, the Irish Volunteers, to counterbalance the Ulster Volunteers, and each side took up arms against the other. Complicating the already incendiary situation was the formation in 1913 of the Irish Citizen Army, initially founded to protect striking Irish workers from the Dublin police force but by 1914 openly talking about the formation of a "workers' republic." Unionists and nationalists were thus poised on the brink of civil war within two years of the introduction of the third Home Rule bill. The British government could not come up with a strategy that would appease both sides. Again, only the outbreak of the Great War averted what looked like imminent disaster.

THE GREAT WAR

The Great War became a "world" war almost immediately upon its outbreak on August 1, 1914, owing largely to the treaties binding together an imperial Europe. Britain's own treaties with Belgium and with France led to a declaration of war against Germany on August 4, a declaration that had broad support even amongst those who had opposed earlier conflicts like the Boer War. Britain, like every other party to the war, thought that victory would be relatively swift; even after the early disasters at Ypres and Mons, it took some months before the British government—like the Germans and the French—began to appreciate that trench warfare meant a war of attrition. It also meant a war of astonishing casualties in the face of infinitesimal gains. Loos, the Somme, Passchendaele—all of these took on meanings of terrible tragedy after calamitous losses to the Germans. In 1915 the shortage of shells and bullets drove the Liberal government out of office in disgrace and ushered in a coalition government under Herbert Asquith. This government was forced to begin conscription in 1916 after the early decimation of the "regular army," the professionally trained military, in Ypres and after the numbers volunteering for Kitchener's New Army proved inadequate.

The war was fought primarily on a small patch of ground in France, but it affected the entire British Empire. Conscription included vast numbers of soldiers from the colonies. At home, issues that had riveted the country—Irish Home Rule, women's suffrage, industrial antagonisms—were temporarily put to one side as most Britons came together to support what was declared to be a just war against an intolerably aggressive "Hun." The Germans began air bombing certain cities, including London, in April 1915; one month later, the sinking of the British ship *Lusitania* off the coast of Ireland represented a further incursion into traditional civilian safety. The government instituted a program of wage and price controls unimaginable at the height of Victorian free trade. Women were hired on a massive scale into traditionally "male" jobs and volunteered in unprecedented numbers to serve as nurses and aides in army hospitals. Control of essential services, such as the railway, passed into the hands of the government, and food rationing became the norm. It was "total war," involving civilians on a scale that would be surpassed only by the Second World War.

The experiences of civilians were difficult, but the suffering of soldiers was almost unimaginable. Letters home, censored by army officials, kept up a cheerful pretense of gamesmanship or "business as usual," but in memoirs and biographies the details of trench warfare—the rats, the mud, the appalling casualties—emerged to haunt generations of readers. Wilfred Owen, the most famous of Britain's "War Poets," wrote home after the battle of the Somme in January 1917 that, "I can see no excuse for deceiving you about these four days. I have suffered seventh hell. I have not been at the front. I have been in front of it."[2] Owen died before he could return home.

In all, British casualties including men from the colonies totaled about 1 million. The wounded accounted for another 2.5 million. The high numbers of the fallen from Australia and New Zealand—primarily at Gallipoli—led to the establishment of April 25 as a national holiday, Anzac Day (after the Australian and New Zealand Army Corps). Canada, South Africa, and India also suffered great losses. The devastation of the war was followed in quick succession by the influenza epidemic of 1918, which carried off between 200,000 and 300,000 men and women—primarily in their thirties and forties—in England and Ireland alone. The demographic cataclysms of the war and the influenza epidemic would take some time to appreciate, but the wartime casualties by themselves automatically increased the number of unmarried women for the decade to come, as an entire generation of husbands and fathers simply disappeared. Those soldiers who survived suffered great bitterness upon their return home, especially the young men who had been officers during the war, for they found that the "old men" who had managed the war from the safety of an office were unwilling to give up any power to those who had actually suffered in the trenches.

THE ESTABLISHMENT OF THE IRISH FREE STATE

The immediate postwar period was a difficult one, both economically and politically. The "Irish problem" had not been defused but had in fact worsened: in 1916 the so-called Easter Rising left several thousand defeated Irish dead or imprisoned. The Rising had been planned by the IRB to take advantage of British involvement on the Continent, and had included the intended use of German munitions that never arrived. The leaders were executed, with the exception of Eamon de Valera, whose American citizenship (his mother was an American citizen) saved him from death.

In the aftermath of the Rising, the British government introduced martial law and began another round of discussions to try to settle the question of Ireland's future status. At the same time, both nationalist and anti-nationalist sentiment hardened, and it became ever clearer that a peaceful end to the conflict was impossible. Sinn Féin emerged as the leading organization of the nationalists, although ties between the organization and the Irish Volunteers made it difficult for Sinn Féin to argue that it remained committed to peaceful and constitutional change. De Valera was elected president of the movement in 1917 and proclaimed the goal of an Irish republic whose citizens would then be able to choose the future form of government—presidential or dual monarchical.

In 1918, after the armistice was signed, a general election included the return of 73 Sinn Féin members and 26 Ulster Unionists to the Parliament in Westminster. The Sinn Féin members refused to take their seats, instead forming a separate Irish parliament—the Dáil Éireann—in January 1919 and declaring an independent Ireland. At the same time, the Irish Volunteers—reconstituting themselves gradually as the Irish Republican Army (IRA)—began a program of armed resistance to British law enforcement officials, whom they saw as agents of a hostile and now foreign state. Michael Collins, a survivor of the Easter Rising and the new leader of the IRA, introduced an era of widespread political assassination with his handpicked "Squad" of guerrilla fighters. The British responded to what it perceived as terrorist activities with increased military and police force, but even the use of the infamous "Black and Tan" soldiers—poorly disciplined and often drunk—tended only to increase support for the new Irish government and for IRA violence.

After several years of guerrilla warfare, an uneasy truce recognized the reorganization of 26 southern and western counties into the Irish Free State in December 1921. The six northern counties that included Ulster were renamed Northern Ireland and remained in union with Great Britain. The Free State was given the same dominion status as that granted to Canada, an act that enraged the republican members of the IRA and Sinn Féin but which negotiators accepted as the only practical option and as a necessary step on the road to complete autonomy. The major sticking point—an oath of loyalty to the Commonwealth—would eventually be dropped after 1932.

The Anglo-Irish Treaty that established these conditions was accepted by a narrow margin in the Dáil, and the close vote prefigured the mood of the country. Although fewer than a third of the seats in the new Provisional Government went to anti-treaty candidates, it was appallingly clear that those who opposed the partition of Ireland would not accept the new reality quietly. De Valera himself refused to acknowledge a partitioned Ireland, walking out of the Dáil after the treaty was confirmed. Even the IRA was divided, with Collins's loyalists accepting the treaty and a vocal minority, known as the Irregulars, providing the militia for the anti-treaty faction. Almost immediately, civil war engulfed the Irish Free State. Several hundred on each side were killed in the fighting, which lasted from June 1922 to May 1923. Collins himself died in an ambush in August 1922. The Provisional Government gained notoriety for its brutal tactics against its opponents, including the suspension of trial by jury for suspected rebels. Some ten thousand individuals were simply thrown in jail without due process during the 12 months of war.

After the civil war ended, new elections placed most power in the hands of the reconstituted Provisional Party, the Cumann na nGaedheal. Sinn Féin remained resolutely anti-treaty and refused to sit in the Dublin parliament. The new government had to reestablish stability in the wake of the war, and also had to attempt to forge relations with the north, where Catholics retained a painful minority status. It became clear that the new administration had neither power nor appetite for more fighting over the boundaries between the Irish Free State and the North, and gradually the prospect of continued conflict began to subside.

POSTWAR BRITAIN AND THE ELECTIONS OF 1918

Much of this played out for Britons only in the newspaper, as "the Irish Question" remained comfortably far from home. The postwar period in

Great Britain as a whole was difficult even without the problems of an independent Ireland. Elections in 1918 returned a coalition government now heavily weighted toward the Conservatives. This set of elections included women voters for the first time: the 1918 Representation of the People Act had expanded the franchise from 8 million to 21 million to include all adult males as well as women property owners over the age of 30. (A further act in 1918 gave women the right to sit in the House of Commons.) David Lloyd George continued as prime minister, but his Liberal party had split among itself during the war over various issues including conscription. The new government in 1918 was therefore primarily a coalition of Conservatives and some so-called "Lloyd George Liberals." The minority position was held by Labour, which attracted the huge influx of new working-class voters. Traditional Liberals found themselves left out of the political conversation, a situation that would endure for many decades.

The new Conservative coalition was heavily oriented toward business and industry, a departure from the prewar Conservative alliance with the old squirearchy of Britain. Future prime minister Stanley Baldwin called them "a group of hard-faced men who looked as if they had done well out of the war."[3] Initially, these M.P.s presided over an 18-month postwar economic boom, a period in which control of essential services was handed back to private capitalists but during which the government also poured significant amounts of money and effort into social programs like subsidized housing and unemployment insurance.

This economic boom did not last. By 1920 the public debt had grown to over £7 billion, pushed upward in part by the period of postwar inflation that had gripped all of Europe in 1918–1919. Unemployment soared, especially in the older industries; by the summer of 1921 over 2 million were out of work. Trade unions turned to the strike again and again as their only real weapon against apparently unresponsive industrial leaders. Women who had entered the workforce by urgent invitation during the war found themselves forced back out as men were given preferential treatment for the jobs that still existed, discovering that suffrage without employment opportunities was a hollow victory indeed.

NEW POLITICAL ALIGNMENTS: RIGHT AND LEFT, CONSERVATIVE AND LABOUR

The government remained divided over how to deal with problems of economics and industry. Lloyd George alienated most of his coalition members through his remote personality and apparent disregard for the sufferings of the country, and the Conservative and Labour parties were deeply suspicious of one another. For the first time, the halls of Parliament were marked not by the sarcastically inflected but sincere friendships immortalized in the novels of Anthony Trollope, but by deeply bitter personal dislike that split the Commons, and politics in general, into Right and Left.

The Right, broadly speaking, included business, the professions, the Church of England, and the landed aristocracy, and adhered to the tenets of modified free trade, a representative democracy run by an educated elite, a belief in empire (including opposition to any form of independent Ireland), an overwhelming distrust of any type of socialism, and a conviction that "British character" would continue to provide ample leadership for the years ahead.

The Left included most Independent Liberals, Labour, the Fabians, and many religious Nonconformists and others unhappy with the status quo. Although the Left split within itself over ideological issues—the emergence of the Communist Soviet Union was only the most prominent of these issues—they did agree that postwar policy must include the nationalization of key industries, the government provision of a broad array of social services that were not linked to any idea of the moral character of the poor, hostility toward the continuation and especially the expansion of empire, and sympathy for the question of independence for India.

Lloyd George's coalition government fell in 1922, ostensibly over the question of war between Greece and Turkey—the so-called Chanak Crisis—but also because it had been seriously divided over the Irish Free State and expenditures for social services. The new elections saw a huge Conservative victory, with Andrew Bonar Law emerging as the new prime minister. Labour remained the main opposition party, with two separate Liberal parties splitting fewer than 25 percent of the seats between them. Bonar Law resigned owing to ill health within months and was replaced by Chancellor of the Exchequer Stanley Baldwin. Baldwin's government took aim at the remnants of free trade as a way to bring down the high unemployment rate—hovering at an apparently immoveable 13 percent by 1923—but this so enraged the Labour and Liberal M.P.s that Baldwin's government was forced out of office in new elections that saw, for the first time, a Labour government under Ramsay MacDonald placed in power. The king, Victoria's grandson, noted in his diary that "Today 23 years ago dear Grandmama died. I wonder what she would have thought of a Labour Government."[4]

MacDonald's Labour government would perhaps have shocked Victoria, but it was by most standards a moderate group of men who subscribed to the "gradualism" of the Fabians. The Chancellor of the Exchequer, Philip Snowden, almost immediately lowered taxes in order to cement ties with industry. While this move was not wildly popular among Labour voters, the main hurdle over which the party eventually stumbled was the official stance of the government toward the newly declared Soviet Union. In 1924 the USSR was formally recognized by the Labour government, which voted a loan to the new regime. In October, just before the 1924 general elections, the so-called Zinoviev letter appeared in the *Times*, in which the president of the Comintern called upon the Communist Party of Great Britain to work for the overthrow of the Crown. Voters flocked to the Conservatives, which won a large majority not only of its traditional party base but also of those who had helped elect Labour just two years previously.

Stanley Baldwin became prime minister again, with Winston Churchill as the new Chancellor of the Exchequer and Neville Chamberlain as Minister of Health, two positions that would prove key in the coming years. Labour had succeeded in demonstrating the weakness of the old Liberal Party, now edged aside by Labour as the recognized opposition, and Baldwin moved to capitalize on this. He also wanted to attract as many working-class voters as possible to the Conservative fold, eliminating the risk that Labour might win again. At the same time, he had to place the country on track to a full postwar recovery.

CHRONIC ECONOMIC PROBLEMS AND THE GENERAL STRIKE OF 1926

This latter task was a difficult one. The hyperinflation of the early '20s gave way to an economic depression, as British industry found itself no longer in command of the international field. Exports dropped dramatically, imports rose, the country's share of world shipping and other "invisible" services fell, overseas investments declined. Before mid-decade, interest rates had settled at an impossibly high level in order to discourage unnecessary spending, and many industries began to call for the reintroduction of protective tariffs and lower wages. By early 1925, a patchwork of measures had brought the pound sterling back up to relative parity with the U.S. dollar, and in April Winston Churchill declared a return to the gold standard.

This move was controversial and certainly did not solve the problems of the older industries, especially coal mining. In June 1925, mine owners argued that the survival of the industry depended on drastic measures and announced that wages would drop and working hours would increase, effective immediately. The miners threatened to strike. Negotiations, presided over by both the TUC and the government, merely forestalled the inevitable: the government's Samuel Commission issued a report after nine months of investigation arguing that the owners had indeed managed the industry poorly, but that no steps should currently be taken to raise wages or restore former hours. Instead, more investigation would be necessary before a gradual move toward nationalization could take place.

Negotiations broke off within weeks and on May 4, 1926, the nation's first general strike began, with miners joined by over a million and a half workers from the railway, transport, and dock unions, the metal and building trades, electricity and gas unions, and the printing unions. The government, which had been planning for such a contingency for weeks and which argued vociferously that a general strike was unconstitutional, called upon military forces and volunteers to take over essential services. For over a week, undergraduates from Oxford and Cambridge drove trams while Winston Churchill edited the national newspaper. On May 13 the strike was ended, much to the distress of many of the strikers, as the TUC accepted overtures by the government.

One year later, the Trade Disputes and Trade Union Act outlawed sympathetic strikes as well as any strike that would "inflict hardship" on the country, and also severely limited the actions of unions, forcing them to get written permission from each member before dues could be used for political activities. The only gesture to workers was the establishment of the Mond-Turner debates, a series of conferences beginning in 1927 that brought together leaders of industry and unions in order to try to define future actions and to determine potential government responsibility, particularly for the older industries. Attempts to establish a formal national industrial council that would include management, union, and government representatives failed.

NEW SOCIAL WELFARE PROGRAMS

At the same time, however, the new Ministry of Health under Neville Chamberlain put in place a set of reforms based upon the notion that the monetary and intellectual resources of the state should be put to work to help those who wanted to help themselves. This was not a move back to the nineteenth-century notion of the "deserving poor," but rather a formal recognition that the government had responsibilities that it alone could fulfill and that the poor often needed a boost in order to leave poverty behind. Chamberlain's ministry rammed through nearly two dozen bills between 1924 and 1929, revising the Old Age Pensions Act, funding new housing, and establishing new health benefits.

Perhaps the most revolutionary action by the ministry came with the 1929 Local Government Act, which abolished the remnants of the old Poor Law and its emphasis on poor relief and introduced instead the idea of public assistance provided by county agencies. From this point on, assistance would be calculated based not upon some subjective notion of moral worth, but rather on objective measures such as age, health status, number of dependents, and employment status. All of these programs were to be paid for through conservative economic policies, and none of them was "socialism" in any sense of the term. Instead, partial monopolies were granted in important services, but the private, profit-seeking individual still had ample room to operate. In addition, there was no talk of eliminating unemployment through "artificial" government intervention. The government should pay unemployment benefits, yes, but the market itself should determine employment levels.

The worldwide depression that began in mid-1929 placed these programs in jeopardy, and the Labour government that took office in the 1929 elections faced terrible economic problems. Unemployment figures rose to 2.5 million by 1930; export levels fell by 1931 to just over half of what they had been in 1929. The predicted deficit for 1932 was estimated at £120 million.[5]

The report of this potentially astronomical deficit level brought down the Labour government, and in the crisis that ensued, a new coalition government, called the National Government, was formed. Ramsay MacDonald remained as prime minister until 1935, when he would be replaced by Stanley Baldwin (until 1937) and then Neville Chamberlain (until 1940). The new government immediately slashed unemployment benefits and state salaries, raised taxes, and removed Britain from the gold standard, causing the pound sterling to fall to about 70 percent of its previous value. More contentiously, at the Ottawa Conference of 1932, the government introduced a general 10 percent duty on all imported goods except for wheat, meat, and some raw materials. A combination of quotas and subsidies protected domestic production of milk and some other agricultural products, so that farm production rose while food prices remained relatively stable. Other actions by the new government included the nationalization of the London transport industry. The government pointed to lowered levels of unemployment to justify its actions: an initial spike in unemployment to 23 percent in January 1933 was followed by a steady decline.[6]

CHANGES TO THE BRITISH EMPIRE

While the focus at home was the economy, changes were afoot in the empire. A working definition of "dominions" had finally been arrived at in 1926. Dominions were "autonomous communities within the British Empire, equal in status, in no way subordinate to one another in any aspect of their domestic or external affairs, though united by a common allegiance to the Crown, and freely associated as members of the British Commonwealth of Nations."[7] This definition applied to the Irish Free State, Canada, Australia, New Zealand, South Africa, and Newfoundland. The office of governor-general in these dominions was gradually emptied of any real powers after 1926. At the 1931 Westminster Conference these dominions were granted power to act without any Crown interference unless requested by the dominion itself.

Other areas of empire continued to provoke conflicting reaction at home and abroad. Britain had participated in the so-called "scramble for Africa" in the 1880s, adding strategically to its existing holdings in South Africa and Egypt. Britain had also, if somewhat unwillingly, placed troops in Egypt in 1882 to protect the Suez Canal, which had been built by the French but whose control had passed to Britain in 1875 when Disraeli directed the government to purchase nearly half of the stock in the Suez Canal Company from the Egyptian Khedive. By 1900 new colonies had been established to protect access to the canal as well as to house new military and trading bases on the continent. None of these was considered to be potentially self-governing in the foreseeable future, and thus military and administrative machinery continued to characterize the British presence in Africa.

In India, as always, the situation was more complex. The notion of self-rule in India as a stepping-stone to full dominion status had been discussed since 1857, but always in terms that painted the colony as insufficiently prepared for such measures. Instead, the Indian Civil Service became an entrenched feature on the subcontinent, even as the borders of the Raj broadened to protect against possible Russian expansionism in the northwest. In 1885 the first meeting of the Indian National Congress (INC) was convened to discuss India's future status. The INC increasingly focused on autonomy and independence, pressuring the government in Westminster to move toward a reconstructed government for India that replaced white British officers and governors with educated Indians, whose numbers had steadily grown during the Victorian period. By the end of the nineteenth century the discussions of an autonomous Indian nation were beginning in earnest, even as religious differences within the

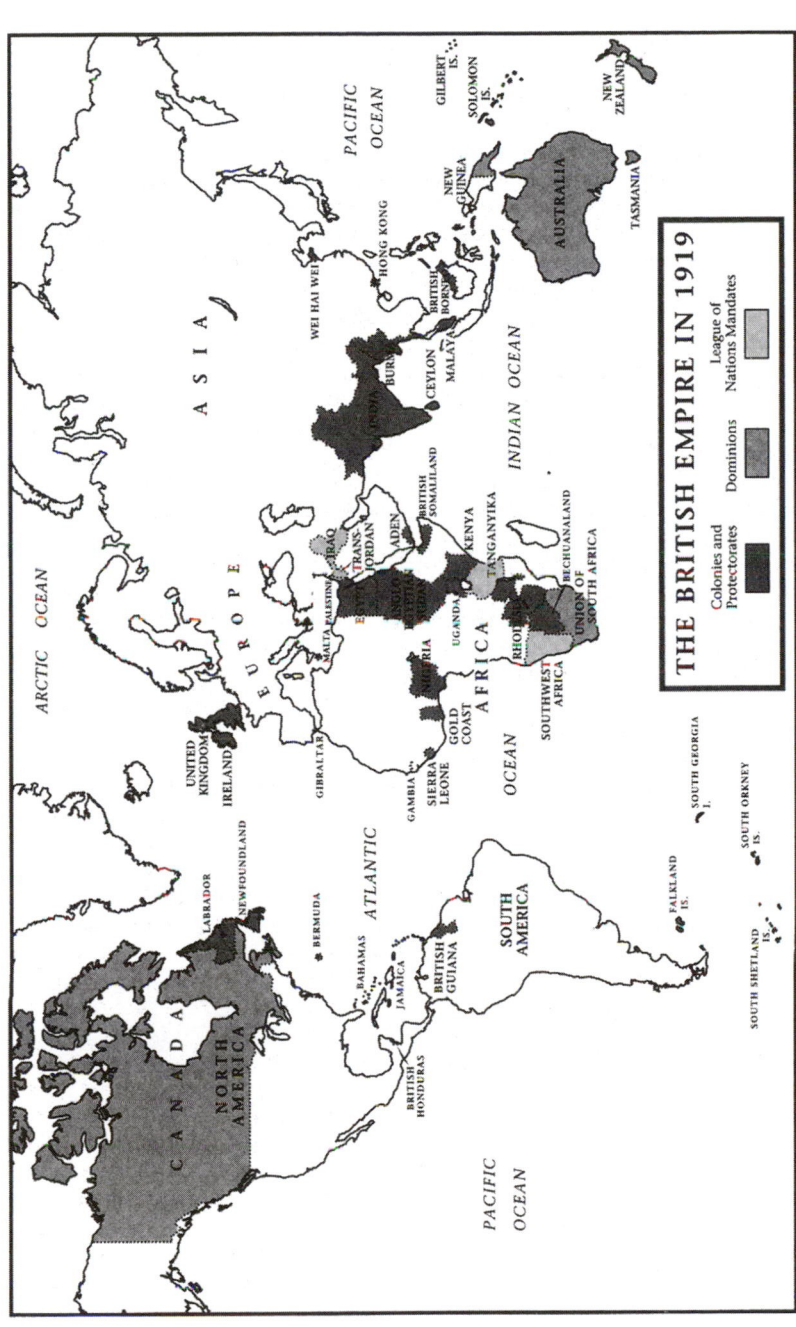

THE BRITISH EMPIRE IN 1919

Colonies and Protectorates

Dominions

League of Nations Mandates

From Walter Arnstein, *Britain Yesterday and Today: 1830 to the Present, Seventh Edition.* Copyright © 1996 by Houghton Mifflin Company. Reprinted with permission.

subcontinent threatened to fracture the fragile unity within the INC. The partition of Bengal in particular polarized both Hindus and Muslims, with each group splitting amongst itself and spawning a violent nationalist subgroup. The Muslims eventually withdrew altogether from the INC to form a separate Muslim League in 1906.

Reforms in 1909 satisfied no one, ignoring as they did the entire principle of self-rule. A decade later, the Crown introduced a constitution that combined provincial self-government with complete British control over the central government. But even as these new measures were implemented, the so-called Amritsar Massacre in April 1919 signaled the beginning of a new era of resistance. Mohandas Gandhi, advocating peaceful noncooperation against the British Crown, was quickly identified with large-scale civil disobedience and was jailed in 1922 for his work. All of this appeared to confirm the worst fears of the doomsayers, that India was simply incapable of self-rule. Others regarded as more dangerous the patchwork of minorities within the subcontinent if they were each granted autonomy, and the INC itself pushed for an autonomous government that would give a central Indian authority vast powers over these minority groups in order to maintain peace and prevent the further eruption of religious violence.

The 1931 Westminster Conference did not apply to the subcontinent, but the Crown recognized that dominion status for India was inevitable. The British government turned for assistance to Gandhi, who had spent the previous decade in and out of prison for his resistance activities, and who by the early '30s claimed to represent the INC and all of India in the move toward autonomy. A 1935 constitution gave full autonomous powers to the provincial government while uniting all the provinces along with the remaining princely states under a federal government. Elections were held for the first time in 1937, but resistance to the structure and powers of the proposed federal government prevented the full transition to a self-governing dominion. The governor-general appointed by the Crown thus retained enormous powers even as this same office had become a figurehead in the other Crown dominions. Further action regarding dominion status was temporarily shelved in 1939 with the outbreak of war against Hitler.

LITERATURE AND CULTURE FROM 1900 TO THE TWENTIES

The golden Edwardian era saw new expressions of culture often targeted to new audiences. For example, children's literature became an immensely rich field, with E. Nesbit providing a model for generations of writers like Noel Streatfeld and C. S. Lewis. Writers like G. A. Henty churned out formula books that invited boys to dream about empire; more sophisticated writers, from H. Rider Haggard to Rudyard Kipling, also used the power of imperialism to shape their fiction and poetry. Often this literature was borrowed by industry to help sell consumer goods that were not necessarily related to the political and economic aspects of the empire: soap, for example, became a consumer good linking the cleanliness of home to the threatening dirt of Africa and Asia in a battle where cleanliness always won.

The deliberately shocking works of the fin de siècle continued to resonate through the first two decades of the new century, but the movements identified with the years just before and after the First World War—the most famous of which was the Bloomsbury movement of Virginia Woolf, Lytton Strachey, E. M. Forster, and Clive and Vanessa Bell—were devoted not only to shifting the boundaries of art and literature but also, in important ways, to reworking the themes of the Victorian period, especially those of family, society, and empire. Novelists experimented with new techniques like the stream-of-consciousness voice made famous by Woolf and Irish writer James Joyce; poets like T. S. Eliot and dramatists like George Bernard Shaw also played with language in new ways that were often grouped together under the rubric of "modernism."

Others, less deliberately modern, applied twentieth-century glitter to nineteenth-century forms, especially the fading aristocracy, often with delightfully fizzy results: the plays of Noël Coward, for instance, were fondly satirical while the novels of Evelyn Waugh were less affectionate and more cynical, if equally funny. P. G. Wodehouse was perhaps the least biting of these writers in his stories and novels about the bumbling young aristocrat, Bertie Wooster, whose very survival depended upon his unflappable butler, Jeeves.

The early twentieth century saw the rise of mass culture in Britain represented by the cinema, the radio, the new British Broadcasting Company, and an increasing number of mass daily newspapers. By the late '20s, this culture began to include consumer goods like washing machines and vacuum cleaners, accessible under "hire-purchase" programs. These goods occupied a hybrid ground as both representatives of "luxury" and as items that redirected women's domestic energies. A washing machine made life easier, true, but it also conveyed expectations of new levels of cleanliness that could be an undisputed burden for housewives.

The rise of mass culture that included women and children as cultural consumers was a phenomenon that would have been unthinkable to Victoria. Yet within three decades of her death, her kingdom had once again changed irrevocably, this time with exponential speed. More changes were waiting in the '30s and '40s.

NOTES

1. Quoted in R. K. Webb, *Modern England: From the 18th Century to the Present*, 2d ed. (New York: Harper and Row, 1980), pp. 464–65.

2. Quoted in Paul Fussell, *The Great War and Modern Memory* (Oxford and New York: Oxford University Press, 1975), p. 81.

3. Baldwin to John Maynard Keynes, quoted in Alfred F. Havighurst, *Britain in Transition: The Twentieth Century*, 4th ed. (Chicago: University of Chicago Press, 1985), p. 181.

4. Quoted in Havighurst, p. 181.

5. Figures are from R. K. Webb, *Modern England*, p. 529.

6. Peter Clarke, *Hope and Glory: Britain 1900–1990* (London and New York: Penguin Books, 1997), p. 178.

7. Webb, *Modern England*, p. 534.

10

Decades of Crisis: 1930–1960

THE 1930S AND LIFE ON THE DOLE

Life in the '30s continued to be marked both by terrible economic problems and by anxious worries over the fragile international peace. In Britain, the 1936 abdication crisis of King Edward VIII provided a temporary distraction, ably managed by Prime Minister Stanley Baldwin. Within a year of his accession, Edward had gone into exile as Duke of Windsor, joined by his new wife, the twice-divorced American Wallis Simpson. Edward's brother took the throne as George VI. His reign, like those of his father and great-grandmother before him, would provide a model of exemplary personal and family behavior.

But absorbing interest in the former king's love life could not balance chronic anxieties over jobs and industry. The serious levels of unemployment that had plagued the country in the '20s appeared irreversible during the '30s, significantly changing the culture of the working classes and the attitudes of the government toward the poor and unemployed. The problem was not the temporarily unemployed, a category that carried with it the assumption that jobs would turn up and that unemployment benefits were simply a short-term solution to a short-term problem. The numbers of temporary unemployed, as well as the newly underemployed, certainly increased in the 1930s, and the bitterness of these men and women increased significantly as it became apparent that "temporarily" might mean "forever." But there was also an entire generation entering adulthood with no prospects of employment. This was the challenge of the 1930s, and it was a problem that no previous government had faced.

Complicating all of this was the undeniable fact that the problems of unemployment and underemployment were localized and industry-based rather than national, affecting most severely the older industries and the rural northwest. Many parts of the economy did quite well after the introduction of protective tariffs. Overall, real wages rose significantly in the 1930s even as many found themselves permanently unemployed. A boom in housing fueled a boom in the purchase of durable consumer goods, while certain industries like the motor industry reshaped whole towns around a new kind of prosperity. This localization of both prosperity and poverty allowed those in the cities and the southern countryside to regard the problems of unemployment as manageable, something that would pass as new industries developed to replace the old.

The National Government, the coalition government elected in 1932 and led by Stanley Baldwin through the abdication crisis and by Neville Chamberlain thereafter, was happy to point to the positives and to argue that the economic recovery of the early '30s would eventually lift all boats, even those in the blighted northwest. No new direct programs to create jobs would be necessary. Thus, the government's solution to the problems of chronic unemployment was to supplement the existing system of unemployment insurance—a benefit for those who had formerly had a job—with a system of unemployment relief, which was to be extended to all those who couldn't qualify for unemployment insurance because they had been out of work for too long or because they were the never-employed.

The main feature, and the most hated part, of this new program was the so-called Family Means Test, which assessed the overall income and resources of the entire family before allocating relief to individuals. This had the unfortunate effect of discouraging thrift; it also persuaded people not to take low-paying jobs, since a family could actually receive more benefits if all members were unemployed and out of savings than if some were employed. It also encouraged a certain degree of "ratting out" the neighbors, as government employees questioned neighbors and friends to determine the true need level of the family.

Despite these problems, by the mid-1930s some 40 percent of the unemployed were receiving their only relief from this program, having exhausted all other sources of benefit such as trade union insurance. "The dole," as it was quickly dubbed, became a fixed part of life for many areas, and in too many towns it was not uncommon to have entire neighborhoods "on the dole." Any vestige of personal shame tended to disappear under such circumstances, since it was impossible to maintain the fiction that individual moral failure was the root of this kind of poverty. Instead, even the most conservative of Conservatives began to question how the state might best begin to develop programs to help its poorest citizens.

Not surprisingly, the problems of endemic poverty—especially its effects on character and morale—colored popular culture during the interwar period. Walter Greenwood's *Love on the Dole* put a human face on the sufferings of decaying northern industry. Victor Gollancz's Left Book Club and its counterpart, the Right Book Club, produced volumes of thoughtful prose for readers interested in the exploration of contemporary political and economic questions.

Many of those writing for the Left and Right Book Clubs were particularly taken up with the developing antagonism between communism and fascism. The Soviet Union's experiment with communism attracted a small but vocal minority that included many former Fabians. At the opposite extreme, Sir Oswald Mosley emerged as the leader of the relatively ineffective British Union of Fascists. Both communist and fascist sympathizers were seeking some measure of order that would resolve the apparent disarray that plagued Britain. A similar impulse propelled many others into what George Orwell famously dismissed as "smelly little isms"—vegetarianism, feminism, and anti-vivisectionism, among others.[1] At the same time, however, because economic decay was relatively localized, many Britons could and did live as though these larger questions of ideology were unimportant. They could pretend that life on the dole, and the deeper issues this reflected, were figments of a particularly ill-tempered and pessimistic imagination.

THE SPANISH CIVIL WAR AND THE QUESTION OF APPEASEMENT

The Spanish Civil War, which began in 1936, served as a wake-up call for many Britons. The Right and Left Book Clubs were among the most prominent cultural voices to use the outbreak of war as a way to intensify discussions about social changes that were already underway. Further, this war warned many Britons that the world was not at peace and that another continental war—perhaps even on the scale of the Great War—was a possibility.

Britain had pursued disarmament during the '20s and early '30s, cutting military expenditures in part to help reduce budget deficits. But in 1935, when secret negotiations to assist Italy in the partition of Abyssinia became public, the sharp outcry against the negotiations and particularly against the appetites of Italian imperialism introduced a note of warning into public discussion. Hitler's drive back into the Rhineland in March 1936 appeared to further threaten any "civilized" commitment to disarmament and peace, and by the outbreak of war in Spain three months later, a small but growing number of men and women had begun to push for a rejection of the official policy of disarmament and a return to a careful and deliberate rearmament of Britain in case the worst should happen. In November, the government voted modest increases for the armed forces as a first step, but Baldwin's administration was reluctant to do more, especially given prevailing financial constraints.

When Neville Chamberlain replaced Stanley Baldwin as prime minister, in the general elections following the coronation of the new king George VI in 1937, his dedication to a "reasonable settlement" to prevent the outbreak of any new world war was still very much the popular option. The Foreign Secretary, Anthony Eden, was the public face of the administration's commitment to preventing war by remedying long-standing grievances, as for instance by acquiescing in Hitler's actions in the Rhineland. But Chamberlain himself was the prime actor behind foreign policy, and Eden resigned, frustrated, in early 1938. Hitler's next actions, to annex Austria and then to demand control of the Sudetenland at the expense of an independent Czechoslovakia, focused public and political attention even more closely on foreign affairs.

At the same time that many prominent public organs, such as the *Times*, came out in support of Chamberlain's commitment to peace and self-determination for Czech Germans, preparations began for what increasingly appeared to be an inevitable military conflict with Hitler. In late September 1938, as the French government in particular raised objections to the imminent partition of Czechoslovakia, the British government distributed millions of gas masks and made plans to evacuate schoolchildren and adults from London should war break out.

The Munich agreement of September 30, 1938 temporarily averted disaster by requiring Czechoslovakia to surrender the Sudetenland to Hitler. But the scare underscored the problems in any long-term policies of appeasement, and in March of 1939 the worst fears of many appeared to be coming true as Hitler annexed the remainder of a supposedly free Czechoslovakia and then turned his attention to Poland. Britain and France quickly put in place treaties with each other and with Poland pledging to come to the aid of the Polish government with military assistance should Germany invade. These treaties were not signed until the literal eve of war: the treaty with Poland, for instance, took effect on August 25, 1939, just a week before Germany's invasion.

WORLD WAR TWO: THE PEOPLE'S WAR

During the Munich crisis of September 1938, the "trial run" for war had forced British urban areas to develop and test bomb shelters and evacuation plans. When actual war broke out a year later, a certain level of preparedness was in place. Winston Churchill became the prime minister in May 1940, setting the tone for the next several years with his famous "blood, toil, tears and sweat" speech: "Victory—victory at all costs, victory in spite of all terror; victory, however long and hard the road may be." In June, the road became particularly long and hard, as France fell and it became "Britain alone" until Russia entered the war in 1941.

This war quickly became "the people's war" in a way that the Great War had not been. This was partly because Hitler's air strikes against London and other cities in the Blitz, which began in June 1940, led to high levels of civilian casualties. Damage to roads, houses, and other parts of the country's infrastructure was also quite high. In one week in April 1941, for instance, Plymouth lost 600 men and women and had 20,000 homes destroyed; a week of bombing in Liverpool killed nearly 2,000. In May 1941, the chamber of the House of Commons was destroyed by a bomb. In all, civilian casualties over the course of six years of fighting would reach 61,000 dead and 86,000 seriously injured, with over a third of the country's housing stock destroyed by bombing. Food rationing became the norm—even the king had a ration book—as did blackout curtains and air raid sirens and huddling for shelter with the neighbors in subway tunnels.

On the front itself, nearly 300,000 soldiers would lose their lives in this war, with unprecedented numbers of men and women drafted into military service. By 1944, approximately 40 percent of eligible men were serving in the armed forces, some 5 million altogether. This meant that the total of 300,000 military dead was very much lower as a percent of total forces than had lost their lives in the Great War. As in the previous war, British soldiers included large numbers of men from throughout the empire.

The costs of the war were astronomical. Much of this was met, at least temporarily, through heavy borrowing from the United States and through heavy taxation at home, nearly 50 percent for those with modest incomes and up to 97 percent in the highest tax brackets. The government was forced to intervene in the economy in unprecedented ways. In what became known as "war socialism," the government directed production, distribution, and labor organization. Government expenditure skyrocketed to an amazing £6 billion in 1945, and unemployment almost disappeared. John Maynard Keynes, an economist associated with the Liberal party in the 1930s, became one of the chief forces behind the war economy, promoting food subsidies and tax increases simultaneously as a way to fund not only the war but also the vast array of social services that, paradoxically, increased in availability and quality during the war years. Keynes argued that, rather than emphasizing thrift and savings, the government should instead promote consumption as a way to stimulate production and wealth. Government programs should be actively interventionist, using consumption as a way to reach full employment and to end deficit spending, and redistributing at least some wealth in order to eliminate deep pockets of poverty.

A POSTWAR ECONOMY AND THE BIRTH OF THE WELFARE STATE

Keynes and others, including the social reformer William Beveridge, began early in the war to plan for Britain's postwar economy. The Beveridge Report of 1942, *Social Insurance and Allied Services,* which became a surprise best-seller among the public, articulated a planned economy that was based upon a broad notion of social progress. Comprehensive social welfare benefits should be the key to any forward movement after the war. These benefits had to be provided through cooperation between the state and the individual, rather than through one or the other. This future program of benefits should provide a "national minimum" that would not eliminate capitalist incentives toward individual achievement. Finally, this national minimum should include guaranteed employment (rather than focusing on unemployment insurance) as well as basic health and welfare coverage. All of this, in Beveridge's proposed scheme, would be funded through compulsory but equitable contributions, so that everyone would be entitled from the start to a flat rate of benefit in exchange for a flat rate of contribution. The hated family means test would be abandoned.

The Beveridge Report was discussed but not adopted by the wartime coalition government. This reluctance was partly because the Labour and Conservative members of that coalition envisioned a postwar political climate in which one or the other party could again dominate and could then take credit for any sweeping changes in the economy. At the same time, the expenses of the war itself prevented any definitive commitment to such a large program.

In 1945, after peace had been declared, Labour swept into office under Clement Atlee and began to implement many of the basic ideas articulated in the Beveridge Report, crafting what would become known as the welfare state. It had the advantage, this time, of being a true Labour government, strong enough to avoid any forced compromises with Liberal, Conservative, or Sinn Féin M.P.s. Atlee's government would endure until 1951, and in the half dozen years after the end of the war it nationalized basic industries (airlines, banking, coal, transport, gas and electricity, iron and steel), extended control over much of the insurance and housing industries, and—perhaps most revolutionary—passed the National Health Service (NHS) Act to provide free health care to all Britons. Private medicine remained an option but "national health" became part of the national vocabulary, along with complaints about endless waits and overcrowded hospitals.

All of this was built upon the concept that full employment was possible and would pay for these benefits, so that Labour could talk about cradle-to-grave services as part of an overall program of economic strength rather than as a new version of life on the dole. Individuals were expected to work in an environment where the government guaranteed opportunities for employment, and working individuals and their families would then receive benefits for which they had indirectly paid. Any unemployment would be temporary. There would be no return to the moral slackness or despair that, for many, had been the worst part of the previous program of unemployment benefits.

This program, taken altogether, would be tremendously expensive to introduce, and it came at a time when the national debt was at its highest level ever. In fact, Britain's indebtedness especially to the United States would endure for years to come, and would shape every attempt to revitalize industry and manufacturing. Taxes were raised on income and on inheritance. Food rationing was continued, with even bread rationed after the war. Controls on production and distribution were extended and limits enforced on consumption of domestic goods with an eye to boosting the level of exports, which had fallen to disastrous lows by the end of the war.

On a day-to-day basis, almost every Briton was affected by the experience of endless lines for basic foods and other goods, and by the lack of any kind of luxury goods. Paradoxically, those who had been mired in poverty before 1939 saw their standard of living increase dramatically, with nearly full employment and at least a minimum of food and fuel available. Seebohm Rowntree revisited York in the late '40s and found that the number of people living in what he had dubbed "primary poverty" had fallen from 30 percent to 3 percent. But the extras were nearly impossible to come by, and the late '40s were a period of austerity and drabness for many. Even the well-to-do could no longer sustain the kind of servant-heavy life they had enjoyed before the war. The chronic problems of indebtedness could not be solved solely by doing without, however, and it was the extension of Marshall Plan aid to Britain and the devaluation of the pound sterling in 1949 by over 30 percent (from $4.03 to $2.80) that finally pushed the British economy into recovery.

DISMANTLING THE EMPIRE

One of the expenses that had to be met after the war was the high cost of preparing for the end of empire. The British Empire had not collapsed after 1939, as many had feared; indeed, even the fully dependent colonies whose peoples had been agitating most strongly for self-government remained loyal to the British flag rather than breaking away and negotiating a separate peace with the Germans. But it was clear to almost everyone after 1945 that the empire could no longer be sustained. Bargains struck during the late '30s and early '40s already pointed toward eventual self-rule for the remaining parts of empire, and the notion that Britain must simply fulfill its duties of "trusteeship," preparing colonies for autonomy, became the official line.

There were, of course, issues of finance: Britain needed its colonial income for as long as possible, and even a Labour government admitted that the economy could not initially sustain itself if the colonies simply disappeared. Morally, as well, the government argued that Britain was obliged to lay the groundwork for successful autonomy, smoothing the way in areas where religious or ethnic or tribal minorities might otherwise suffer great persecution.

The problem was that the empire still covered so many different types of colonies. Further, many British settlers felt that their own interests demanded the continuation of a strong British administrative and military presence, especially in East Africa, where the hope of a new white dominion held great attraction for those Britons in Kenya, Uganda, and neighboring areas. Some parts of the empire were especially touchy—Palestine, for instance, which had been under British control since 1922, was the site of increasing postwar conflict between Palestinian Arabs and the Jews who looked to Britain to fulfill its 1917 promises to help create a Jewish state in the Middle East.

In 1945 the Labour government's Colonial Development and Welfare Act appropriated £120 million to the colonies—all of them together—to be used to build roads, schools, houses, colleges, and other structures and to develop potentially lucrative agricultural and manufacturing bases. While these funds appeared to be tied to rapid transitions to self-government in Asian colonies, in Africa even the most optimistic and anti-imperialist voices agreed that it would be "at least a generation" before African colonies were ready for any measure of autonomy.

In India, the path to independence was complicated by religious conflict. The Muslim League, formed in 1906, increasingly feared that the formation of an independent India would immediately put the Muslim minority at risk from the Hindu majority, a risk that had been tempered under British control. Agitation for a separate Muslim state had been at the top of the League's agenda for decades, and in the immediate postwar period, as it became increasingly clear that Britain no longer wished nor could afford to maintain control over the Raj, violence erupted throughout the subcontinent. The Muslim demand for a separate Pakistan appeared in the end the only way to resolve the crisis without starting a full-fledged civil war, and even then millions lost their lives in riots and localized fighting. The "jewel in the crown of empire" became two separate states in August 1947, with both India and Pakistan surprisingly choosing to remain members of the Commonwealth.

Indian independence was quickly followed by independence for other colonies and clearer autonomy for members of the informal empire. Burma and Ceylon gained independence in 1948, Palestine was cut loose from its mandate status in the same year, and portions of the Arab peninsula asserted increasing control over British interests, as seen in the nationalization of the Anglo-Iranian Oil Company in the early 1950s. But the British colonies in Africa, running from South Africa in an unbroken line north to Egypt, were still regarded as candidates for independence only at some vague future date.

THE SUEZ CRISIS

Egypt in particular proved embarrassing to Britain in the 1950s. Although Egypt had gained nominal independence in 1936, British interests dictated the presence of a significant military presence in and around the Suez Canal. Egyptian nationalists agitated for the withdrawal of those

troops, which was accomplished in 1954 with the Baghdad Treaty. However, two years later Egyptian President Nasser nationalized the Suez Canal Company, still owned by France, and invited the entire Arab Peninsula
to join Egypt in pushing all remaining British and other European interests
out of the region.

Because the canal remained key to international shipping, this action
was viewed as alarming and even incendiary. Protest against what was
seen as a deliberate destabilization of the Middle East cut across party
lines in Britain, with Conservative and Labour M.P.s agreeing that British
influence should be asserted even more clearly and that Nasser's actions
had been both illegal and dictatorial. Some, including Conservative Prime
Minister Anthony Eden, argued that Nasser must have ties to the Soviet
Union.

Eden, working secretly with France and the new state of Israel (created
in 1948), authorized the military invasion of Egypt and the use of force to
capture the canal and oust Nasser, despite the fact that negotiations with
Nasser were well underway. In a planned series of events, Israel invaded
Egypt in late October and Eden's government sent troops in to "assist,"
at the same time preparing the public for a long war to "protect" Israel.
But Egyptian forces were defeated within days, and the ministry was
forced to agree to the replacement of British troops by United Nations
forces. International public opinion, especially in the United States whose
financial aid continued to be crucial to the British economy, rapidly turned
against Eden's administration. Even many members of the Commonwealth joined in the censure. Domestic opinion was no kinder. Eden's
government suffered humiliation and Eden himself was driven by ill
health to resign. More importantly, Britain lost any remaining status as a
major world power that could continue to act with impunity.

DOMESTIC STABILITY AND THE WELFARE STATE

As the limits of British influence and control steadily contracted, life at
home was stable and predictable at last. Domestic life turned to the rearing
of babies as the birth rate rose after 1945 to levels not seen since before
the Great War. Age at marriage dropped, giving couples more fertile years,
and by the early 1960s there were nine babies born for every 100 women
of childbearing age—a level that guaranteed ample use of Labour's cradle-
to-grave program of services, especially the child allowance that supple-
mented family incomes for those with two or more children.

The first real blow to the uninterrupted continuation of welfare benefits
came with Britain's involvement in the Korean War (1950–1953). Labour,

still in office, undertook an expensive program of general rearmament, sharing the fears of many in this new era of Cold War that the outcome of the Korean conflict might destabilize the entire European continent if the balance of powers shifted toward the Soviet Union. Chancellor of the Exchequer Hugh Gaitskell raised the basic income tax to 47.5 percent, with another 50 percent levied in a surtax on the highest incomes. However, it was not this action but rather his introduction of charges for NHS–supplied dentures and glasses that split Labour, a split that would give the Conservatives the opening they had pined for since 1945. Aneurin Bevan, who had created the NHS during his stint as Minister of Health, was now Minister of Labour, and he resigned in early 1951 in disgust over what he perceived as Gaitskell's mishandling of the health service. Bevan and his followers formed a left-wing splinter group within Labour that pressed hard to reduce dependence upon the United States and to push further toward nationalization of all services. The 1951 general elections were won by the narrowest of margins by the Conservatives, and Winston Churchill once again became prime minister.

Churchill almost immediately turned to one of the most pressing of domestic issues, that of housing. Half a million houses had been damaged or destroyed during the war and the immediate postwar focus had been on rebuilding industry, with the result that by 1951, given the steady rise in the birth rate, many families were crammed into substandard housing. Churchill created a new Ministry of Housing under Harold Macmillan, which easily met its goal of 300,000 new units of housing by 1953. Much of the housing built under Macmillan's tenure was so-called "council housing," owned and operated by local authorities and let at low rates to families with low incomes.

The Conservatives also took aim at another nagging issue, that of education. The Butler Education Act passed in 1944 had raised the school-leaving age to 15, and had established a system that "streamed" children into three types of schools based upon exams at the age of eleven: some children would continue on to secondary grammar schools to prepare for university, some to technical schools for vocational training, and some to secondary modern schools for all other needs. (Similar acts were passed in Scotland in 1945 and in Ireland in 1947, although in Scotland the division into grammar/technical/modern schools tended to be much less concrete and class-bound.) By the 1950s, however, it was clear that secondary modern schools were simply a dumping ground for the 65 percent or so of working-class children who were unprepared for the eleven-plus exams. They were merely being "trained" for working-class jobs with no real hope for any upward mobility, whether social or intellectual. The

Conservative administrations under Churchill and his successors pushed to combine these various tracks, or streams, of education into comprehensive schools. Such comprehensives would not solve all of the problems of class-based public education, by any means, but they did help reduce some of the worst abuses of the secondary modern system.

POPULAR CULTURE IN THE 1950S

By the mid-1950s, although the costs of the military and defense continued to slow the overall economic recovery, the standard of living for most of the population was undeniably higher than it had been at any time in memory. Postwar consumer culture now included not simply canned food and cheap clothing but also household appliances and automobiles. Average weekly earnings rose 50 percent between 1950 and 1955, during which the cost of living rose by 30 percent. And because full employment was the norm, this rise in standards of living was not limited to certain areas or certain industries. Until 1970, in fact, the level of unemployment rarely rose above 2 percent. As Harold Macmillan told an audience in 1957, "Most of our people have never had it so good."[2]

Popular culture both reflected and challenged this statement. The 1951 Festival of Britain, a deliberate echo of the Great Exhibition a century before, celebrated the arts and industry in six permanent installments in London and the Midlands, as well as with a traveling exhibition designed to reach as many Britons as possible. It was a huge success, attracting over 10 million to the exhibition sites and many more to the 22 arts festivals associated with the event. Those who could not attend could listen and watch as the BBC—the British Broadcasting Corporation, founded as a radio corporation in 1922 and expanding into television in 1936–1937—broadcast special programming about and from the festival. The entire event was designed to mark the end of the long and difficult postwar period and to signal a new era in British life and culture.

The involvement of the BBC was significant, because more and more the broadcasting company and its rivals, including the new ITV, were becoming a central part of daily life for most Britons. Radio had been crucial in keeping up morale during the Second World War, but in the '50s it was being eclipsed by television—owned by 5 million families in 1956.[3] The BBC as a whole was committed to a particular kind of moral and educational programming, exemplified for many in its so-called Third Programme of arts and classical music. Its television offerings were similarly designed.

Television itself radically changed the ways in which culture was experienced. The coronation of Elizabeth II in 1953 drew millions of viewers to the BBC, giving the event a unique sense of immediacy. Other effects were less uniformly positive: for example, coverage of public sporting events led many to experience football and rugby and tennis from their armchairs, rather than on the field, so that the number of patrons at local sports clubs declined precipitously in the '50s and '60s. And the popularity of television led, as it did elsewhere, to a decline in filmgoing. The postwar film studios produced popular and important films but audiences continued to shrink, even after film itself had gained credence as an important cultural tool and even as filmmakers began using the medium for biting social criticism and experimental art.

In drama and literature, there was a similar outburst of anger, as the so-called "angry young men" filled pages with brutal descriptions of a declining post-imperial Britain. Whereas in the '40s Evelyn Waugh had written frothy if nasty satires about the problems of postwar England, these newer writers—including John Osborne, whose *Look Back in Anger* epitomized the bitterness of the movement—focused on kitchen-sink realism, substituting squalor for satire and fury for cynicism. All of this emotion was driven by two warring perceptions: first, that Britain was changing beyond recognition, not only through the continuation of the welfare state but also through various advances in the sciences and industry (Britain detonated its first atomic bomb in 1951, and Watson and Crick began their work on DNA in the early '50s). Second, that Britain was not changing at all, but was instead mired in its past and was therefore class-bound, rigid, industrially backward, and without any outlet for the creative and chaotic impulses of its young men and women. Both perceptions were correct, at least in part.

NOTES

1. George Orwell, *The Road to Wigan Pier* (1937; reprint, San Diego, Calif.: Harcourt Brace and Co., 1958).

2. Peter Clarke, *Hope and Glory: Britain 1900–1990* (London and New York: Penguin Books, 1997), p. 255.

3. Clarke, *Hope and Glory*, p. 250.

11

Consensus, Antagonism, and Decay: Britain 1960–1979

CONSERVATIVES AND LABOUR IN THE 1960S

The Conservative lock on power continued well into the 1960s, with Winston Churchill and Anthony Eden followed by Harold Macmillan and Sir Alec Douglas-Home. Conservative policies continued to be based upon strong support for the welfare state crafted by Labour, so that the period up to 1964, when Labour was restored by a narrow margin under Harold Wilson, was characterized by a general consensus about domestic policy. The continuing strong economy made such consensus relatively easy. Unemployment was low, remaining at a level between 2 percent and 3 percent, and periods of inflation were brought under control through government intervention. Jobs and prices remained stable. Most men and women came to expect that they would always have enough, even if they would never be rich. All of this meant that the Labour Party had no major issues upon which to challenge the Conservatives.

This period of Conservative power was briefly shaken in 1960–1961 when an economic crisis prompted a so-called "pay pause," a halt in wage increases. Macmillan, the prime minister, used this moment to argue unsuccessfully for Britain's membership in the European Common Market or, more formally, the European Economic Community (EEC). Neither the pay pause nor the EEC membership was a popular measure. Further trouble for the Conservatives came in mid-1963, when the Minister of War John Profumo was forced to resign after the public learned that his mistress was sharing a bed, and presumably also state secrets, with a Soviet attaché. But Labour was unable to move into power in the midst of these scandals, partly because of the untimely death in January 1963 of party leader Hugh Gaitskell. Gaitskell's replacement as leader of the party was Harold Wilson, the man who would lead a new Labour administration in 1965.

Labour under Wilson continued to be a party of consensus, but it was also a party forced to address serious economic issues that had been papered over by the Conservatives. For one thing, the deficit was as large as it had been since the end of the Second World War, and Labour was reluctant to turn to either deflation or devaluation of the pound, which stood at $2.80 by 1964. Labour had presided over the 1949 devaluation of the pound and Wilson wanted to avoid linking his party once again to that unpopular move. Instead, income taxes and import duties were raised and the cost of borrowing money went up as well, and this temporarily halted the economic crisis. But Labour had campaigned on the platform of continued economic growth and an expansion of welfare services, and Wilson was determined to carry out these promises.

New methods of measuring poverty and wealth in the 1960s had forced the government and many individuals to radically reconsider the measures of poverty and affluence in use since Seebohm Rowntree's groundbreaking studies of York, with the result that many families considered out of poverty under the old guidelines were newly rediscovered as poverty-stricken by the mid-1960s. Part of this rested on the widespread acceptance as "normal" of what were previously considered luxury goods, such as televisions and even cars; families without a television in the '60s were no longer viewed as eccentric but rather as too poor to afford this basic consumer item.

Labour's response to these new levels of poverty was to raise spending on welfare programs by an average of 5 percent per year between 1965 and 1970. The Conservatives, back in office after 1970, continued this spending until 1975. Interest groups devoted to the elderly, the homeless, the immigrant, the child, and other specific populations kept up continual pressure for more government services. Paying for these required financial creativity, especially in the period of worldwide inflation that characterized the late '60s and early '70s. Labour continually had to balance calls for more expenditure with the problems of chronic monetary crises. Periods of wage and price freezes alternated with periods of voluntary cutbacks; all of this provided an odd counterpoint to rising levels of welfare benefits. Complicating the picture was the reality of Britain without empire, without the markets and the resources that would have helped boost the domestic economy.

A POST-IMPERIAL BRITAIN

As Britain entered the 1960s it also entered a new period of post-imperialism. India's independence in 1947 had been the turning point in the empire, but there were still many colonies, especially in Africa, waiting to receive independence in the '50s and early '60s. Compared to the trials of France, Belgium, and the Netherlands, the dismantling of the British Empire ran relatively smoothly. But there were still major problems, such as those in Cyprus, where British troops had been reassigned before the Suez crisis in Egypt and where Turks and Greeks continued to battle for dominance.

The problems in eastern Africa were especially daunting because of the reluctance of white settlers in Kenya and in Rhodesia to recognize or accept change. To solve these problems, the government proposed two loose federations that would be built around each of these white-settled colonies, with Kenya buoyed up by Uganda and Tanganyika and white Southern Rhodesia surrounded by Northern Rhodesia (eventually Zambia) and Nyasaland (eventually Malawi). In Kenya, the proposed federation never got a chance: the Mau Mau uprising in the late 1950s was the start of a bloody civil war that pitted nationalists against white settlers. In Rhodesia, a military-supported federation limped into the '60s, helping keep control of valuable northern copper reserves in the hands of southern whites. Any discussion of shared power and responsibility between whites and blacks remained only talk until the federation itself finally dissolved in 1963 amidst bloody turmoil, with Ian Smith leading a white majority that wanted no part in shared power with blacks. In 1965 Smith led the Rhodesian parliament in a unilateral declaration of independence from Britain; Britain responded with trade sanctions but refused to back these sanctions with any show of force. The situation in Rhodesia was similar to that in South Africa, where minority white rule was also the bitter norm.

By the early '60s, little was left of the former "map of red." Direct British rule continued in Hong Kong, the Falkland Islands, Gibraltar, the British Honduras, and a few other scattered areas, but the notion of Britain as an imperial presence was long gone. In its place was a new set of issues arising from decolonization. Many of these issues had to do with finance—how was Britain to replace the revenue and the markets lost with the end of empire? Less was spent on defense after the colonies were granted independence, but these cuts did little to balance the economic losses. Other issues were even more difficult than the economic problems faced by both Britain and the former colonies. How would Britain, the so-called Old Commonwealth of white settlement (including Canada, Australia, and New Zealand), and the New Commonwealth (India, Pakistan, the West Indies, and former African colonies) define the status and privileges of these former colonies and their peoples, both white and black? Many of these individuals maintained ties of emotional attachment and family connections to those in the British Isles.

More than 1 million immigrants from these former colonies flooded into Britain in the '50s and early '60s, until the 1962 Commonwealth Immigrants Act limited immigration to those who could prove they had a job. In many cities, nonwhite immigrants replaced working-class whites as the owners of corner shops and the residents of downscale housing. Race tensions became commonplace in urban areas, with race riots in Nottingham and in London in 1958. The passage of the 1965 Race Relations Act outlawing discrimination did little to ease the anxieties caused by large numbers of families coming to Britain from the New Commonwealth. In 1968, a Labour government tightened immigration restrictions once again, this time setting up a practice of specifically race-linked controls that gave preferential treatment to white rather than nonwhite holders of British passports. Despite these controls, racist fears grew as these immigrant families—most with more children than non-immigrant families—placed new burdens on the welfare state. And these fears were molded into racist and nationalist propaganda by men such as Enoch Powell, a Conservative M.P. who was driven from the party in 1968 and went on to find a new home in the Irish Unionist party.

PROTEST AND DISSENT IN A NEW YOUTH CULTURE

Racial tensions and the fight against discrimination did not shape Britain's youth in the same way as they did in the United States. Instead, the youth culture in Great Britain tended to focus around two other issues, one domestic and the other international: generalized cultural dissent and protest over nuclear weapons. On the home front, young people of all classes began to chafe against the trappings of that very affluence that appeared to characterize all levels of the British economy: abundance fueled discontent among the young, articulated in a youth culture that appeared to reject all restraint in behavior, dress, and entertainment. The Beatles and the Rolling Stones changed the face of music; Mary Quant and Twiggy changed the look of fashion. The development of the birth control pill did not in itself significantly change sexual behavior, as many had feared, but it did symbolize a new openness toward sex and intimacy as well as toward marriage and family. These new attitudes were noisy and often frightening to the middle-aged and middle class. And the availability and wide use of hashish, marijuana, and LSD among the young, along with a simultaneous if unrelated rise in working-class juvenile crime, merely intensified these fears. The generation born after the Second World War appeared to have lost all moral restraint.

The cultural aspects of the British youth movement were loose enough to draw in many individuals whose interests differed widely but whose age and rebellion seemed to link them together. However, without a focal point like the Vietnam War in the United States, youth culture in Britain did not automatically mean noisy and disruptive protest: 1968, that year of wonders in most countries, passed in relative peace in Britain.

The other main focus of cultural protest, however, was directed at a target that was terrifyingly specific: Britain's and the world's accumulation of nuclear missiles. Nuclear weapons had appeared the obvious and logical—and much less expensive—substitute for massive defense spending, and as traditional military expenditures dropped in the 1950s and '60s, money was funneled into research into the bomb. An agreement with the United States, negotiated under Macmillan, guaranteed the provision of U.S. Polaris submarines as the means of launching British warheads, making the British program curiously and irrevocably dependent upon the United States but allowing the government to claim that it was autonomous.

The movement against nuclear weapons attracted not only the young and disaffected but also a large cross section of middle-class housewives who had never considered themselves protesters. But these women found the government's arguments of mutual deterrence completely unconvincing, and viewed the growth of nuclear arms as an immediate threat to home and family. The outcome of these two different sets of concerns— young men and women protesting against the establishment, and mothers fighting for the safety of their children—was the Campaign for Nuclear Disarmament, founded in February 1958. It grew rapidly throughout the '60s, hosting marches to the laboratory in Aldermaston that housed research into nuclear weapons.

SOCIAL REFORMS UNDER LABOUR

The challenges of youth culture and the active campaigns against nuclear arms were only a small part of the changing cultural landscape of 1960s Britain. Labour remained in office under Wilson until 1970, enduring chronic and increasingly frequent financial crises but at the same time successfully implementing a number of social reforms that included the abolition of the death penalty, more relaxed laws governing obscenity and pornography, the end to laws against homosexual behavior, and abortion reform. Many of these changes distressed older Britons but they attracted support across party lines, as did divorce reform and the lowering of the voting age to 18.

Other major social reforms included education, where the comprehensive school continued to replace the tripartite system of grammar, technical, and secondary modern schools and the eleven-plus examination was abolished. New universities and colleges were built at a rapid pace—seven in England in the 1960s, one new and several redesigned universities in Scotland, expanded polytechnic colleges in Wales, and a new university in Ireland. In addition, the innovative system of the Open University was launched in 1969, where students pursued degrees by correspondence and via programs on radio and television (often at very wee hours in the morning, a practice in dedication that ended only with the coming of the VCR).

Of particular concern to many was the wide gap between the sciences and the humanities, in what novelist and scientist C. P. Snow famously dubbed "The Two Cultures" in 1959: British students appeared to excel in the latter at the direct expense of the former, and in a society that was struggling to remain internationally competitive, this gap was a troublesome one. Educators and legislators wrung their hands and proposed any number of solutions to a problem that had a long history in the culture of British—especially English—higher education. The Labour government poured money into secondary schools, especially into science and language laboratories, as an apparent resolution of this problem.

LABOR AND INDUSTRY: CONTINUED ANTAGONISMS

Even as technical and scientific education for the future received increased funding and attention, the problems of present-day manufacturing continued to challenge legislators and union leaders. The sterling crises and the serious balance-of-payments problems that dogged the Labour government forced unions to accept "pay pauses" and the like, but workers' attitudes toward industrialists and government hardened with every concession. By the late '60s, many unions had become highly suspicious of a Labour government that supposedly held dear the interests of the working classes but which was apparently willing to sacrifice those interests whenever industry called. Labour, under Wilson, had tried various ways to solve the economic problems of the late '60s: the pound was devalued again in 1967 (from $2.80 to $2.40), and Chancellor of the Exchequer Roy Jenkins drastically raised taxes on consumer goods and on high incomes. But when these actions were not enough, the government began to propose significant limits on the powers of trade unions.

The government could argue that it was merely reflecting the popular mood: productivity lost to strikes had skyrocketed in 1968 and by 1969 the general public's view of unions was much less positive than it had been just a few years before. Fewer than 60 percent of those polled said that unions were "good," while 27 percent identified them as "bad" for the country.[1] The new tendency of local shops to strike without the sanction of the national union was especially singled out for criticism. However, the 10 million Britons who belonged to unions, as well as many committed to the ideals of Labour, found the government's proposals for restructuring deeply offensive. The twin proposals of mandatory cooling-off periods and mandatory ballots before a strike could be called were particularly resented. The Wilson administration was eventually forced to withdraw both proposals in the face of deep resentment by unions and by the left wing of the party. It was an embarrassing defeat for the government, but it also left many non-union workers and professionals angry at the continued power of organized labor.

THE CONSERVATIVES TAKE CONTROL

Labour lost the general election in 1970 and the Conservatives, under Edward Heath, came into power once more. The new regime pledged itself to reduce the power of both big government and big unions, and moved to legally restrict the power of trade unions while committing itself and Britain to a renewal of free trade and market forces. Britain as part of a larger European economy was high on the list of Heath's priorities, and he successfully persuaded the EEC to include Britain in 1973 even as he worked to ratchet down the country's dependent relationship with the United States. Other aspects of Conservative economic policies included the dismantling of Labour's income policies and wage freezes and a new Industrial Relations Act. This act called for the same mandatory ballots and cooling-off periods that Labour itself had unsuccessfully proposed. But the bill applied only to those unions registered with the government, and the TUC immediately advised its member unions to refuse to register so they could remain outside the power of the new Industrial Relations Court. This proved tremendously embarrassing to Heath's new government, and early attempts to invoke the new powers of the court were disastrous.

The commitment to free trade and market forces also suffered early setbacks, as Heath's administration stepped in to nationalize the bankrupt Rolls-Royce company and then to save the Upper Clyde Shipbuilders. Other embarrassments included a 1972 coal miners strike. Miners' wages had actually risen ahead of inflation, but the miners as a group had a long and well-publicized history of suffering at the hands of government and mine owners, and public opinion in 1972 was largely on the side of the striking men. British industry, heavily dependent upon coal rather than oil, spun into a temporary decline as the government declared a state of emergency; and the miners eventually wrung major concessions out of the nationalized coal industry.

Heath's Conservative ideology was sacrificed to administrative necessity in other areas as well, as the government intervened in various aspects of daily life. For example, the old counties and localities of the country were reorganized in a fit of tidiness that eliminated many traditional boundaries in the name of more efficient delivery of services. Protest was unavailing. Similarly confusing to many was the decimalization of money, replacing the old guinea, half-crown, shilling, and pence with 100 "new pence" in each pound beginning in 1971.

Fewer people initially resisted the Conservatives' reduction of the income tax rate to 30 percent, although this ushered in a level of deficit spending that had not been seen since the Second World War. Inflation had reached epic proportions, mainly because of the oil crisis in the Middle East and the formation of OPEC (Organization of Petroleum Exporting Countries). Britain was less dependent upon imported oil than other European or North American countries, and quickly moved to exploit oil reserves in the North Sea. However, these oil reserves did not shield the country from international economic pressures, and by the third year of Heath's administration inflation had outstripped even the nominal lending rate of the banks so that, in effect, banks were paying borrowers to borrow. Credit boomed, with predictable results: housing prices skyrocketed as consumers scrambled to purchase and hold onto real property.

Prices rose rapidly for all goods, but in these early years of rampant inflation pay raises more than compensated, and for a short time inflation was undeniably beneficial for many ordinary men and women. At the same time, unemployment temporarily fell to 2.6 percent by 1974 but rose steadily thereafter; it would reach 6.2 percent by 1977. Inflation continued apace, at levels averaging over 17 percent between 1974 and 1978, with an all-time high of 27 percent in 1975.[2] Deficit spending soared to £1 billion in 1973 and £3 billion in 1974.[3] A second coal strike, this one in late 1973 and early 1974, led up to a general election in February 1974, where to no one's surprise, the Conservatives were ousted. Voters blamed them for runaway inflation, a mandatory three-day workweek, and a new era of candles and making do. Heath hoped for a coalition with the Liberals, who had their first really strong political showing in decades, but he was disappointed, and Labour returned under Wilson for another try. Wilson would resign in April 1976 owing to ill health, and James Callaghan would serve for three years as Labour prime minister during a very difficult time.

ANOTHER LABOUR GOVERNMENT: MORE ECONOMIC WOES AND THE "WINTER OF DISCONTENT"

Labour moved immediately to repair relations with industry, repealing Conservative legislation on wage limits and settling the coal miners' strike. Industrial earnings skyrocketed, initially pleasing workers but forcing the government to institute wage and price controls after realizing that it would be literally impossible to sustain the inflationary pay hikes that drove the cost of living up by nearly 25 percent in 1975. These measures in and of themselves were insufficient to resolve the economic crises that continued to dog Britain. By late 1976 another sterling crisis was in full swing, with inflation at 16 percent, unemployment at over 5 percent, the interest rates hovering at 15 percent, and the pound down to $1.57.[4] Labour presided over huge levels of deficit spending, continuing to try to support welfare programs that had been designed in the mid-1940s to operate on full employment and an expanding economy. These programs were now impossible to sustain. The International Monetary Fund offered a loan on harsh terms; Labour was forced to cut many parts of the budget to the bone and to reinvigorate controls on wages and prices.

Union membership surged during this crisis to 13 million, and days lost to strikes soared as well. Unions and Labour were supposed to be on friendly terms, but after several years of reluctant cooperation, the winter of 1978/79—the so-called "winter of discontent"—witnessed paralyzing strike activity by organized labor in response to a Labour government's mandate that wage increases be held to 5 percent. Workers in all sectors of the economy walked out, leaving patients untreated at the NHS, garbage piling up in the streets, corpses unburied, merchandise stranded. The presence of television cameras at these selective strikes brought home the extent of the disruptions, even to those who had escaped most personal experience of the walkouts. A general election was inevitable, as was the result: the Conservatives, campaigning on the slogan "Labour Isn't Working," captured an astounding one third of the votes of union members, and swept into office with promises of a fresh start.

"THE TROUBLES": UNIONISTS AND CATHOLICS IN NORTHERN IRELAND

While the problems of industry and inflation were the most pressing matters left unresolved by Labour, the late '70s also witnessed new levels of nationalism and activism by Britons who felt themselves or were treated by others as inferior to "the English." English attitudes toward their fellow subjects in Ireland, Scotland, and Wales, and certainly toward those in the colonies and former colonies, had always been complicated by feelings of superiority and personal mistrust, but the decade of the '70s saw these relationships take on new bitterness. Enoch Powell and his National Front continued to be loudly active in their protests against "the coloured," but expanded their protests to include a new sense of nationalist pride as well as racialist prejudice.

Much of this nationalism was voiced in regard to Ireland. The Free State, created in 1921, had gradually moved toward independent republican status, becoming Éire in 1937 and the Republic of Ireland in 1948. Éire had remained neutral during the Second World War, choosing this means of underscoring autonomy from Britain, but postwar economic ties continued to link the Republic to the United Kingdom. The Dáil, the Irish parliament, sought to minimize other links: Irish was declared one of the country's official languages, Catholicism was recognized as the majority religion, and Irish membership in the EEC was gained in 1973 (the same year in which Great Britain joined). The economy of Ireland continued to lag behind the economies of both Britain and much of the rest of the world, but the Republic had emerged and survived despite the naysayers who believed that the extreme nationalism of Sinn Féin and the IRA could not lead to a true parliamentary democracy.

In Northern Ireland, the problems of nationalism were much more difficult than they were in the south. "The Troubles," the period of murderous conflict between Catholic and Protestant, tormented the six counties governed by the Home Rule administration at Stormont Castle, Belfast. Northern Ireland was bound to England not only by ties of culture and religion—two-thirds of the region was Protestant, and most of these men and women continued to regard their Scots-Presbyterian heritage as infinitely superior to the "backward" Irish Catholic culture to the south— but also by economic dependence, as the Ulster counties were forced to rely upon Westminster for aid. An early boycott of Belfast manufactures by the Irish Free State, as a protest against the treatment of the Catholic Northern Irish, showed just how vulnerable the northern economy was. Other weaknesses were exploited by the IRA, which continued its attack on the borders of Northern Ireland and stepped up violence against unionist M.P.s.

The Protestant government responded with draconian laws directed at Catholics, which only intensified the religious and political antagonisms of the region. Protestant unionists claimed that Catholics refused to participate fully in the national life of Northern Ireland, and that this refusal was treasonous. To protect the dominion, therefore, unionists argued that it was necessary to deny basic voting rights and other privileges to the minority. Catholics, a large minority at 33 percent, argued that their withdrawal into a specifically Catholic subculture was largely a response to widespread discrimination by Protestants in employment, housing, education, and most other aspects of daily life.

These two antagonistic cultures were enshrined in separate schools, separate clubs, separate neighborhoods, and separate parades in which, for instance, Protestant marchers swarmed into Catholic neighborhoods to celebrate historic Protestant victories. Chronic economic problems worsened a situation that could have been at least partially eased by lower unemployment and higher wages. Ongoing threats by the IRA did nothing to lower the temperature of the region. And Whitehall, busy elsewhere, was generally happy to let Northern Ireland govern itself, refusing to interfere in the domestic activities of the dominion.

By the '60s, activists in Northern Ireland had formed several nonsectarian civil rights organizations to protest the discrimination aimed primarily at Catholics. Most of these activists were not seeking unification with the south, but rather a new status for Northern Irish Catholics within the dominion. British pressure from Westminster encouraged the discussion of new laws and new attitudes. However, the continued presence of hard-line unionists in every government made it nearly impossible for the two sides to agree on reform.

In late 1968, a civil rights march in Derry (Londonderry) by the Northern Ireland Civil Rights Association (NICRA) forced the government in

Belfast to agree to pursue political and social reforms after television cameras caught Protestant police attacking the marchers. But the administration refused to grant the demand for one-man, one-vote representation in local elections. This enraged Catholics, who argued that the government really had never intended any true reforms. It also infuriated unionists, who felt that any political reform would merely compromise the autonomy of Northern Ireland and move the country away from closer relations to the rest of the UK and toward a dreaded union with the Republic of Ireland. A march in January 1969, also near Derry, signaled the complete breakdown in any peaceful move toward conciliation; unionist mobs ambushed civil rights marchers and ignited a series of violent confrontations that raged through Derry and Belfast for months.

By August 1969, the British army had taken up residence in Northern Ireland, in response to continued and escalating violence that increasingly involved fatalities. By 1971, the situation had become so difficult that the army and the Northern Irish police forces—all Protestant—began to imprison IRA members and collaborators without trial. Protest against the new internment camps and the torture used against prisoners led in turn to renewed violence by law enforcement officials against civilians, and by 1972 the British government was forced to intervene and dissolve the Northern Irish parliament.

The period between 1969 and 1972, when Whitehall officially prorogued the Stormont government and decreed that Northern Ireland would be ruled directly from Westminster, was marked by chronic violence, and this violence did not decline once British forces entered Ulster. Both the IRA and the Ulster unionist paramilitaries—the Ulster Volunteer Force and the Ulster Defence Association—were engaged in an acknowledged war to the finish, and British troops strove in vain to keep the peace. New political parties were formed in the hopes of capitalizing on the atmosphere of chaos and desperation, including the Democratic Unionist Party of the Reverend Ian Paisley. Paisley represented the hard right, turning against moderate unionists and characterizing any discussion of compromise as the eventual end of independent Northern Ireland and the virtually guaranteed slaughter of northern Protestants by southern Catholics, all led by the pope.

Paisley and others also argued that any Catholic protest in Northern Ireland had to be the work of the IRA, even though there was ample evidence that many of the early protests in and around Derry had no links at all with the IRA or with Sinn Féin. However, by the time the Stormont government was suspended, the IRA had become deeply involved in "The Troubles." The IRA itself had split in 1969, forming the Provisional IRA (holding fast to the early rigid agenda of the original body, including a refusal to participate in parliament and the advocacy of guerrilla violence when necessary) and the Official IRA (which advocated a peaceful end to the fighting and also called for parliamentary action as a vehicle for future reform). The Official IRA declared a ceasefire in 1972, but the Provisional IRA continued to escalate its use of force throughout the next two decades.

The Provisional IRA—known to the public simply as the IRA—claimed that its victims were "legitimate," that is, official representatives of a repressive regime. On the other side, the unionist paramilitaries that were formed in response frankly declared their intention of terrorizing Catholic civilians into denouncing the IRA and withdrawing any support, emotional or financial, from the organization. Thus, the unionists in Northern Ireland targeted Catholic men, women, and children with no apparent links to Sinn Féin or the IRA, claiming hundreds of such victims in the years of violence. The use of terror by both sides would provide a chilling picture to the outside world; in 1972, for instance, 258 of the 496 victims of unionist and IRA violence were civilians. Periodic cease-fires never held. Between 1969 and 1976, more than 1,500 people were killed in "The Troubles."

The British government, viewing direct rule of Northern Ireland as a temporary measure, attempted in the 1973 Northern Ireland Constitution Act to find a solution acceptable to all parties. The act recognized that a united Ireland could come only through the will of the people of Northern Ireland rather than from above, but even this was too much for die-hard unionists. They especially protested against any inclusion of a Catholic minority in any future Northern Irish parliament, a condition that the British argued was nonnegotiable. Unionists as a group were divided into three camps: one favored devolution, or a form of Home Rule, although they wished for such devolution to exclude Catholics; the second argued for complete absorption into the United Kingdom; and the third pushed for the formation of a completely autonomous Ulster. None wished for a unified Ireland. "Shared power" was the basis for the so-called Sunningdale agreement of 1974, where a governing council that included both Catholics and Protestants was established in the hopes that Home Rule might resume, but it was short-lived and direct rule remained the order of the day.

"The Troubles" thus punctuated the already pressing problems of both Labour and Conservative regimes at Westminster. No matter what party was in power, however, the administration refused to agree to any action that might signal the defeat of British troops by the IRA, and thus the guerrilla war continued. The IRA attempted to carry the war into England, planting bombs in pubs and parking lots in English towns and cities, and assassinating Lord Mountbatten, the uncle of Queen Elizabeth's husband, in 1979. Imprisoned IRA members also adopted a policy of hunger strikes, focusing media attention on the slow deaths of inmates such as Bobby Sands, who won a by-election while in prison and whose funeral in May 1981 drew 100,000 people. "The Troubles" spilled southward as well, with IRA bombings in Dublin and other cities of the Republic, and as a result the Dáil began its own campaign against the terrorists.

At the same time, however, recognizing the bonds between southern and northern Irish Catholics, the Dáil began to make overtures designed to lower the temperature between the two areas: in 1972, for instance, the constitutional article endowing the Catholic Church with "special status" was struck down, and in 1980 the Republic officially recognized Northern Ireland as a province of Britain, rather than as a misplaced limb of a unified Ireland. Reunion of north and south remained the goal, but the Dáil formally agreed that any such unification must be the result of free choice on the part of the Northern Irish. Any such choice appeared very far away in 1979, when Margaret Thatcher took office under a new Conservative regime.

NATIONALISM IN WALES AND SCOTLAND

The other members of the United Kingdom were as restive, if not as violent, as the Irish during the '60s and '70s. Wales and Scotland had both experienced movements of cultural nationalism in the late nineteenth and early twentieth centuries, but in each case the rediscovery of Welsh and Scots identity had developed amicably alongside of, rather than in place of, a larger British identity. In Wales, for instance, the lack of separate political institutions meant that any Welsh nationalist movement was necessarily a movement focused on language and culture. Religious nonconformity formed one strand of Welsh culture; other expressions included the eisteddfodau, annual celebrations of Welsh poetry and song, which were often dominated by Nonconformist clergy, and the glorification of a traditional Welsh peasantry which had, in fact, ceased to exist.

Despite such unpopular decisions at Westminster as the mandate that schoolchildren be taught only in English—one result was that by the 1930s, less than a third of the Welsh actually spoke their native language—movements for political independence continued to be weak and short-lived. One of the earliest and most successful, the Young Wales (Cymru Fydd) movement, lasted only from 1894–1896. Continual pressures to disestablish the Anglican Church were finally successful in 1914. Similar pressures to end exclusive land ownership practices were helped along by the income and inheritance taxes of the inter-war administration.

By the early 1920s, Wales was a land of small farmer-owners, with industry centered on the coal mining regions in the south. These areas became centers of working-class solidarity rather than any specifically local or national identity. Workers in Wales were both workers and Welsh, but they were also British, and found common cause with the Labour party. In the '40s, this allegiance began to pay off, as Atlee and then the Conservatives poured resources into the development of new industry in Wales, including steel and oil, to replace the dependence on the area's old coal mines. Despite the encouragement of alternative industry, however, Wales remained economically depressed. The oil crisis of the early 1970s turned attention back to coal, but Welsh coal miners were unable to win concessions from the government and by the late 1970s unemployment was once again appallingly high.

It was in this atmosphere of economic distress and industrial decay that Welsh nationalism enjoyed a resurgence. This time, however, instead of a limited focus on language and culture, the Welsh Nationalist Party, or Plaid Cymru, mounted a political challenge to Labour and forced the Wilson administration to address the crises of Wales. The establishment of a Welsh Office in 1964 was followed by the Welsh Language Act of 1967, and in the 1970s television broadcasts in Welsh were introduced. The issue of devolution, already a source of passionate discussion in regard to Northern Ireland, began to be raised for Wales as well, with many in Wales pushing for a new constitution and significant autonomy. In 1974, Labour went so far as to propose elected assemblies for both Wales and Scotland, but without giving these assemblies any legislative powers. Welsh nationalists tended to oppose the idea of such a toothless institution; others feared that any measure of autonomy would lead to further economic decline; and in 1979, when devolution was on the ballot, it was overwhelmingly defeated. This did not mean the end to nationalist sentiment, but when the Conservatives regained office in 1979, the political issue was temporarily dead.

In Scotland, devolution was more ardently pursued, in part because the same oil crisis that crippled England and Wales led to the development of North Sea oil refineries that were, in the words of the Scots, "our oil." American companies contracted to develop the oil used Northern Scotland as the base for storage and refineries, and the activities of the '70s poured money into the Scottish economy. But there were problems. Financially, Scotland saw few of the profits, as Whitehall viewed the North Sea oil wells as "British" rather than "Scottish" and acted accordingly.

Environmentally, Scotland bore the brunt of the damage to land and sea. Industrially, the ships and equipment used to extract and move the oil were not built in Scotland but were contracted out to cheaper international firms. Thus, despite the fact that North Sea oil staved off significant disaster for all of the British Isles during the 1970s, Scotland's benefits were dramatically fewer than many had hoped.

This disillusionment with the ways in which oil profits were parceled out helped intensify a campaign for devolution that had already emerged. Since the union of 1707, Scotland had maintained many important institutions quite separate from those of England: a Scottish state church, or kirk; a separate and in important ways different legal system and judiciary; a Scots civil service; a Scottish Office in Westminster; a secretary of state for Scotland. These institutions provided an infrastructure for autonomy that was lacking in both Wales and Northern Ireland. And while Welsh nationalists focused most heavily on reviving and preserving Welsh language and literature, in Scotland the focus was more pragmatic. The Scottish National Party, earliest of the parties devoted to devolution, began early in the '60s to talk openly of Home Rule and a devolved parliament, using as part of their campaign message, "It's Scotland's Oil." By 1970, devolution was one of the main issues occupying Scottish voters. It attracted support across the political spectrum in Scotland, from Conservative and Labour alike, as well as from the church and the trade unions.

Wilson bowed to the inevitable, as he had done with Wales, and allowed the question of Home Rule to be placed on a referendum in 1979. But the referenda for both Wales and Scotland were carefully worded to tip the scales against devolution. For one thing, at least 40 percent of all eligible voters had to vote yes for devolution to be effective; this in and of itself was designed to kill the bill, as voter turnout was by this point always very low. Wilson calculated that a majority of voters who showed up at the polls might vote in favor, but he also knew that getting out the entire electorate would be impossible; and he was correct. In Wales, less than 12 percent of the eligible voters chose devolution, although 80 percent of those who voted were in favor of it. In Scotland, 32.9 percent of eligible voters chose devolution, and although this amounted to a majority of the votes cast, it still was insufficient to meet the standards of the referendum. Thus Wilson was able to talk about devolution and offer it as an option, and then point to low voter turnout to justify the status quo.

THE END OF AN ERA

By the end of 1979, it was clear that Labour was no longer able to remain in power. Year after year had seen desperate economic measures fail in the face of intractable inflation and a stagnant economy. The "intimate members" of the United Kingdom were chafing, and the defeat of devolution in both Wales and Scotland appeared to many to be the result of a shell game rather than a true reflection of popular sentiment. "The Troubles" in Northern Ireland had become an unending tragedy, again with no apparent way out. The remnants of empire remained, true, but the Commonwealth countries were often lukewarm in their support of Britain. On many fronts, but especially in terms of the domestic economy, the Conservatives pointed out trenchantly in their 1979 campaign posters that "Labour Isn't Working. Britain's Better Off With the Conservatives." The question for many was, who would rule the Conservatives?

NOTES

1. Peter Clarke, *Hope and Glory: Britain 1900–1990* (London and New York: Penguin Books, 1996), p. 316.

2. Arthur Marwick, *British Society Since 1945*, 3d ed. (London and New York: Penguin Books, 1996), p. 185.

3. Clarke, *Hope and Glory*, p. 338.

4. Clarke, *Hope and Glory*, p. 352.

12

Britain since 1979: The Thatcher Revolution and the Rise of New Labour

THE IRON LADY COMES TO POWER

In 1979, Margaret Thatcher—soon to be known as the "Iron Lady," a nickname coined out of spite but adopted by Thatcher herself with enthusiasm—emerged as the first woman prime minister of Great Britain. She had earned her political credentials through hard work: she served in the so-called "shadow cabinet" of the Opposition during Wilson's administration, and became Education Secretary under Heath in the '70s. Her work there included the elimination of milk for schoolchildren as a way to maintain funding for the Open University system, a decision that led the press to portray her as "Thatcher, the Milk Snatcher."[1]

Thatcher's 11 years as prime minister saw what some have claimed as a "revolution" in British government. Thatcher herself was committed to revolutionary changes in the relations between government and the people, and committed as well to very specific changes in the ways in which "the people" ought to govern themselves. Her administration demonstrated almost at once a dedication to long-term change even at great personal cost to certain segments of the British population.

Thatcher's own moral and emotional fiber made her impatient with those who disagreed with her, whether voters or M.P.s. Her moral rectitude, developing as it did out of her upbringing as the daughter of a grocer who demonstrated the so-called Victorian values of thrift, hard work, and self-help, was expressed in a belief that the government had an obligation to push people to help themselves. Her disdain and impatience for the welfare state found expression in a renewed discussion of the "undeserving" poor and the elimination of policies that supposedly cushioned the lazy and incorrigible.

REVOLUTIONARY ECONOMIC POLICIES

Thatcher's willingness on behalf of Britons everywhere to embrace short-term pain for long-term gain, like a nanny administering a dose that tasted awful but promised to restore sound health, was evident in her treatment of the economy. Thatcher's economic policies were monetarist, focusing not on consumption and employment but rather on control of the money supply: the government should take specific steps to limit inflation, and allow wage levels and employment to take care of themselves. Under Thatcher, this meant lowering interest rates and income taxes, eliminating wage and price controls, and removing state interference in what should be private business decisions. All of this would infuse the economy with vigor and would teach Britons to be disciplined and self-reliant—economic policy with moral value. Thatcher's first moves in this direction were to lower the income tax—from 83 percent to 60 percent at the very top (eventually down to 40%), and from 33 percent to 30 percent at the low end—and to begin reducing government services in order to curtail state spending.

At the same time, indirect taxation rose. The VAT—value-added tax, a sales tax of sorts—was raised to 15 percent, which critics immediately noted was punitively harsh for the poor. Indeed, many critics accused Thatcher's policies of favoring the rich, a charge that would also be applied to her close personal friend and colleague U.S. president Ronald Reagan. But Thatcher was convinced that a short period of adjustment, uncomfortable as that might be, would ultimately do more to bring inflation down than any simple Keynesian model of economic management.

In this, at least on the surface, she was correct. Inflation ramped up sharply early in the Thatcher years but then dropped precipitously, from 18 percent in 1980 to 4.5 percent in 1984 and further to 3 percent in 1986. At the same time, however, unemployment rose sharply, from 1.4 million in May 1979 to 3.3 million in the winter of 1982/83.[2] Jobs disappeared from the older industries and from the northern cities, so that the experience of displacement was uneven, as it had been in the 1930s. Once again, the southeast and the counties surrounding London were relatively insulated from the recession, while the old north suffered disproportionately. Riots over unemployment and distress reached violent levels, especially in the poorer parts of London and Liverpool. But Thatcher was absolutely determined to prevail, despite the problems in a contracting economy; she wanted to avoid at all costs the reversals of previous administrations. "You turn if you want to; this lady's not for turning," she told the more reluctant Conservatives, in direct reference to Edward Heath's notorious U-turn to interventionist economic policies.

Thatcher's revolution was to include other sweeping ideological shifts as well. Her rejection of trade union power was, after the "winter of discontent," not an unpopular stance. Thatcher intended to impose legal restraints upon the unions, but was determined to avoid the farce of sweeping legislation that contained embarrassingly obvious loopholes, as in the case of Heath's Industrial Relations Act. The mood of the country in 1979 was on her side: many concurred in the Conservatives' call for new controls on "lawless" unions.

Thatcher's administration introduced a series of stair-step laws to limit the powers of unions. Between 1980 and 1984, new laws outlawed secondary picketing (picketing at places other than the site of the strike itself), placed limits on closed shops, held unions accountable for a broadened list of illegal actions, called for a mandatory secret ballot before any strike actions, and further increased the powers of individual members against union leadership. This gradual expansion of government control over unions went hand in hand with Thatcher's monetarist policies. She believed that abandoning wage and price controls would make industries and services more responsive to the pressures of a capitalist economy, and these pressures would in turn bring unions more in line with other segments of the economy.

None of this was without pain. The unemployment that ravaged Britain in the later years of Thatcher's reign would be more effective than any legislative policy in weakening unions, as membership dropped by several million during the worst period of economic stagnation. But Thatcher was determined that "the people" would endure short-term pain for long-term prosperity, and she showed this during the coal strike of 1984–1985. As talks between the government and the National Union of Mineworkers (NUM) broke down, the administration made sure that it had enough coal on hand to keep the country going during a walkout. When the coal miners left their jobs they found that the combination of a mild winter and this hoarded coal made it impossible to force industry and government to make any wage or workplace concessions. The strike eventually ended after 12 long months, during which miners and their families suffered tremendously but during which Thatcher refused to budge. The defeat of the NUM signaled that the Iron Lady would not bend in the way that previous governments, Labour and Conservative, had done.

Thatcher's economic radicalism carried through in the privatization of many nationalized companies. She regarded this as a necessary step in reinvigorating the overall economy by reducing state spending and subjecting industries to the pressures of competition; more importantly in some ways, she wanted to reinfuse the British soul with the values of small-scale capitalism by making it easy for the "average" Briton to buy shares and follow the market. The road to privatization was not without its bumps, but her goal of undoing the Atlee government's huge project of nationalization was clearly underway within a few years of taking office. "Popular capitalism" found expression in the rapid if partial privatization of British Rail, British Airways, British Aerospace, BP (British Petroleum), Rolls-Royce, and others. The gas industry, the water industry, and the telephone industry all followed.

Much of the sales money immediately enriched the state coffers; half of British Telecom went for £3,900 million in 1984, with much of that sold in small shares to private individuals.[3] Thatcher's intuition was borne out by the enthusiasm with which the not-so-well-off participated in the stock sales, but her contention that privatization would in and of itself lead to healthy competition was less well founded. The government was forced to reintroduce some regulation into the utilities and transportation industries in order to keep the country's infrastructure healthy.

INROADS ON LOCAL GOVERNMENT AND THE POLL TAX

One of the issues most annoying to Thatcher was the autonomy of local government. Thatcher's Conservatism combined individual responsibility with a very strong state government, and within this equation there was no room for independent towns and counties. Thatcher did not want power to move from the central authority into the local authority. She was suspicious of any governmental agency that would siphon decision-making away from Westminster and especially from Downing Street. However, she did want individual men and women to reassert themselves within their own small spheres, to stop being coddled by a welfare government, and to exercise the kind of moral rectitude and self-improvement that she had grown up with.

Thus, even as Thatcher was building a central government that enjoyed unrivalled authority, she was constantly telling the average man and woman to shake off what she saw as the learned helplessness of the post-war state and instead to exercise decision and judgment. Britons who wanted to could pull themselves up by their bootstraps. They were hindered, in Thatcher's mind, by town and county authorities that were fat and soft with overfunding and too much power. Her target during the second half of her administration, therefore, was the local council that exercised power over education, housing, and the provision of welfare services.

Thatcher's feeling, shared by many, was that local councils—especially in London and other large cities—were in the hands of free-spending Labourites whose ideological convictions were squarely in opposition to those of Whitehall. At the same time that her administration was arguing for streamlining government services, her parliaments were also passing bills limiting the powers of local authorities to spend money. Her dislike for local, and especially Labour, councils was so intense that seven metropolitan authorities, including the Greater London Council, were simply abolished in 1986.

Other measures for limiting the power of local government focused on spending caps for local services. Local councils depended upon rates as well as on grants from the central government to fund local services. Thatcher's administration reduced these grants and then, as heavy-spending councils simply raised rates to make up the difference, capped the rates. Given the structure of government, local councils were helpless to protect themselves against these actions. In 1985 came the next step: abolishing the rates altogether and replacing them with a new "Community Charge." Rates had been based on property and on rental values and could be raised; the Community Charge would be, in essence, a poll tax levied on every adult. Unlike the rates, any increase in the Community Charge would affect all adult residents of a locality, and thus all voters would have a vested interest in maintaining controls on local government.

The poll tax, as it soon became known, was perhaps the most disastrous misstep of Thatcher's administration. Even Thatcher's Chancellor of the Exchequer, Nigel Lawson, objected strenuously to the idea, arguing that the tax was unfair because it placed an undue burden on the poor. The press had a field day, not only because so many voices were raised against the tax but also because Thatcher's own government was split over if and how to modify it for the poor. Despite the protests, Thatcher was determined to carry on, and the poll tax was introduced in Scotland in April 1989 and in England a year later. Estimates that nearly 50 percent of all men and women simply refused to pay the tax bore out the doomsayers' predictions, and the costs of attempting to collect the tax ran the government's own bills up considerably. Thatcher, however, refused to make any U-turn and the poll tax remained, to be abolished in 1991 by her successor, John Major.

HOUSING, EDUCATION, AND HEALTH CARE REFORMS

Other domestic reforms were designed to reduce the culture of dependency that Thatcher saw throughout Britain. In 1980 her administration introduced a program providing low-cost mortgages to those who wanted to buy their own council house. Over a million such homes were sold to their occupiers by 1987, at reduced costs depending on how long they had lived there. Similar measures promoted small business, and the number of self-employed rose to 15 percent of the total workforce—from 8 percent—in the 11 years of Thatcher's tenure.[4] The gratitude of these new homeowners and small businessmen helped keep Thatcher's popularity levels high, at least through her first two terms of office.

A new Education Act in 1988 placed national standards at the heart of the school curriculum. If the school system in Britain did not immediately begin to "teach to the test" in the way the schools in the United States already had begun to do, teachers had to reach "attainment targets" in the classroom. The act also introduced open enrollment and per capita funding into local schools, forcing schools to compete for students and thereby for state funds. Competition was reintroduced in higher education as well through the abolition of the tenure system at universities, a move that reflected Thatcher's suspicious distrust of the traditional professions. University educators, lawyers, journalists, and even the Anglican Church all were lumped into "the chattering classes" in Thatcher's universe.

Other professionals, including physicians, also came in for new programs of competition. The NHS was subject to market forces as local hospitals were forced to buy services not only from the state but also from private health care providers. General practitioners were given limited budgets and issued the same mandate to choose their laboratories and other ancillary services with an eye to economy. On the other hand, medical service continued to be free to the public and provided to all, so even those who disliked this introduction of market forces had to acknowledge that Thatcher's radicalism was, in the field of health care at least, under some restraint.

THE FALKLANDS WAR AND POLITICAL VICTORY

While many of these domestic reforms were not difficult for the average Briton to understand or appreciate, they took place against the backdrop of continued widespread economic distress. How, then, did Thatcher win reelection not once but twice, in 1983 and in 1987? In 1983, Thatcher's victory came from the remnants of empire in the form of the tiny collection of Falkland Islands off the coast of South America. Argentina claimed sovereignty over the islands despite Britain's continual occupation of the Falklands since 1833 (by the 1980s, these Britons were primarily sheep farmers). One ship, the HMS *Endurance*, provided protection to the islanders. In 1982 this token of military power was called home as part of an overall effort to reduce defense spending. Shortly thereafter, Argentine military dictator Leopoldo Galtieri sent forces in to capture the islands. An emergency meeting of the Commons on a Saturday morning saw Thatcher enlist the support of the entire House in military action against Argentina, and behind-the-scenes maneuvering obtained a UN Security Council resolution condemning Argentina's actions. The United States, balancing established ties with Britain against potential friendships in South America, served as mediator in the ensuing crisis, but it was clear that diplomacy would not be persuasive. British ships attacked their Argentine counterparts in April. The British military recaptured the islands in May, with relatively small loss of life. By the middle of June, Argentina had surrendered.

Thatcher's decisiveness and determination to retain one of the last outposts of British colonialism were warmly welcomed by the public, and she was able to schedule the general election to take advantage of this new popularity. In addition, her opponents were in a particularly weak state. Labour had responded to the losses of 1979 by fracturing into two distinct groups. The radical left gained control of the party and in 1980 elected Michael Foot as the party leader. Many observers were surprised by the choice of Foot over Tony Benn, the Labour M.P. who appeared to be the obvious leader, especially since Benn's menu of Labour policies formed the basis of the party's platform for the 1980s. These policies included repudiation of the EEC and a call for unilateral nuclear disarmament, as well as further nationalization of British industries.

Foot's elevation alienated the moderates, who formally split and formed the Social Democratic Party (SDP) in 1981. The SDP formed an alliance with the still-surviving Liberal Party and made small but impressive gains in local by-elections. By 1983 the SDP-Liberal alliance was firmly cemented, and within Labour itself even Foot's supporters admitted he was too radical to realistically compete for the office of prime minister.

Labour's chaotic state, added to the upsurge in popularity coming from the Falklands War, guaranteed Thatcher's victory. And Labour's split would continue to work for the benefit of the Conservative Party. Foot resigned in favor of the more moderate Neil Kinnock in 1983, but that was not enough to reunite the party. The SDP-Liberal Alliance was uneasy at best; Labour remained in the hands of the militant left; the Conservatives won again, handily, in the general election of 1987. This time, they were able to take advantage of an overall 4 percent growth in the economy. Much of this growth occurred in and around the large urban areas of the south and Midlands, and centered on financial services and computers. It helped offset the loss of jobs in traditional manufacturing and industry, but did little to lift the mood in the decaying northern centers.

BRITAIN ALONE OR AS PART OF EUROPE? THATCHER AND THE EUROPEAN COMMUNITY

One of the issues polarizing Labour, and enraging Thatcher, was Britain's relationship to continental Europe. Britain as an imperial power was long gone. The Falklands War had been fought for the livelihood of, in the words of one historian, "1,800 people, 650,000 sheep, and 10 million penguins,"[5] and it had inspired emotional rather than rational support. Other remainders of empire were equally problematic. Britain's involvement in the transition of a Rhodesia ruled by a racist white minority to the majority-ruled Zimbabwe in 1980 had been necessary, but it also showed how significantly Britain's former power had eroded. The passage of the 1981 British Nationality Act seemed a further repudiation of former colonial responsibilities: it seriously limited immigration of citizens from the former Commonwealth countries into Britain, essentially eliminating the notion that Commonwealth membership had carried with it full British citizenship. When Thatcher's administration in 1989 agreed to transfer power over Hong Kong back to China in 1997, the end of empire appeared complete. Britons both at home and abroad turned their attention to their continental neighbors, albeit reluctantly.

Britain's entrance into the EEC in 1973 had gained lukewarm approval, but any further contractual agreements with continental governments appeared to promise only more expensive food and fewer jobs. Indeed, Thatcher spent much of her first administration badgering the European Community (EC) to lower the amount of Britain's monetary contributions, a campaign that eventually ended with success.

Thatcher herself was ardently opposed to Britain's eventual acceptance of the European Exchange Rate Mechanism (ERM), arguing that any control over exchange rates would cripple the British economy and subject the country to undue international interference. She was equally dismissive of any move toward a common currency and a central European bank that would make decisions about the overall European economy. But pressures from within the cabinet, specifically from Chancellor of the Exchequer Nigel Lawson and Foreign Secretary Geoffrey Howe, persuaded Thatcher to agree to the Single European Act of 1985 as a commitment to closer integration into the European community.

Neither Lawson nor Howe was able to convince Thatcher of the benefits of the ERM, however, and both resigned in protest—Lawson in 1989, Howe a year later—over what they regarded as her misguided resistance to practical reality. They were especially concerned that Thatcher continued to block any integration into a Europe that by now had a vigorous and reunified Germany positioning itself to take control. Thatcher's isolationism appeared to be a disastrous response to this development. By the end of 1990, Thatcher was forced to agree to sign off on the ERM, but by then the flight of top advisors from the cabinet was seen as a symptom of a larger problem within Thatcher's government.

This is not to say that membership in the European Community (EC) and the proposed acquiescence in the formation of a federated Europe with a single currency were unequivocally welcomed by Thatcher's opponents. Indeed, one of the issues splitting the Labour party was the question of relations with Europe. The hard-line Labourites had argued for years that isolationism was preferable to any relations with countries whose governments were unfriendly to unions and workers. They criticized membership in the EC because it hobbled attempts by British unions to win higher wages for British workers, and instead advocated a program of industrial nationalization that would by itself have guaranteed Britain's ejection from the EC. The SDP-Liberal alliance, on the other hand, continued to argue for membership in the EC and, eventually, full participation in whatever model of federated Europe might emerge.

NORTHERN IRELAND, SCOTLAND, AND WALES

Closer to home even than continental Europe was the ongoing problem of Northern Ireland, and in this area Thatcher also proved that "the lady's not for turning." The IRA's intensification of terrorist acts against civilians, and against government officials outside of Ireland and Northern Ireland, included the attempted assassination of Thatcher in the 1984 bombing of the Brighton Grand Hotel, which killed five and injured many others. Thatcher and her cabinet were there negotiating what would eventually become the 1985 Anglo-Irish Agreement, or Hillsborough Agreement. This treaty, between Britain and Ireland, included clauses that acknowledged both British sovereignty over Northern Ireland and also the vested interests of the Republic of Ireland in its neighbor to the north. The treaty called for renewed efforts to protect and reconcile the two cultures of Northern Ireland without violence and to set up new levels of border security, and established an office outside of Belfast devoted to the protection of Dublin's interests in Northern Ireland. The unionists repudiated the treaty but were unable to come to any alternative agreement as to how to proceed, and the Hillsborough agreement, although far from perfect, at least established a framework for further discussion. Thatcher had argued from the outset that acknowledging the interests of Ireland in Northern Ireland was the only practical way to move forward, and her refusal to cave in to terrorist pressures gave new hope to the eventual establishment of peace in the region.

As for Scotland and Wales, the defeat of the devolution referenda in 1979 imposed a temporary silence on those who wanted Scots and Welsh independence, but it did nothing to assist in the economic recovery necessary to guarantee continued good relations among the various members of the United Kingdom. Labour continued to win in Scotland and Wales throughout Thatcher's administrations, as it did in the depressed north of England. Economic depression led to emigration, with the result that population levels in Scotland and Wales declined significantly as young men and women left home for the cities in the south of England where employment prospects were much brighter. In Wales, resentment of southern English prosperity took the form of arson, as the summer homes of a number of prosperous English visitors were burnt to the ground. In Scotland, where Thatcher's poll tax was introduced a year before it became the law in England, antagonism tended to take more political shape, primarily in the resurgence of the Scottish National Party. But the problem of unemployment, especially among the young, appeared unresolvable even as Thatcher was claiming victory against inflation and even as the overall British economy continued to expand.

POPULAR CULTURE AND DISAFFECTED YOUTH

One result of this continued unemployment was an upswing in "hooliganism," violence primarily by young men and often concentrated around public sporting events such as football (American soccer). Banning the sale and consumption of alcohol at football matches at home helped, but the international football championships were often the scenes of particularly loutish and violent behavior that resulted in destruction, death, and an overall distaste among Europeans generally for the British fan. The tendency toward alcohol-related violence among the young was not limited to sporting events; the '80s saw an upsurge in so-called "lager louts," and observers were divided over whether to place the blame solely on high unemployment among the young or to pin it upon the moral decline resulting from years of what Thatcher had early on dubbed "dependency culture." No matter who was at fault, the social fabric of Britain was certainly strained, and neither economic growth nor Thatcherite imprecations to behave seemed to make much headway against the phenomenon of disaffected youth.

It was this disaffection that colored much of popular culture after 1970, which pushed the boundaries of acceptable behavior as the rock and roll music of the '60s had done. This time, however, the goals of musicians and writers appeared to be not just celebration of youth but rather a cynical and often nasty rejection of contemporary and established culture. This rejection could be intellectual and witty in nature: musicians like Elvis Costello, for instance, provided a constant commentary on the Thatcher years through songs that were often melancholy and always satirical. More often, the rejection was less topical but more overtly shocking, as the bizarre performance techniques and the private behaviors of performers like Sid Vicious became grist for the media mill. The longevity of popular musical figures from the early '60s—the Rolling Stones, Paul McCartney and other former Beatles, Eric Clapton—provided a certain odd continuity to a period of musical innovation that ranged from heavy metal and punk rock to disco and new wave, all counterposed to the less lyrically and tonally difficult pop music of the Top 40s. Jamaican reggae and Indian bhangra represented important influences of the former empire within the musical culture. Similar influences would creep into the film and theater of the '80s and '90s, with movies like *My Beautiful Laundrette* and the 2003 hit *Bend It Like Beckham* specifically grappling with the issues of New Commonwealth immigrants and their lives in urban Britain—issues that the government often chose not to address.

JOHN MAJOR COMES TO POWER

By 1990, it was clear that the Thatcher years were drawing to a close. Margaret Thatcher had served three successive terms, the first prime minister to do so since Lord Liverpool in the early 1800s, but she was losing

support within her party. The main problem for her Conservative col-
leagues was Thatcher's unbending opposition to the EC, and this time
there was no international war that could boost her ratings. Thatcher's
offer of support to the United States after the 1990 invasion of Kuwait by
Saddam Hussein failed to distract voters from domestic issues. At the
same time, Neil Kinnock had begun to successfully revitalize the Labour
Party, so that Labour won several by-elections. All of this spelled the end
to Thatcher's leadership in the party. In late 1990 she was replaced by
John Major, a man with close ties to Thatcher but who had managed to
avoid the personality problems that increasingly plagued the Iron Lady.
In the general election of 1990, the Conservatives clung to power, but it
was Major, not Thatcher, who would preside over seven more years of
Conservative reign.

Major inherited an economy in recession, with interest rates in the double digits and unemployment at 1.75 million. While Nigel Lawson's exit
from Thatcher's cabinet had done her no good in the public's eye, his
years of slashing taxes had done significant long-term harm that only
began to emerge in the 1990s, placing Britain's balance of payments once
again firmly in the red and shrinking economic growth to about half a
percent annually. Even more difficult, perhaps, was the nature of British
society, which had become more polarized than before around issues of
class and race. Major proclaimed in 1990 that he wanted Britain to be "a
country that is at ease with itself"—never mind that he was now speaking
for four countries, not one—and that Britain would and should transform
itself into "a genuinely classless society."[6]

The problems in the economy were met with a number of steps that
included the abolition of the hated poll tax and a consequent increase in
the VAT—including, in 1993, a tax on fuel. Public borrowing increased as
well in order to continue and to expand the social services that had been
neglected under Thatcher. In 1992, Britain left the ERM, devaluing the
pound in the process. It was a painful retrenchment and one that appeared
to undercut all the talk of economic management and fiscal responsibility
of previous years.

The problems of social relations were equally difficult. Thatcherite policies of privatization had not, as she had promised, resulted in a society
imbued with the moral rectitude and practical values of small capitalism.
Instead, privatized companies came under fire as charges of cronyism
and greed were leveled at their new CEOs, many of whom had been
personal or professional friends of Thatcher. Excessive corporate salaries
appeared to be possible only at the cost of layoffs and downsizing, on the
one hand, and increased prices, on the other. By 1994–1995, even the most

Conservative newspapers were running exposés on sleaze in corporate life and corruption in the so-called "quangos"—"quasi-autonomous non-governmental organizations," the agencies staffed by political appointees who were charged with overseeing governmental functions such as health and housing.

Alongside these reports on corporate mismanagement and dishonesty, there were many stories on the sufferings of the man on the street. The press focused on the all-too-plentiful families who simply fell through the cracks as the NHS and other government agencies were trimmed and realigned. Families who could no longer afford water supplied by now-privatized water companies, families whose members had to wait years for necessary health care, families whose council housing was dilapidated and condemnable, families who finally owned their own homes but who could no longer meet the mortgage payments as interest rates hovered above 12 percent—all of these provided ample material for the media. Stories about individuals harried over nonpayment of the now-defunct poll tax also received wide attention, written as they were to illustrate what appeared to be a growing and now deeply dangerous divide between rich and poor. British society was not at all "at ease with itself" or "classless"; instead, reading the papers, it appeared increasingly fragmented and at odds with itself.

BRITAIN AND EUROPE UNDER MAJOR

Despite these very serious problems, however, the Conservative government remained in power until 1997. Major and the Conservatives used the issue of Britain's relationship with the rest of Europe to distract public and political attention away from the problems of private individuals. This time, however, the party roles were reversed. The Conservatives were increasingly the voice of isolationism, while Labour called for renewed ties to the Continent. Major's role in the passage and ratification of the Maastricht Treaty in 1991 had included two components crucial for Conservative support: first, Britain retained the right to opt out of a future European currency, to be introduced in 1999; and second, Britain also could refuse to accept the package of workers' rights and social benefits—the so-called "social chapter" of the treaty—that would go into effect throughout Europe.

But these concessions were not enough to prevent the Conservatives from polarizing around pro- and anti-European positions. Thatcher had not been the only rabidly anti-European party member, and her fellow isolationists found the Maastricht treaty much too threatening to British independence and autonomy. They argued that the right to opt out of a European currency would not necessarily preserve the strength of the pound, and that any further economic ties to the Continent would inevitably weaken the position of British manufacturing and industry. Further, a federated Europe of whatever composition would threaten the strength of the Crown and of Parliament. Voices raised against European union became more and more strident as the introduction of the euro, the single European currency, loomed. All of this in-fighting took place against the backdrop of unquestionably closer ties to Europe, symbolized most potently by the Channel Tunnel, or Chunnel, which opened between Paris and Dover in 1994.

Relations with the Continent were complicated by several difficult incidents. The increase in bovine spongiform encephalopathy (BSE), or "mad cow disease," an illness fatal to humans as well as cattle, led to an international scare in which British beef was banned on the Continent. Farmers feared for their livelihood, and many of them blamed not the relaxation of feed regulations under Thatcher but rather a powerful German lobby that, in the minds of many Britons, sought any opportunity to weaken the British economy. The spread of foot-and-mouth disease in sheep and other livestock in early 2001 had the same effect, with bans against the export of animals and animal products and with farmers forced to slaughter entire herds in order to contain a disease that threatened to destroy the wool and lamb industries.

Relations within the Isles themselves were relatively peaceful, at least on the surface. Not until Labour's 1997 victory did devolution become a byword in Scotland and Wales; until then, economic malaise and slow but steady depopulation continued to dog the so-called Celtic fringe. In Northern Ireland, the Hillsborough Agreement paved the way for incremental movement toward peace. As with everything in Northern Ireland, this process was not a simple one; an IRA bombing in 1987, for instance, killed 11 Protestants in Enniskillen but also turned public opinion even more firmly against the IRA and placed increasing pressure on Sinn Féin to move away from its tacit approval of terror as a political weapon. By 1994, the IRA had been brought to declare "a total cessation of operations,"[7] a move that was echoed in the voluntary cease-fires of other paramilitary organizations on the unionist side.

In 1996, the cease-fire was broken with an IRA bombing incident in London's Canary Wharf district, resulting in two fatalities and over 100 casualties. Within two years, however, the historic Good Friday Agreement was reached, brokered between Sinn Féin's Gerry Adams and the unionist Donald Trimble through the combined efforts of new prime minister Tony Blair and U.S. senator George Mitchell. The agreement established an elected assembly based on proportional representation, thus guaranteeing a Catholic presence that reflected the population of Northern Ireland; it also established a north-south ministerial council responsible for security and other measures. At the same time, it gave the devolved government the ability to veto any north-south policies it found offensive.

NEW LABOUR COMES TO POWER

Blair's involvement in the formation of this agreement and the devolved government it established reflected his own, and Labour's, wider commitment to the ideal of devolution. Labour had remade itself vigorously in the years of Major's administration. Tony Blair, M.P. since 1983, emerged as the face and voice of "New Labour," taking over the leadership of the party in 1994 and steering it to a new and identifiably different set of ideals than those of the still-fractured old Labourite left.

Blair and his followers were primarily targeting not the traditional Labour voters in the working classes, but rather the broader middle classes, who generally felt that Conservative policies were lacking in social conscience and who appeared to wish for less nannying and more real assistance for the less fortunate. In December 1993, the *Observer* had published poll results showing that of those polled, 68 percent felt that the government had not "made Britain more prosperous" and 70 percent felt it had not "begun to create a classless society"—the two main goals of the Major government. More damning, perhaps, was the fact that only 12 percent felt that the Conservatives were "fair with people" or even "sincere"; a mere 9 percent felt that the government was "in touch with ordinary people."[8] These numbers appeared to show that a new kind of Labour Party could attract voters across party lines.

Blair, using media with more skill than any of his predecessors, shaped New Labour for public consumption in ways that capitalized on the underlying sense that Thatcherite Britain, continued under Major, had gone wrong both socially and economically. New Labour was deliberately not Old Labour; it was more inclusive and less committed to the socialist policies of the past, voting in 1995 to eliminate the party's commitment to nationalization of industries and services. It was also willing to acknowledge that privatization was not in and of itself evil, and that Thatcherite policies promoting home ownership and reigning in the powers of trade unions had been beneficial to the nation. New Labour projected itself as younger, more modern, more European, more innovative than any other party, and in 1997 the voters seemed to agree: Blair became prime minister in a landslide victory for Labour, after the long "wilderness years." Along with Blair came a record number of 120 women M.P.s, 100 of them representing Labour—the largest influx of women into the House of Commons in its history.

Blair appeared to many to take as his model the American presidency of Bill Clinton, with whom he was often compared, and he was accused by opponents and even a number of supporters of seeking to strengthen the powers of the prime minister and cabinet at the expense of Parliament. One of his most controversial proposals was the dissolution of the House of Lords. Partially successful, he managed to end the practice of hereditary peers sitting in the House of Lords in 1999. Other pledges made in 1997 included devolution in Wales and Scotland; acts establishing the Welsh National Assembly and the Scottish parliament were passed in 1998. At the same time that he was pledging to "reform" the upper house and "modernize" the lower house in ways that appeared to gather more power to the office of the prime minister and his cabinet, however, Blair was also committing significant resources to regional assemblies throughout England, as a counterpart to the devolution of government in Scotland and Wales. Thus, his government continued to consolidate certain kinds of central authority within the offices of Downing Street, as Thatcher had done, but began to reverse Thatcher's anti-locality campaigns with new initiatives for regional and London government.

Blair's administration emphatically did not reject all of Thatcher's economic policies, refusing to re-nationalize the companies privatized in the 1980s, but New Labour did return to policies of wage guarantees and renewed funding for programs for children and the elderly. Nor did Blair abandon the caution with which previous administrations had regarded the coming of the euro. Britain remained wedded to the pound even when much of the rest of Europe adopted the euro in 2002. However, the practical fact of membership within the EC gained legal strength in the late 1990s with several new laws, including some enforcing the use of the metric weights in place of the old imperial weights. The Human Rights Act of 1998 also brought British courts under the aegis of the European Convention on Human Rights and added new guarantees of protection not necessarily included in British law. In the wake of the terrorist bombings in the United States on September 11, 2001, the British courts were forced to recognize that the treatment of terrorist suspects had to conform to international law rather than English common law, a realization that came as a shock to many Britons who had always held British law as sufficient and all-encompassing.

The debates over sovereignty and autonomy, fueled by integration into the EU, appeared to call into question the very existence of a monarchy that appeared outdated and unnecessary. The personal travails of the royal family—dogged by marital scandal among Elizabeth's children—contributed to an overall sense that perhaps it was time to transform Britain into a republic. The death of Prince Charles's ex-wife, Diana, princess of Wales, in an automobile accident in 1997 ironically reawakened a dormant affection for the monarchy. Diana had represented a "real person" amongst the royals, with her publicly discussed eating disorders, her unhappiness within the Windsor family, her obvious love for her two sons, and, eventually, her advocacy of international relief efforts for victims of land mines, AIDS, and other tragedies. The outpouring of public grief at her death struck many onlookers as excessive, but signaled to others that the rumblings of republicanism were premature at best. Blair himself was able to use that moment of public emotion to cement his hold on the nation's attention, representing a Britain that was both a traditional monarchy and a youthful and energetic member of the world community.

Labour enjoyed a second major victory at the polls in 2001, providing the party with a second term in office for the first time in history. Blair's domestic policies have remained relatively popular, although his moves to raise university tuition and increase taxes to expand the NHS caused some grumbling. Only with Blair's decision to involve Britain in the U.S. invasion of Iraq did his popularity begin to significantly suffer. Blair justified his willingness to send British troops to oust Saddam and to look for weapons of mass destruction in part by citing the hundreds of British casualties in the attacks of September 11, but his poll numbers slipped in October 2002 to new lows. When the vote to send troops into war was taken, Blair found that 139 of his party members voted against him, and three of his ministers resigned. The practical fact of victory—Saddam's regime fell quickly and with very few British casualties—helped temporarily boost his popularity again, but rumors of manipulated intelligence data that exaggerated the possibility of weapons of mass destruction and evidence of mistreatment of Iraqi prisoners once again forced Blair on the defensive, a situation that at the time of this publication continues to dog the prime minister.

NOTES

1. Quoted in Anthony Seldon and Daniel Collings, *Britain under Thatcher* (Edinburgh: Longman Press, 2000), p. 1.
2. Peter Clarke, *Hope and Glory: Britain 1900–1990* (London and New

York: Penguin Books, 1996), p. 372; Seldon and Collings, *Britain under Thatcher,* p. 66.

3. Seldon and Collings, *Britain under Thatcher,* p. 67.

4. Clarke, *Hope and Glory,* p. 381.

5. Thomas William Heyck, *The Peoples of the British Isles: A New History. From 1870 to the Present* (Belmont, Calif.: Wadsworth Publishing Company, 1992), p. 351.

6. Quoted in UKPol Magazine 2000–2003 at http://www.johnmajor.co.uk.

7. Quoted in Senia Pašeta, *Modern Ireland: A Very Short Introduction* (Oxford and New York: Oxford University Press, 2003), p. 122.

8. Statistics reprinted in Marwick, *British Society Since 1945,* p. 415.

Notable People in the History of Great Britain

Atlee, Clement (1883–1957), Labour prime minister, 1945–51. Atlee served as deputy prime minister under Winston Churchill in the wartime coalition government, 1940–45. He joined first the Fabians and then the Independent Labour Party, and after serving in World War I was elected to Parliament. As prime minister after World War II, he shaped the welfare state that became the hallmark of postwar Britain, as well as the nationalization of key industries and the dismantling of much of the British Empire.

Baldwin, Stanley (1867–1947), Conservative prime minister, 1923–24, 1924–29, 1935–37. Baldwin entered Parliament in 1908; as prime minister he worked to end free trade and introduce protectionist tariffs. During the General Strike of 1926 he pursued a line of conciliation, although by 1927 his cabinet was able to force through the Trades Disputes Act, which contained harsh measures toward strikers. He helped avoid a constitutional crisis when Edward VIII abdicated, and retired two weeks after the new king, George VI, was crowned.

Bevan, Aneurin (1897–1960), creator of the National Health Service after 1945. Born into a Dissenting Welsh family, Bevan became known as the "socialist soul" of the Labour party. He broke with the left wing of Labour over the issue of unilateral disarmament in 1957.

Beveridge, William H. (1879–1963), author of the Beveridge Report, a runaway best-seller in 1942 outlining the future of a social welfare state in Britain, and a supplementary report in 1945 arguing for full employment as the basis for the welfare state. A social reformer who was closely associated with the Fabians and with the London settlement house of Toynbee Hall, he joined the Board of Trade in 1908 and significantly shaped both the Labour Exchanges Act of 1909 and the National Insurance Act of 1911. He served as director of the London School of Economics from 1919 to 1937.

Blair, Tony Charles Linton (b. 1953), Labour prime minister, 1997–   . Blair entered Parliament in 1983. He became leader of the Labour Party in 1994 and began to shape the party into a modernized "New Labour." In 1997 he led Labour in an overwhelming victory at the polls, and since becoming prime minister has made significant changes to government, in part in an effort to undo the Thatcherite revolution of the 1980s. The reforms of New Labour include the devolution of government for Scotland, Wales, and the localities; an elected Lord Mayor for London; and the abolition of most hereditary peers as members of the House of Lords.

Chamberlain, Arthur Neville (1869–1940), prime minister, 1937–40. A son of Joseph Chamberlain, Neville Chamberlain also entered politics through service on the Birmingham City Council and won election as M.P. for Birmingham in 1918. His years as Minister of Health in 1924–29 included social services projects such as pensions for widows and orphans, affordable housing, and school meals for poor children. In the '30s, first as Chancellor of the Exchequer and then as prime minister, he ended free trade and lowered the income tax. He was the public face of appeasement toward the Nazi regime in the '30s, a policy that was enormously popular throughout the entire British public, and his signature on the Munich accords was at first widely acclaimed. By 1939, however, Chamberlain had lost public support and was widely seen as having been outmaneuvered by Hitler; he resigned in 1940 and died shortly thereafter.

Chamberlain, Joseph (1836–1914), politician and imperialist. Initially a Liberal, Chamberlain began his political career in 1874 as city councilman and then as mayor of Birmingham, where he introduced a program of reforms dubbed "gas-and-water socialism." He was a tireless advocate of social programs that included slum clearance, free art galleries and libraries, free elementary and secondary education, and municipal ownership of essential services. After 1875 he served as M.P. for Birmingham.

In 1886 he formed the Liberal Unionist party to oppose Home Rule in Ireland and to support a stronger British presence in Africa and Asia. In 1895, he became colonial secretary under the Conservatives, talking openly about the "white man's burden" in the colonies.

Churchill, Sir Winston Leonard Spencer (1874–1965), prime minister, 1940–45, 1951–55. One of Britain's most beloved figures, primarily for his work in maintaining British spirit during World War II. A war correspondent in the Boer War, he served in both world wars. He entered Parliament in 1900, becoming First Lord of the Admiralty in 1911 and authoring the disastrous Dardanelles campaign in 1915. His work in the 1920s as Colonial Secretary included a treaty with the Irish Free State. He spent the years from 1929 to 1939 out of office, working on his military histories, and in the early '30s emerged as a voice of opposition to the Nazis and a counterbalance to appeasement. After the resignation of Neville Chamberlain he became prime minister of a wartime government. When peace was declared, he served as leader of the Opposition and in 1951 returned as prime minister. He resigned the premiership in 1955 but remained in office, where he died as a sitting M.P. in 1965.

Collins, Michael (1890–1922), Irish revolutionary leader. After participating in the Easter Rising of 1916, he became one of the leaders of the Irish Volunteers. Under his direction the group became the Irish Republican Army and began a guerrilla campaign against British politicians and others who opposed Irish independence. He helped negotiate the Anglo-Irish treaty that established the Irish Free State in 1922, but was assassinated that same year.

Cromwell, Oliver (1599–1658), M.P., general of the New Model Army during the English Civil War, and later Lord Protector of Britain. One of the most prominent of the parliamentarians or "roundheads" during the civil war, Cromwell signed the death warrant of King Charles I and spent the years until 1651 in continuous and ruthless military campaigns in Ireland and Scotland. In 1653, he and his army council ejected the remaining M.P.s and he became the leader of a military regime. By 1654, he had become Lord Protector. His regime was characterized by military discipline and military expense, an emphasis on godly living, and growing resentment by the common man. In 1660, as part of the Restoration settlement, the bodies of Cromwell and the other regicides were dug up and displayed as traitors by the new king, Charles II.

Cromwell, Thomas (c. 1485–1540), minister under Henry VIII, he was the man most responsible for the break with Rome and the formation of the English church. He used Parliament to formulate the series of laws establishing the royal supremacy, thereby giving Parliament a strong sense of political importance. Cromwell managed not only the end of Henry's marriage to Catherine of Aragon but also the conviction and execution of Anne Boleyn, Henry's second wife. His matchmaking for wife number three, Anne of Cleves, was carried out in pursuit of alliances with Protestant powers on the Continent, but led to his downfall and execution when Henry found the candidate distasteful and the political policies treasonous.

Darwin, Charles (1809–1882), natural scientist and author of the 1859 *Origin of Species,* which outlined the theory of evolution by natural selection. Darwin's voyages on the HMS *Beagle* in 1831–36 provided him with ample evidence of evolutionary change. Not until 1881 did he address the role of evolution in human history, in his *Descent of Man.*

Dickens, Charles John Huffam (1812–1870), novelist and social critic. Dickens was a prolific author, producing journalism, drama, and fiction mostly about London. He combined realism and vivid expressionism in his novels, often choosing a social problem—the law, the prison system, the civil service—as an organizing focus for his work. His first big success was *The Pickwick Papers,* and his early, more sentimental novels such as *Nicholas Nickleby* were followed by darker, more complex works such as *Bleak House* and *Little Dorrit.* Many of his novels were serialized in journals edited by Dickens (*Household Words*) or his friends, catering to the growing reading public and especially to the novel-reading habits of middle-class men and women.

Disraeli, Benjamin, first earl of Beaconsfield (1804–1881), politician, prime minister (1874–80), and novelist. Disraeli is famous for referring to Victorian politics as "a climb to the top of the greasy pole," but it took him many years to reach the top. His early adulthood was spent in writing "silver fork" novels about the aristocracy. In 1837 he became a Conservative M.P., but did not succeed in gaining significant influence within the party until the mid-1840s. He served as the leader of the Conservative party in the Commons under the earl of Derby, serving as Chancellor of the Exchequer in Derby's governments of 1852, 1858–59, and 1866–68. As prime minister, he presided over the acquisition of the Suez Canal and the declaration of Victoria as empress of India. Despite his lifelong membership in the Anglican Church, his Jewish heritage made him suspect to many Britons, and his flair for self-aggrandizement was further proof that he was in many ways more exotic than English.

Gladstone, William Ewart (1809–1898), politician, prime minister (1868–74, 1880–85, 1886, 1892–94), and author. Gladstone entered Parliament in 1832, beginning a long parliamentary career that included several terms as Chancellor of the Exchequer. By the mid-1860s he was an identified radical within the Liberal party, supporting such measures as an expanded franchise, the abolition of church rates (taxes), the disestablishment of the state church, and eventually Home Rule for Ireland. His administrations also pushed through sweeping reforms in education, the military, and land ownership in Ireland, as well as the secret ballot. His moral rectitude informed both his domestic and foreign policies, as seen in his Midlothian campaign, where he called for recognition of the equal rights of all nations. Despite his own personal convictions, he was pressured by his party to support the expansion of the British Empire into Africa and the Pacific.

Heath, Sir Edward (b. 1916), prime minister, 1970–74. Heath entered Parliament as a Conservative M.P. in 1950, holding various offices in the shadow cabinet during Labour's long tenure. As prime minister, he had to deal with such difficult issues as the escalation of violence in Northern Ireland, the international oil crisis, rampant inflation and unemployment, and the controversial decision to enter Britain in the European Economic Community (EEC).

Hogarth, William (1697–1764), artist. Hogarth was an engraver and illustrator of "scenes of contemporary life," most of which were situated in London. He became famous for his narrative sequences that carried moral and social messages, among which were *The Rake's Progress, Marriage a la Mode,* and *Beer Street/Gin Lane.*

Lloyd George, David (1863–1945), prime minister, 1916–22. As leader of the coalition government during the First World War, Lloyd George made sweeping changes in the role of government in the life of the ordinary citizen, increasing centralized control and direction in order to marshal military and other resources. As Chancellor of the Exchequer before the war, his "People's Budget" introduced the progressive income tax to fund old-age pensions and military expansion. He presided over the 1918 Representation of the People Act enfranchising women, as well as the settlement with the Irish Free State.

MacDonald, James Ramsay (1866–1937), prime minister, 1924, 1929–31, 1931–35. MacDonald helped shape the modern Labour party as a party working to build a socialist future through parliamentary means. He joined the Independent Labour Party in the 1890s, and in 1903 helped form the coalition with the Liberals that enabled the Labourites to win 24 seats, including his own, in the 1906 election. MacDonald opposed Britain's entry into the First World War and lost his seat, but reentered Parliament in 1922 and was subsequently elected leader of the Labour party. He became the first Labour prime minister.

Major, John (b. 1943), prime minister, 1990–97. Major replaced Margaret Thatcher as leader of the Conservative Party and as prime minister, continuing most of Thatcher's policies but ending such hated innovations as the poll tax. Under his administration, Britain was forced to leave the ERM (Exchange Rate Mechanism) and suffered new highs in unemployment, tax increases, and deficit spending. Major signed the Maastricht Treaty in 1992 despite the Conservatives' ambivalence about closer relations with Europe, an ambivalence that continued to grow during such crises as the BSE episode, where Europe closed its doors to British beef over fears of "mad cow disease." Even the peace talks he brokered in Northern Ireland broke down when Ulster unionists feared betrayal by Westminster. And the public reacted negatively to changes in the National Health Service under Major. All of these episodes helped spell a disastrous defeat for the Conservatives in 1997.

Mill, John Stuart (1806–1873), Utilitarian and liberal philosopher. Mill was the product of a peculiar childhood, educated by his father in accordance with the tenets of "philosophical radicalism" first postulated by Jeremy Bentham. He served in the East India Company for 35 years, then was elected as M.P. in 1865; during his three years in Parliament he unsuccessfully worked for women's suffrage. He advocated a combination of free market philosophy and some governmental controls on the economy, and also, in *On Liberty* (1859) wrote eloquently about the uses of personal freedom to ensure the overall health of a society. He argued for controlled participatory democracy, calling for the extension of education in order to prepare an intelligent electorate.

Newton, Sir Isaac (1642–1727), scientist. Newton's 1687 *Principia Mathematica* was the basis for what was later dubbed "the Newtonian synthesis," working out the laws of space, time, and motion in order to form a unified theory of physics that included the notion of gravity as a force that operated across empty space to hold the universe in place.

O'Connell, Daniel (1775–1847), Irish politician who campaigned for Catholic emancipation. He was elected to Parliament in 1828 but could not take his seat because he was a Catholic; the following year, the government ended discrimination against Catholics.

O'Connor, Feargus (1794–1855), Chartist. O'Connor was an Irish politician elected to Parliament in 1832; he helped lead the Chartist movement during its most active phase. He edited the national Chartist newspaper, *The Northern Star,* and supported the Chartist Land Plan, which called for the relocation of urban working people to small holdings in the countryside.

Parnell, Charles Stewart (1846–91), Irish nationalist and politician. Parnell entered Parliament in 1875 and became president of the Irish Land League in 1879. His work helped shape Gladstone's first Home Rule bill in 1886. Parnell's political career ended disastrously with the divorce case brought against him by a former colleague, the husband of his long-time mistress Kitty O'Shea.

Peel, Sir Robert (1788–1850), prime minister, 1834–35, 1841–46. Peel entered Parliament in 1809 as a Tory. He opposed Catholic Emancipation personally but ushered through the bill which ended disabilities for Catholics; he also opposed the Reform Act of 1832 but conceded that cautious reform under a Tory ministry was necessary. He lowered the tariffs on imported foodstuffs, eventually spearheading the repeal of the Corn Laws in 1846.

Rowntree, Benjamin Seebohm (1871–1954), author of the influential 1901 *Poverty: A Study of Town Life.* Rowntree examined the presence of poverty in 1900 York and concluded that it could be divided into two categories: primary poverty, defined as the lack of some necessity of life such as fuel, clothing, food, or shelter, occurring no matter how careful the family was about expenditure; and secondary poverty, defined as the lack of money for anything beyond the four necessities, such as medicine. His study helped change the thinking about poverty, eroding the notion that the poor were only poor because they did not work hard enough or save carefully enough.

Shakespeare, William (1564–1616), playwright and poet, and author of over 40 plays and numerous sonnets and sonnet cycles. His history plays explored the ways in which the Tudors and Stuarts used power and myth as tools of governance; his tragedies and comedies became increasingly complex reflections of an often violent Elizabethan and Jacobean culture.

Smith, Adam (1723–1790), economist and philosopher. Smith's 1776 *Wealth of Nations* condemned the economic theories and practices of mercantilism and instead advocated a relatively "laissez faire," or free market, economy, devoid of unnecessary government interference. Smith postulated an "invisible hand" directing the marketplace, the result of competition among individuals and healthy self-interest as a motivating force among consumers and producers.

Thatcher, Margaret (b. 1925), prime minister, 1979–90. Thatcher, the first woman prime minister of Britain, presided over a series of radical changes in government known as the "Thatcher Revolution." Her economic policies focused on lowering interest rates and taxes, and she systematically worked to undo the welfare state created by Clement Atlee after 1945, privatizing nationalized industries and advocating what she called small-scale capitalism through the purchase by ordinary men and women of shares in these former nationalized industries. A Europhobe, Thatcher opposed entry into any formal European community, although she was forced to accede to demands for entry into the European Exchange Rate Mechanism at the end of her administration. Her popularity soared during the Falklands War (1982) but plummeted at the introduction of the poll tax (1989–90).

de Valera, Eamon (1882–1975), Irish nationalist, taoiseach (prime minister) (1932–48, 1951–54, 1957–59), and president (1959–73) of the Irish Free State. De Valera was the only surviving leader of the Easter Rising of 1916, and after release from jail began working toward the complete independence of Ireland from Great Britain. He became president of the Irish Dáil, or parliament, in 1919 but refused to attend the peace talks with Britain at the end of the Anglo-Irish War, instead insisting that any partition into a southern republic and a British Northern Ireland was unacceptable. He won the 1932 elections as leader of the Fianna Fail party, after which the Irish constitution was altered to omit allegiance to the British Crown.

Victoria (1819–1901), queen of the United Kingdom of Great Britain and Ireland (1837–1901) and empress of India (1877–1901). Victoria was the first woman since Elizabeth I to ascend to the throne, and like Elizabeth's, her rule spanned several generations. Direct royal authority had diminished by 1837 but Victoria's influence was significant. She represented the moral and domestic side of Britain to itself and to the outside world, and at the same time presided over an expanding empire at the pinnacle of its strength. Her marriage to her cousin Albert produced 9 children and 40 grandchildren, so that she was, by the time of her death, truly the "grandmother of Europe."

Walpole, Sir Robert (1676–1745), chief minister and First Lord of the Treasury (1721–41). Walpole entered Parliament in 1701 and became a valued member of the Whig party, serving as Secretary of War and Treasurer of the Navy. He was impeached and expelled by the Tories, then regained office when George I ascended. Walpole was known for his financial acumen (he helped rescue the country from the financial disaster of the South Sea Bubble) as well as his skillful use of patronage; he helped develop the cabinet system; and he fought viciously against the continued threat of Jacobitism.

Wesley, John (1703–1791), founder of Wesleyan Methodism. Raised as a high-church Tory, he was dissatisfied with his own spiritual life and used "methodical" rituals and practices to enhance his piety and his emotional relationship with God. Based upon his own conversion experience, he was unswerving in his belief that religious experience should be emotional as well as rational. He evangelized all over England for decades, holding tent meetings and preaching in open fields. Wesley managed to keep his Wesleyan fellows within the Anglican Church until he died, but the formation of a separate Methodist sect followed soon after his death.

Wolsey, Thomas (c. 1472–1530), cardinal and minister to Henry VIII. Wolsey rose quickly from humble beginnings through the hierarchy of the Catholic Church and became archbishop of York as well as cardinal, papal legate, and eventually Lord Chancellor of England. He expanded the court system, endowed new colleges, and involved England in expensive wars with France. He was charged with treason after failing to secure the king a divorce from his first wife, Catherine of Aragon, but died on his way to appear before the court to answer these charges.

Bibliographic Essay

Much of the most interesting recent work on Great Britain can be loosely categorized as having to do with the question of identity. That is, what does it mean to be British, to be English, to be Scots or Welsh or Irish or Northern Irish? Further, what does it mean to be a member of a Commonwealth country? These questions build upon important work since the 1960s on the question of class in Britain, a question that is still being explored. Perhaps the most famous of these works on class, and certainly the classic starting point for any subsequent work, is E. P. Thompson's *Making of the English Working Class* (New York, 1966). Gareth Stedman Jones's *Languages of Class: Studies in English Working Class History 1832–1982* (Cambridge and New York, 1983) provocatively explores class and the ways in which language shapes identity. Other more recent works on the question of class include David Cannadine, *The Rise and Fall of Class in Britain* (New York, 1999); Dror Wahrman, *Imagining the Middle Class: The Political Representation of Class in Britain, c. 1780–1840* (Cambridge and New York, 1995); and F. M. L. Thompson, *The Rise of Respectable Society* (London, 1988), which is particularly accessible to the general reader. *The Cambridge Social History of Britain 1750–1950* (Cambridge and New York, 1990) includes essays on various aspects of class identity. Jose Harris, *Pri-*

vate Lives, Public Spirit: Britain 1870–1914 (London and New York, 1994) places class relationships within an evolving British society.

Works exploring the notion of national identity include Linda Colley, *Britons: Forging the Nation 1707–1837* (New Haven and London, 1992); Paul Langford, *Englishness Identified: Manners and Character 1650–1850* (Oxford and New York, 2000); and Catherine Hall et al., *Defining the Victorian Nation: Class, Race, Gender and the Reform Act of 1867* (Cambridge and New York, 2000). Hall's book incorporates questions of nationality as defined within a growing empire, and for books on empire the best starting place is indisputably the four-volume *Oxford History of the British Empire* (Oxford and New York, 1998–99). The crown of the British Empire, India, has been treated at length in a number of books; one starting point would be *Raj: The Making and Unmaking of British India* (New York, 1998). Readers should also look at P. G. Cain and A. G. Hopkins, eds., *British Imperialism*, 2d ed. (New York, 2001) and the *Cambridge Illustrated History of the British Empire* (Cambridge and New York, 1996). David Reynolds's *Britannia Overruled: British Policy and World Power in the Twentieth Century*, 2d ed. (New York, 2000) addresses post-imperial Britain within the overall context of foreign policy; John Darwin and Geoffrey Warner, *Britain and Decolonization: The Retreat from Empire in the Post-War World* (New York, 1988) focuses on the post-1945 dismantling of empire. Niall Ferguson's *Empire: The Rise and Demise of the British World Order and the Lessons for Global Power* (Boulder, Colo., 2003) links British imperial history to the largely unacknowledged present-day imperial power of the United States. Among the works that look at empire through a narrower lens are P. S. Gupta, *Imperialism and the British Labour Movement, 1914–1964* (Thousand Oaks, Calif., 2002) and John MacKenzie, ed., *Imperialism and Popular Culture* (Manchester, UK, 1998), part of Manchester University Press's excellent "Studies in Imperialism" series.

Other types of identity receiving a great deal of attention in recent years focus on gender, including Judith Walkowitz, *City of Dreadful Delight: Narratives of Sexual Danger in Late-Victorian London* (Chicago, 1992); Leonore Davidoff and Catherine Hall, *Family Fortunes: Men and Women of the English Middle Class 1780–1850* (Chicago, 1987); and Sandra Gilbert and Susan Gubar, *The Madwoman in the Attic: The Woman Writer and the Nineteenth-Century Literary Imagination* (New Haven and London, 1984). Recent work on masculinity includes John Tosh, *A Man's Place: Masculinity and the Middle-Class Home in Victorian England* (New Haven and London, 1999) and Michael Roper and John Tosh, eds., *Manful Assertions: Masculinities in Britain Since 1800* (London, 1991). Work on the family includes the old but excellent Peter Wilmott and Michael Young, *Family and Kinship in East London* (Berkeley, Calif., 1954; repr. 1992) and their *Family and Class in a London Suburb* (New York, 1984).

For political and economic histories, Eric J. Hobsbawm's series places Britain in an international context. See *The Age of Revolution 1789–1848* (New York, 1996); *The Age of Capital 1848–1875* (New York, 1996); *The Age of Empire 1875–1914* (New York, 1989); and *Age of Extremes: The Short Twentieth Century 1914–1991* (London, 1994). For specifically British studies, see David Cannadine, *The Decline and Fall of the British Aristocracy* (New York, 1990; repr. 1992); Martin Pugh, *The Making of Modern British Politics, 1867–1939*, 3d ed. (Oxford, 1982, 2002); Peter Clarke, *A Question of Leadership: Gladstone to Thatcher* (London and New York, 1991).

Works on a Britain now firmly redivided into separate nations are appearing in great numbers. A few of the most recent include Paul Chaney et al., *New Governance, New Democracy? Post-Devolution Wales* (Cardiff, Wales, 2000); Richard Rawlings, *Delineating Wales: Legal and Constitutional Aspects of National Devolution* (Cardiff, Wales, 2003); Neal Ascherson, *Stone Voices: The Search for Scotland* (New York, 2003); Christopher T. Harvie: *Scotland and Nationalism: Scottish Society and Politics, 1707–Present* (New York, 1999); David McKittrick and David McVea, *Making Sense of the Troubles: The Story of the Conflict in Northern Ireland* (Chicago, 2002); and Jack Holland, *Hope Against History: The Course of Conflict in Northern Ireland* (New York, 1999).

For general histories, the most effective of the textbooks available is the three-volume work by Stanford E. Lehmberg and Thomas William Heyck, *The Peoples of the British Isles: A New History* (Belmont, Calif., 1992; an updated edition is currently underway). The authors do an excellent job of incorporating information on Wales, Scotland, and Ireland within the overall narrative rather than appending it as an afterthought. The massive one-volume work by Norman Davies, *The Isles: A History* (Oxford and New York, 1999) can be idiosyncratic in its approach. Less enormous and more satisfying are Peter Clarke, *Hope and Glory: Britain 1900–1990* (London and New York, 1996) and Arthur Marwick, *British Society Since 1945* (London and New York, 1996). Edward Royle, *Modern Britain: A Social History 1750–1997*, 2d ed. (London, 1997) is organized by categories such as class, education, and religion, treating each category for the entire period under study. Also helpful is Keith Robbins, *The Eclipse of a Great Power: Modern Britain 1870–1992*, 2d ed. (London and New York, 1994).

Finally, among the Internet sites devoted to British history, these deserve special mention: The Spartacus Encyclopedia of British History

1500–1950 (http://www.spartacus.schoolnet.co.uk/industry.html); The Internet Modern History Sourcebook (http://www.fordham.edu/halsall/mod/modsbook.html); and Victoria Research Web (a superb and always-growing site) (http://www.victorianresearch.org).

Index

About the Author

ANNE BALTZ RODRICK teaches modern European history at Wofford College. She is the author of *Self-Help and Civic Culture: Citizenship in Victorian Birmingham*.

Other Titles in the Greenwood Histories of the Modern Nations
Frank W. Thackeray and John E. Findling, Series Editors

The History of Argentina
Daniel K. Lewis

The History of Australia
Frank G. Clarke

The History of Brazil
Robert M. Levine

The History of the Baltic States
Kevin O'Connor

The History of Canada
Scott W. See

The History of Chile
John L. Rector

The History of China
David C. Wright

The History of Congo
Didier Gondola

The History of Cuba
Clifford L. Staten

The History of Egypt
Glenn E. Perry

The History of France
W. Scott Haine

The History of Germany
Eleanor L. Turk

The History of Holland
Mark T. Hooker

The History of India
John McLeod

The History of Iran
Elton L. Daniel

The History of Ireland
Daniel Webster Hollis III

The History of Israel
Arnold Blumberg

The History of Italy
Charles L. Killinger

The History of Japan
Louis G. Perez

The History of Mexico
Burton Kirkwood

The History of New Zealand
Tom Brooking

The History of Nigeria
Toyin Falola

The History of Poland
M. B. Biskupski

The History of Portugal
James M. Anderson

The History of Russia
Charles E. Ziegler

The History of Serbia
John K. Cox

The History of South Africa
Roger B. Beck

The History of Spain
Peter Pierson

The History of Sweden
Byron J. Nordstrom

The History of Turkey
Douglas A. Howard